MW00764849

The Class of '93

*How One Baseball Team
Wrecked An Entire League*

ANDREW LINKER

ISBN-10: 1986602613
ISBN-13: 978-1986602617

DEDICATION

To Michelle, my bride who before ever meeting me in person in 1996 said, "By the way, I really like baseball." After hearing 87,284 or so baseball stories since then, I hope she still feels the same way.

TABLE OF CONTENTS

The Class of '93

INTRODUCTION

As the 20th century melted into the 21st, the well-meaning folks at Minor League Baseball made plans to celebrate the 100 greatest teams in the history of the minors since 1901.

A hundred teams for 100 years.

Assigned to rank the teams were highly respected baseball historians Bill Weiss and Marshall Wright. The job — as with all efforts like this — was a thankless one for Weiss and Wright.

Really now, who could say for sure if the 1920 St. Paul Saints, who were No. 6 on their list, were that much better than, say, the 1990 West Palm Beach Expos, who checked in at No. 89?

C'mon, were the 1903 Jersey City Skeeters appreciably better at No. 7 than the 1983 Reading Phillies were at 62?

How does one differentiate between teams? The teams ranked in the Top 100 played in different classifications in dramatically different eras with demographics that kept teams in the minors from being nothing more than a whites-only club until 1946, when Jackie Robinson made his debut with the Brooklyn Dodgers' top farm team in Montreal.

These variables made the rankings flawed from the outset, when the 1944 Milwaukee Brewers were the first team announced at No. 100.

Eventually, the countdown reached 73, and that was where Minor League Baseball placed the 1993 Harrisburg Senators.

Seventy-freaking-third.

Anybody who saw that team knew better.

More than 15 years after its release at the turn of the new millennium, the MiLB Top 100 list — specifically, Harrisburg's ranking — still irked Jim Tracy, the Senators' manager in 1993.

"I would put the nucleus of my club against any of them," Tracy said a quarter-century after leading the '93 Senators to exactly 100 victories from Opening Night through the final game of the Class AA Eastern League playoffs.

"I don't know who these other 72 teams are," he said, "but we'll play a short series against any of them, and we'd win most of them. I don't think I'm going out on a limb here. That's just how good this team was."

Just how good?

The numbers tell only part of the story.

Tracy's team graduated 22 of its 41 players to the major leagues with eight of those 22 playing in the majors for at least 10 seasons.

Phenomenal numbers.

Even more extraordinary when considering that of every team on MiLB's Top 100 list only the '93 Senators had as many as eight of their players spend at least 10 seasons in the majors after first playing with them.

The 1937 Newark Bears, who were ranked third on the list, and 1992 Columbus Clippers, at No. 72, were next with seven each.

Only 19 of the 72 teams that were ranked ahead of the '93

JIM TRACY

Senators played in the post-segregation era. That era started in 1946 with Jackie Robinson's arrival in Montreal for his one-year stay there before reaching Brooklyn as the majors' first black player since Fleet Walker played in 42 games for Toledo in 1884.

Of those 19 post-segregated teams, only eight played either at the Class AA or AAA level, and none of those eight teams had an average age younger than the '93 Senators.

In some ways, the '93 Senators were an experiment, one devised by the Montreal Expos for their Class AA affiliate well before the start of spring training that year.

What would happen, the Expos wondered, if they stashed most, if not all, of their top prospects in one place at one time?

Would they dominate their league or would they collapse under the weight of their own alpha male egos?

The timing was perfect for such an experiment, given the Expos' top prospects in 1993 ranged in age from 19 to 22.

Age-wise, many of them were too young for Class AA.

Talent-wise, most of them were too good for it.

The Expos knowingly planned to set loose a team talented enough to obliterate the Class AA Eastern League.

First, they had to find the right person to manage the team.

That person was Jim Tracy.

Since Class AA tended to be baseball's last level on which players often faithfully took on the persona of the manager, the always-confident-but-never-cocky Tracy was the perfect fit.

His clubhouse in Harrisburg was one in which the top prospect in Cliff Floyd was treated no differently than a former prospect like Darrin Winston, a pitcher whose career by 1993 was hanging on the surgically rebuilt ligaments of his left elbow.

His clubhouse in Harrisburg also was where another of the Expos' top prospects, Rondell White, was assigned a corner locker beneath a balky, sometimes-dripping air conditioning unit that occasionally made postgame interviews both noisy and wet.

To White's left was Floyd, whose locker was bordered on the other side by outfielder Tyrone Woods — a mostly soft-spoken but sometimes smoldering, barrel-chested man who believed he was an everyday player but knew his playing time always was going to be impeded by the presence of top prospects like Floyd, White and Glenn Murray.

Woods could have griped and aired his complaints in public.

He rarely did.

Nor did Chris Martin, the Senators' everyday shortstop in 1991 and second baseman in '92 who often watched from the bench in '93. The playing time he expected at shortstop instead went to a better all-around player in Tim Barker, whom the Expos acquired in an offseason trade from the Los Angeles Dodgers for onetime All-Star third baseman Tim Wallach. No room at second base for Martin, either, not after the slick-fielding Mike Hardge arrived a month into the season from Class A West Palm Beach.

Martin, like Woods, was good enough to start for most, if not all, of the other seven teams that season in the Eastern League.

So were other bench players who either started the season with the Senators or finished the summer with them. Accomplished hitters like Oreste Marrero and Randy Wilstead, a pair of left-handed first basemen who batted from the same side of the plate as Floyd, often sat because no one was replacing Floyd. Period.

Ten of the 11 pitchers who started games for the '93 Senators would become major leaguers.

The No. 4 starter in the rotation was Kirk Rueter, who for a decade after leaving Harrisburg would become one of the most consistent left-handers in the majors.

The No. 5 starter was Miguel Batista, who outlasted everyone from the Class of '93. He pitched in the majors until 2012 and then for three more seasons in the Dominican Winter League before finally retiring at 43 years old — 26 years after first signing with the Expos in 1988.

The '93 Senators were that talented, that deep, that good.

They were not, however, perfect.

More than a few members of the Class of '93 enjoyed the nightlife both in Harrisburg and around the league, and they often did so with a beer in one hand and a groupie or two nearby.

They were 20-something years old, and young 20-somethings at that. They were ballplayers, not saints. Well, except maybe for first baseman Randy Wilstead, the happily married, soda-sipping Mormon from St. George, Utah.

They were, as team broadcaster Mark Mattern called them a quarter-century later, "a group of rock stars."

The Class of '93 also lost some games they should have won. Then, too, so has every great team since the game was first played.

They had some instances when someone did not run hard to first base — OK, one time — but, not to mention any names, Mike Hardge never again coasted down the line.

They also had some less-than-happy campers.

Early in the season, two of those frustrated players, backup catcher Miah Bradbury and infielder Ron Krause, abruptly quit. They opted to retire — Bradbury inexplicably after being told he was promoted to Class AAA Ottawa and Krause when he started losing playing time.

And, every now and then, Woods — a self-proclaimed "suspect" instead of a prospect — would be dusted off for a start, hit a ball halfway toward Harrisburg's West Shore and then after the game wonder aloud what he needed to do for more playing time. Woods always knew exactly when he was talking, like whenever Montreal general manager Dan Duquette and his staff were in Harrisburg to evaluate their Class AA team. Woods knew they would read his comments in the next morning's newspaper.

Toward the end of the season, Tracy had some sit-downs with a couple of players who thought they already should have been promoted to Ottawa, but still were in Harrisburg.

Tracy's biggest challenge was Derrick White, the Senators' first baseman in 1992 who had reached the majors midway through the 1993 season only to grumble his way back to the minors late in the season. Not back to Class AAA Ottawa, but to City Island, where White inherited Kirk Rueter's uniform number, Cliff Floyd's batting helmet and Rondell White's locker, the one in the corner of the clubhouse under the dripping air conditioner.

If the demotion two levels from the majors to the Eastern League did not humble Derrick White, then that perspiring AC did.

"We had to overcome clubhouse tangles and fights, as expected in a long season with close quarters," catcher Lance Rice said of sharing such a small-time clubhouse with so much big-time talent.

"We genuinely liked each other," Randy Wilstead remembered 25 years later. "There were the typical arguments in the clubhouse over what music got played and girls ... but for the most part we enjoyed being around each other."

Disagreements stayed in the clubhouse, never aired in the daily newspaper and never evident on the field.

There, on the field, the Class of '93 played with a singular focus, and that was to beat the crap out of the Eastern League.

They fought together on the field and rarely lost, whether in a game or in one of a handful of bench-clearing brawls they had against teams tired of being bludgeoned by the league's most potent offense and of being fooled by its best pitching staff.

At times, they seemed to win games hours before the first pitch.

Typically, teams set up batting practice groups to allow starters to hit in quartets for each of the first two rounds before letting their bench players scramble for pitches to hit during the final round.

Not the Senators. Especially for home games, and this was where the gamesmanship began.

Regardless of his lineup on a given night on City Island, Tracy arranged his hitters so the final quartet would take their batting practice close to 5 p.m. — the same time visiting teams would congregate in deep left field to stretch before taking their own BP.

A couple of Harrisburg pitchers stood as sentries, ostensibly to protect those stretching and presumably unaware players from being struck by balls hit toward them.

The pitchers, though, did nothing to shield those players from the balls being rocketed over their heads and off the painted wood of the billboards in left field or simply launched over the fence.

Four of the Senators' most powerful right-handed hitters — Rondell White, Shane Andrews, Glenn Murray and Tyrone Woods, who arguably was the greatest 5 o'clock hitter in team history — routinely joined Tracy's final group of BP hitters to take aim at the left-field wall and beyond.

The '93 Senators lost a lot of baseballs that way.

In doing so, they also won the pregame battle of wits by giving opposing teams, especially opposing pitchers, an up-close look at what awaited them in the game.

"Can you imagine as word traveled throughout the league about the Harrisburg club and how powerful they were, and then to walk out when you came to the island to play and have to stretch, and watch that last group of guys," Tracy remembered 25 years later.

"How much of an intimidation factor do you think that was, especially if you were a starting pitcher on the opposing club? Or a reliever for that matter," Tracy said. "I can't tell you how many times we finished BP early in the season and had to send for more balls because there would be like four left in the bucket.

"And to try to find the ones that were no longer in the park, you were either going to have to walk a helluva long way or be one really good swimmer."

This went on for six months, starting from the time the Senators first gathered in mid-March for spring training in Lantana, Florida, and ending in mid-September with the most decisive comeback in Eastern League playoff history.

The Harrisburg *Patriot-News*, in its annual preseason section on the team, proclaimed in the first line of the lead story on the Senators' upcoming season that "this should be fun."

Those four words — "this should be fun" — rankled the older, stuffier shirts in the newsroom as they grumbled about an editorial comment being injected into what was supposed to be an objective story. *Well*, the editors muttered, *we can't have that, you know.*

They were wrong, because those four words turned out to be a prediction of the absolute, unvarnished truth of the season that was to follow.

The Class of '93 was all about fun, the kind of fun that came with winning, overcoming adversity both on and off the field, and winning again. Not just winning, either, but dominating.

The Class of '93 did all of that.

This is their story.

Enjoy.

Andrew Linker
April 2018

Before The 'Burg

They all came from someplace else to get to Harrisburg, each coming to an island in the middle of the Susquehanna River during the summer of '93 with the hope of one day reaching the majors.

Most did. Others came close.

Their stories are on the pages that follow, but first some background information on the 41 players, two coaches and one manager who in 1993 formed one of the greatest teams in minor league history.

THE MANAGER

JIM TRACY. Position as player: Outfielder-first baseman. **Born:** Dec. 31, 1955 in Hamilton, Ohio. **Height:** 6-foot-3. **Weight:** 205 pounds. **Batted:** Left. **Threw:** Right. **How acquired by Montreal:** Signed by Expos in fall 1992 after four seasons in Cincinnati Reds' system as minor league manager and field coordinator. **Major League experience:** Played 87 games for Cubs in 1980-81. **Before the 'Burg:** Reds' minor league field coordinator before being fired after the 1992 season.

THE COACHES

CHUCK KNIFFIN. Pitching coach. **Position as player:** Pitcher. **Born:** Oct. 28, 1950 in Rockville Centre, New York. **Height:** 5-11. **Weight:** 185. **Threw:** Left. **Batted:** Right. **How acquired by Montreal:** Joined Expos in 1992 after spending four seasons as Class A pitching coach with Seattle Mariners. **Major League experience:** None. **Before the 'Burg:** Pitching coach in 1992 at West Palm Beach in Class A Florida State League.

GREG FULTON. Coach. **Position as player:** Infielder. **Born:** Feb. 20, 1963 in Quincy, Massachusetts. **Height:** 6-4. **Weight:** 195 pounds. **Batted:** Right. **Threw:** Right. **How acquired by Montreal:** Signed as minor league free agent in July 1990. Retired as player in March 1993 and assigned to Senators coaching staff. **Major League experience:** None. **Before the 'Burg:** Spent 1993 training camp trying to win a roster spot at AAA Ottawa.

THE BALLPARK

RIVERSIDE STADIUM IN 1993: SEATS FOR 5,600 FANS, HOME TO 41 PLAYERS

THE PLAYERS

 **SHANE ANDREWS.** Third baseman. **Born:** Aug. 28, 1971 in Dallas, Texas. **Height:** 6-1. **Weight:** 215. **Bats:** Right. **Throws:** Right. **How acquired by Montreal:** First-round pick (11th overall) in the 1990 amateur draft. **Before the 'Burg:** Spent the 1992 season with Class A Albany, Georgia, in the South Atlantic League, where he batted .230 in 136 games with 25 homers, 87 RBIs, 107 walks and, gasp, 174 strikeouts.

 **JOE AUSANIO.** Pitcher. **Born:** Dec. 9, 1965 in Kingston, New York. **Height:** 6-1. **Weight:** 205 pounds. **Throws:** Right. **Bats:** Right. **How acquired by Montreal:** Claimed off waivers from Pittsburgh on Nov. 12, 1992. **Before the 'Burg:** Called up July 20 from the rookie-level Gulf Coast League, where he opened the '93 season rehabbing his right elbow. Replaced pitcher Rick DeHart on the Senators' roster for the rest of the season.

THE PLAYERS

TIM BARKER. Shortstop. **Born:** June 30, 1968 in Baltimore, Maryland. **Height:** 6-0. **Weight:** 175. **Bats:** Right. **Throws:** Right. **How acquired by Montreal:** Trade from Los Angeles Dodgers for Tim Wallach on Dec. 24, 1992; originally ninth pick of Dodgers in 1989 amateur draft. **Before the 'Burg:** Arrived from AAA Ottawa on April 26, replacing shortstop Edgar Tovar on the roster.

MIGUEL BATISTA. Pitcher. **Born:** Feb. 19, 1971 in Sano Domingo, Dominican Republic. **Height:** 6-1. **Weight:** 170. **Throws:** Right. **Bats:** Right. **How acquired by Montreal:** Signed as non-drafted free agent Feb. 29, 1988. **Before the 'Burg:** Opened the 1992 season in majors with Pittsburgh as a Rule V pick, returned to Expos April 23, 1992; went 7-7 in 24 starts at Class A West Palm Beach.

MIAH BRADBURY. Catcher. **Born:** Jan. 30, 1968 in San Diego. **Height:** 6-4. **Weight:** 210. **Bats:** Right. **Throws:** Right. **How acquired by Montreal:** Player to be named later from the Nov. 20, 1992 trade that sent former Senators pitcher Dave Wainhouse to Seattle. **Before the 'Burg:** Spent 1992 with Seattle's Peninsula affiliate in the Class A Carolina League, batting .280 in 111 games with 7 homers.

MARIO BRITO. Pitcher. **Born:** April 9, 1966 in Bonao, Dominican Republic. **Height:** 6-3. **Weight:** 179. **Throws:** Right. **Bats:** Right. **How acquired by Montreal:** 45th overall pick in the 1985 Dominican draft. **Before the 'Burg:** Split 1992 season between the Senators and Class AAA Indianapolis in first full season as a relief pitcher, posting 2.29 ERA and three saves in 48 games.

ARCHIE CORBIN. Pitcher. **Born:** Dec. 30, 1967 in Beaumont, Texas. **Height:** 6-4. **Weight:** 190. **Throws:** Right. **Bats:** Right. **How acquired by Montreal:** Purchased from Milwaukee on Feb. 5, 1993; originally a 16th-round selection of the New York Mets in the 1986 amateur draft. **Before the 'Burg:** Appeared in 27 games in 1992 for Class AA Memphis, going 7-8 with a 4.73 ERA.

THE PLAYERS

 **REID CORNELIUS.** Pitcher. **Born:** June 2, 1970 in Thomasville, Alabama. **Height:** 6-0. **Weight:** 185. **Throws:** Right. **Bats:** Right. **How acquired by Montreal:** 11th-round pick in 1988 amateur draft. **Before the 'Burg:** Limited by injury in 1992 to four starts for Senators, going 1-0 with 3.13 ERA after posting 10-4 record in 1991 in 20 starts for Class A West Palm Beach and Senators.

 **MIKE DANIEL.** Catcher. **Born:** Sept. 21, 1969 in Weatherford, Oklahoma. **Height:** 6-1. **Weight:** 200. **Bats:** Right. **Throws:** Right. **How acquired by Montreal:** Fifth-round pick in 1991 amateur draft. **Before the Burg:** Called up from Class A West Palm Beach on May 22, 1993. Spent eight days with the Senators while catcher Rob Fitzpatrick was on the disabled list with a sprained ankle.

 **RICK DeHART.** Pitcher. **Born:** March 21, 1970 in Topeka, Kansas. **Height:** 6-1. **Weight:** 180. **Throws:** Left. **Bats:** Left. **How acquired by Montreal:** Signed as non-drafted free agent on March 24, 1992. **Before the 'Burg:** Started '93 season at Class A San Bernardino, going 4-3 in nine starts there before joining the Senators on May 27 when pitcher Kirk Rueter was promoted to AAA Ottawa.

 **RAFAEL DIAZ.** Pitcher. **Born:** Dec. 12, 1969 in Quades, Mexico. **Height:** 6-1. **Weight:** 178. **Throws:** Right. **Bats:** Right. **How acquired by Montreal:** 15th-round pick in 1988 amateur draft. **Before the 'Burg:** Spent the 1992 season at Class A West Palm Beach, going 8-4 with a 2.18 ERA, three complete games, two shutouts and two saves in 24 appearances.

 **JOEY EISCHEN.** Pitcher. **Born:** May 25, 1970 in West Corvina, California. **Height:** 6-1. **Weight:** 190. **Throws:** Left. **Bats:** Left. **How acquired by Montreal:** In trade with Texas Rangers for pitcher Dennis "Oil Can" Boyd on July 21, 1991. **Before the 'Burg:** Spent '92 season at Class A West Palm Beach, going 9-8 with 3.08 ERA, three complete games and two shutouts in 27 games.

THE PLAYERS

ROB FITZPATRICK. Catcher. **Born:** Sept. 14, 1968 in Ridgewood, New Jersey. **Height:** 5-11. **Weight:** 190. **Bats:** Right. **Throws:** Right. **How acquired by Montreal:** Seventh-round selection in 1990 amateur draft. **Before the 'Burg:** Spent 1992 at West Palm Beach, hit .256 in 96 games with eight homers and 37 RBIs before playing in prestigious Arizona Fall League.

CLIFF FLOYD. First baseman-left fielder. **Born:** Dec. 5, 1972 in Chicago. **Height:** 6-4. **Weight:** 220. **Bats:** Left. **Throws:** Right. **How acquired by Montreal:** First-round pick (14th overall) in 1991 amateur draft. **Before the 'Burg:** Spent 1992 at Albany, Georgia, in the Class A South Atlantic League, batting .304 in 134 games with 24 doubles, 16 triples, 16 homers, 97 RBIs and 32 stolen bases. Was named South Atlantic League's MVP.

MARC GRIFFIN. Outfielder. **Born:** Sept. 15, 1968 in Quebec City, Quebec Provence, Canada. **Height:** 6-0. **Weight:** 170. **Bats:** Left. **Throws:** Right. **How acquired by Montreal:** Trade with L.A. Dodgers for pitcher Ben VanRyn on Dec. 10, 1991. **Before the 'Burg:** Hitting .319 at Class A West Palm Beach with a team-high 23 steals when he was promoted to Senators on Aug. 9, 1993.

MIKE HARDGE. Second baseman. **Born:** Jan. 27, 1972 in Fort Hood, Texas. **Height:** 5-11. **Weight:** 185. **Bats:** Right. **Throws:** Right. **How acquired by Montreal:** Second-round pick in 1990 amateur draft. **Before the 'Burg:** Hitting .228 in 27 games at Class A West Palm Beach before joining the Senators after infielder Ron Krause retired on May 18.

HEATH HAYNES. Pitcher. **Born:** Nov. 30, 1968 in Wheeling, West Virginia. **Height:** 6-0. **Weight:** 180. **Throws:** Right. **Bats:** Right. **How acquired by Montreal:** Signed as non-drafted free agent on June 10, 1991. **Before the 'Burg:** Split the 1992 season between Class A Rockford and Senators, going 5-1 in 48 games with 1.90 ERA, 15 saves and 84 strikeouts in 62 innings.

THE PLAYERS

ROD HENDERSON. Pitcher. **Born:** March 11, 1971 in Greensburg, Kentucky. **Height:** 6-4. **Weight:** 193. **Throws:** Right. **Bats:** Right. **How acquired by Montreal:** Second-round pick in 1992 amateur draft. **Before the 'Burg:** 12-7 with 2.90 ERA in 22 starts at Class A West Palm Beach. Joined Senators Aug. 3, 1993 when pitchers Gabe White and Joey Eischen were promoted to AAA.

TYRONE HORNE. Outfielder. **Born:** Nov. 2, 1970 in Troy, North Carolina. **Height:** 5-9. **Weight:** 190. **Bats:** Left. **Throws:** Right. **How acquired by Montreal:** Expos' 44th-round pick in 1989 amateur draft. **Before the 'Burg:** Hitting .295 with 10 homers in 82 games at Class A West Palm Beach before joining Senators July 24, 1993 after outfielder Rondell White was promoted to Ottawa.

CHRIS JOHNSON. Pitcher. **Born:** Dec. 7, 1968 in Chattanooga, Tennessee. **Height:** 6-8. **Weight:** 215. **Throws:** Right. **Bats:** Right. **How acquired by Montreal:** Signed by Expos as free agent on June 13, 1991. Originally selected in second round by Milwaukee in 1987 amateur draft. **Before the 'Burg:** Spent the 1992 season with the Senators, going 9-10 with 3.98 ERA in 28 games.

RON KRAUSE. Second baseman-shortstop. **Born:** Dec. 27, 1970 in Euclid, Ohio. **Height:** 6-1. **Weight:** 175. **Bats:** Left. **Throws:** Right. **How acquired by Montreal:** Third-round pick in 1989 amateur draft. **Before the 'Burg:** Spent the 1992 season at Class A West Palm Beach, batting .250 in 108 games with eight doubles, eight triples and two homers.

BRIAN LOONEY. Pitcher. **Born:** Sept. 26, 1969 in New Haven, Connecticut. **Height:** 5-10. **Weight:** 180. **Throws:** Left. **Bats:** Left. **How acquired by Montreal:** Expos' 10th-round selection in 1991 amateur draft. **Before the 'Burg:** Was 4-6 with 3.14 ERA and 109 strikeouts in 106 innings over 18 appearances at West Palm Beach before joining the Senators July 16, 1993.

THE PLAYERS

ORESTE MARRERO. First baseman-designated hitter. **Born:** Oct. 31, 1969 in Bayamon, Puerto Rico. **Height:** 6-0. **Weight:** 195. **Bats:** Left. **Throws:** Left. **How acquired by Montreal:** In trade with Milwaukee on Jan. 20, 1993 for Todd Samples and Ron Gerstein. **Before the 'Burg:** Spent the 1992 season with Milwaukee's Class A team in Stockton, batting .276 in 76 games with 51 RBIs.

CHRIS MARTIN. Shortstop-second baseman. **Born:** Jan. 25, 1968 in Los Angeles. **Height:** 6-1. **Weight:** 170. **Bats:** Right. **Throws:** Right. **How acquired by Montreal:** Second-round pick in 1990 amateur draft. **Before the 'Burg:** Spent the 1991 and '92 seasons on City Island, batting .227 in 1992 with five homers and 31 RBIs in 125 games after hitting .224 in 87 games for Senators in 1991.

GLENN MURRAY. Outfielder. **Born:** Nov. 23, 1970 in Manning, South Carolina. **Height:** 6-2 **Weight:** 225. **Bats:** Right. **Throws:** Right. **How acquired by Montreal:** Second-round pick in 1989 amateur draft. **Before the 'Burg:** Played the 1992 season at Class A West Palm Beach, batting .232 in 119 games with 13 home runs, 14 doubles, five triples, 41 RBIs and 26 stolen bases.

YORKIS PEREZ. Pitcher. **Born:** Sept. 30, 1967 in Bajos de Haina, Dominican Republic. **Height:** 6-0. **Weight:** 180. **Throws:** Left. **Bats:** Left. **How acquired by Montreal:** Signed by Expos as free agent on Feb. 15, 1993. **Before the 'Burg:** Only appeared in three games in 1992, all with the Yomiuri Giants of the Japan Central League, going 0-1 with a 7.11 ERA over 6 1/3 innings.

CURTIS PRIDE. Outfielder. **Born:** Dec. 17, 1968 in Washington, D.C. **Height:** 5-11. **Weight:** 195. **Bats:** Left. **Throws:** Right. **How acquired by Montreal:** Signed as free agent on Dec. 8 1992; originally 10th-round pick of N.Y. Mets in 1986 amateur draft. **Before the 'Burg:** Spent the 1992 season with Class AA Binghamton, batting .227 in 118 games with 15 doubles, 10 homers and 42 RBIs.

THE PLAYERS

ED PUIG. Pitcher. **Born:** Oct. 16, 1965 in Michigan City, Indiana. **Height:** 5-10. **Weight:** 185. **Throws:** Left. **Bats:** Left. **How acquired by Montreal:** Signed by Expos as free agent Aug. 9, 1993 from Saltillo in Mexican League. **Before the 'Burg:** Posted six saves for Arecibo in the Puerto Rican League before joining Saltillo. Replaced reliever Darrin Winston on Senators' roster Aug. 9, 1993.

LANCE RICE. Catcher. **Born:** Oct. 19, 1966 in Salem, Oregon. **Height:** 6-1. **Weight:** 195. **Bats:** Both. **Throws:** Right. **How acquired by Montreal:** Signed by Expos as free agent on May 7, 1993. **Before the 'Burg:** Spent three seasons with the Los Angeles Dodgers' Class AA affiliate in San Antonio before being released. Joined the Senators May 7, 1993 as player-coach Greg Fulton was deactivated.

KIRK RUETER. Pitcher. **Born:** Dec. 1, 1970 in Hoyleton, Illinois. **Height:** 6-3. **Weight:** 190. **Throws:** Left. **Bats:** Left. **How acquired by Montreal:** 18th-round selection in 1991 amateur draft. **Before the 'Burg:** Spent the 1992 season with Rockford of the Class A Midwest League, going 11-9 in 26 starts with a 2.58 ERA, six complete games and two shutouts.

MATT RUNDELS. Utility player. **Born:** Aug. 26, 1970 in Columbus, Ohio. **Height:** 5-11. **Weight:** 175. **Bats:** Right. **Throws:** Right. **How acquired by Montreal:** Expos' 13th-round pick in 1992 amateur draft. **Before the 'Burg:** Split 72 games at Class A Burlington and West Palm Beach before joining Senators July 29, 1993 after shortstop Tim Barker's promotion to AAA Ottawa.

MITCH SIMONS. Infielder. **Born:** Dec. 13, 1968 in Midwest City, Oklahoma. **Height:** 5-9. **Weight:** 172. **Bats:** Right. **Bats:** Right. **How acquired by Montreal:** 23rd-round pick in 1991 amateur draft. **Before the 'Burg:** Made a couple of trips between Harrisburg and Class A West Palm Beach, batting .256 in 45 games in Class A before sticking with Senators on Aug. 4, 1993.

THE PLAYERS

MIKE THOMAS. Pitcher. **Born:** Sept. 2, 1969 in Sacramento, California. **Height:** 6-2. **Weight:** 200. **Throws:** Left. **Bats:** Left. **How acquired by Montreal:** Trade with New York Mets for pitcher Tim Burke on July 15, 1991. **Before the 'Burg:** Was 1-3 with nine saves and a 3.29 ERA in 25 appearances. Joined Senators on July 7, 1993 after reliever Yorkis Perez was promoted to Ottawa.

EDGAR TOVAR. Shortstop. **Born:** Nov. 28, 1973 in Aragua, Venezuela. **Height:** 6-1. **Weight:** 170. **Bats:** Right. **Throws:** Right. **How acquired by Montreal:** Signed as non-drafted free agent on Jan. 25, 1992. **Before the 'Burg:** Spent the '92 season at Jamestown in the short-season, Class A New York-Penn League, batting .270 in 72 games with 31 RBIs and 13 stolen bases.

UGUETH URBINA. Pitcher. **Born:** Feb. 15, 1974 in Caracas, Venezuela. **Height:** 6-2. **Weight:** 184. **Throws:** Right. **Bats:** Right. **How acquired by Montreal:** Signed as non-drafted free agent on July 2 1990. **Before the 'Burg:** Was 10-1 with a 1.99 ERA in 16 starts at Burlington in the Class A Midwest League. Joined Senators on July 5, 1993 when reliever Mario Brito was promoted to AAA Ottawa.

DERRICK WHITE. First baseman. **Born:** Oct. 12, 1969 in San Rafael, California. **Height:** 6-1. **Weight:** 220. **Bats:** Right. **Throws:** Right. **How acquired by Montreal:** Sixth -round pick in 1991 draft. **Before the 'Burg:** Reached the majors in '93 after playing '92 in Harrisburg. Was batting .224 in 17 games with Expos when sent to Senators on Aug. 12, 1993, swapping roster spots with Oreste Marrero.

GABE WHITE. Pitcher. **Born:** Nov. 20, 1971 in Sebring, Florida. **Height:** 6-2. **Weight:** 200. **Throws:** Left. **Bats:** Left. **How acquired by Montreal:** First-round pick (28th overall) in 1990 amateur draft. **Before the 'Burg:** Spent the '92 season with Rockford of Class A Midwest League, going 14-8 with a 2.84 ERA, seven complete games and 176 strikeouts in 187 innings over 27 starts.

THE PLAYERS

 **RONDELL WHITE.** Outfielder. **Born:** Feb.23, 1972 in Milledgeville, Georgia. **Height:** 6-1. **Weight:** 205. **Bats:** Right. **Throws:** Right. **How acquired by Montreal:** First-round pick (24th overall) in 1990 amateur draft. **Before the 'Burg:** Spent 1992 at West Palm Beach in the Class A Florida State League, batting .316 in 111 games with 10 doubles, 12 triples, 41 RBIs and 42 stolen bases.

 **RANDY WILSTEAD.** First baseman. **Born:** April 5, 1968 in Salt Lake, Utah. **Height:** 6-1. **Weight:** 195. **Bats:** Left. **Throws:** Left. **How acquired by Montreal:** 16th-round pick in 1990 amateur draft. **Before the 'Burg:** Started 1993 season at Class A West Palm Beach, hitting .333 in 60 games there before joining Senators on June 21 after Curtis Pride was promoted to Class AAA Ottawa.

 **DARRIN WINSTON.** Pitcher. **Born:** July 6, 1966 in Passaic, New Jersey. **Height:** 6-0. **Weight:** 195. **Throws:** Left. **Bats:** Right. **How acquired by Montreal:** 18th-round pick in the 1988 amateur draft. **Before the 'Burg:** Joined the roster April 16, 1993 from extended spring training when Chris Johnson was traded to Chicago Cubs. Missed all of the 1992 season after elbow surgery.

 **TYRONE WOODS.** Outfielder. **Born:** Aug, 19, 1969 in Dade City, Florida. **Height:** 6-1. **Weight:** 204. **Bats:** Right. **Throws:** Right. **How acquired by Montreal:** Fifth-round pick in 1988 amateur draft. **Before the 'Burg:** Spent the 1992 season at Rockford in the Class A Midwest League, batting .291 in 101 games with 12 homers, 47 RBIs and 15 stolen bases.

THE GENERAL MANAGER

 **TODD VANDER WOUDE.** General manager. **How acquired by Senators:** Team's second hire before the franchise's reboot in 1987 — following newly named general manager Rick Redd from Richmond, Virginia, where they worked for the Atlanta Braves' Class AAA team. Promoted to GM in June 1992 when Redd resigned.

From Whence They Came

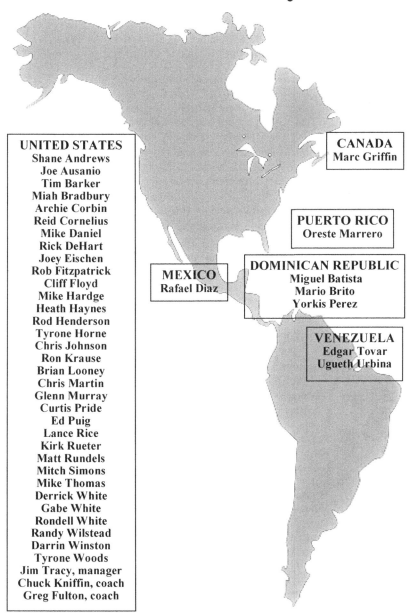

UNITED STATES
Shane Andrews
Joe Ausanio
Tim Barker
Miah Bradbury
Archie Corbin
Reid Cornelius
Mike Daniel
Rick DeHart
Joey Eischen
Rob Fitzpatrick
Cliff Floyd
Mike Hardge
Heath Haynes
Rod Henderson
Tyrone Horne
Chris Johnson
Ron Krause
Brian Looney
Chris Martin
Glenn Murray
Curtis Pride
Ed Puig
Lance Rice
Kirk Rueter
Matt Rundels
Mitch Simons
Mike Thomas
Derrick White
Gabe White
Rondell White
Randy Wilstead
Darrin Winston
Tyrone Woods
Jim Tracy, manager
Chuck Kniffin, coach
Greg Fulton, coach

CANADA
Marc Griffin

PUERTO RICO
Oreste Marrero

DOMINICAN REPUBLIC
Miguel Batista
Mario Brito
Yorkis Perez

MEXICO
Rafael Diaz

VENEZUELA
Edgar Tovar
Ugueth Urbina

From Sea To Shining Sea

Thirty-six of the 44 players, manager and coaches who comprised the Class of '93 were born in the United States, representing 22 states and the District of Columbia.

California (5): Miah Bradbury, catcher, San Diego
Joey Eischen, pitcher, West Covina
Chris Martin, infielder, Los Angeles
Mike Thomas, pitcher, Sacramento
Derrick White, first baseman, San Rafael

Ohio (3): Ron Krause, second baseman, Euclid
Matt Rundels, infielder, Columbus
Jim Tracy, manager, Hamilton

Texas (3): Shane Andrews, third baseman, Dallas
Archie Corbin, pitcher, Beaumont
Mike Hardge, second baseman, Fort Hood

Florida (2): Gabe White, pitcher, Sebring
Tyrone Woods, outfielder, Dade City

Illinois (2): Cliff Floyd, first baseman-left fielder, Chicago
Kirk Rueter, pitcher, Hoyleton

New Jersey (2): Rob Fitzpatrick, catcher, Ridgewood
Darrin Winston, pitcher, Passaic

New York (2): Joe Ausanio, pitcher, Kingston
Chuck Kniffin, pitching coach, Rockville Center

Oklahoma (2): Mike Daniel, catcher, Weatherford
Mitch Simons, infielder, Midwest City

Alabama (1): Reid Cornelius, pitcher, Thomasville
Connecticut (1): Brian Looney, pitcher, New Haven
Georgia (1): Rondell White, outfielder, Milledgeville
Indiana (1): Ed Puig, pitcher, Michigan City
Kansas (1): Rick DeHart, pitcher, Topeka
Kentucky (1): Rod Henderson, pitcher, Greensburg
Maryland (1): Tim Barker, shortstop, Baltimore
Massachusetts (1): Greg Fulton, coach, Quincy
North Carolina (1): Tyrone Horne, outfielder, Troy
Oregon (1): Lance Rice, catcher, Salem
South Carolina (1): Glenn Murray, outfielder, Manning
Tennessee (1): Chris Johnson, pitcher, Chattanooga
Utah (1): Randy Wilstead, first baseman, Salt Lake
West Virginia (1): Heath Haynes, pitcher, Wheeling
Washington, D.C. (1): Curtis Pride, outfielder

Building A Perfect Beast

Montreal Expos general manager Dan Duquette was asked midway though the summer of '93 if he was surprised by the early season runaway success of his Class AA team in Harrisburg.

Not really, he said with a shrug. This was, after all, what he had envisioned for the Senators when he first considered sending most, if not all, of the Expos' top prospects to Harrisburg that season.

This was how he built the team that would win 100 games from Opening Night through the Eastern League playoffs.

AMATEUR DRAFT (22 players)
First Round
Shane Andrews, third baseman, 1990 (11th overall pick)
Rondell White, center fielder, 1990 (24th overall)
Gabe White, pitcher, 1990 (28th overall)
Cliff Floyd, first baseman-left fielder, 1991 (14th overall)
Second Round
Glenn Murray, outfielder, 1989   Mike Hardge, second baseman, 1990
Chris Martin, infielder, 1990   Rod Henderson, pitcher, 1992
Third Round
Ron Krause, second baseman, 1989
Fifth Round
Tyrone Woods, outfielder, 1988   Mike Daniel, catcher, 1991
Sixth Round
Derrick White, first baseman, 1991
Seventh Round
Rob Fitzpatrick, catcher, 1990
10th Round
Brian Looney, pitcher, 1991
11th Round
Reid Cornelius, pitcher, 1988
13th Round
Matt Rundels, infielder, 1992
15th Round
Rafael Diaz, pitcher, 1988
16th Round
Randy Wilstead, first baseman, 1990
18th Round
Darrin Winston, pitcher, 1988   Kirk Rueter, pitcher, 1991
23rd Round
Mitch Simons infielder, 1991
44th Round
Tyrone Horne, outfielder, 1989

ACQUIRED THROUGH TRADES (6 players)

Mike Thomas, pitcher, from N.Y. Mets, 1991 for Tim Burke
Joey Eischen, pitcher, from Texas, 1991 for Oil Can Boyd
Marc Griffin, outfielder, from L.A. Dodgers, 1991, for Ben VanRyn
Tim Barker, shortstop, from L.A. Dodgers, 1992 for Tim Wallach
Miah Bradbury, catcher, from Seattle, 1992, for Dave Wainhouse
Oreste Marrero, first baseman, from Milwaukee, 1993, for two players

SIGNED AS NON-DRAFTED FREE AGENTS (5 players)

Miguel Batista, pitcher, 1988
Ugueth Urbina, pitcher, 1990
Heath Haynes, pitcher, 1991
Edgar Tovar, shortstop, 1992
Rick DeHart, pitcher, 1992

SIGNED AS MINOR LEAGUE FREE AGENTS (5 players)

Chris Johnson, pitcher, 1991
Curtis Pride, outfielder, 1992
Yorkis Perez, pitcher, 1993
Lance Rice, catcher, 1993
Ed Puig, pitcher, 1993

DOMINICAN DRAFT (1 player)

Mario Brito, 1985 (45th overall)

CLAIMED OFF WAIVERS (1 player)

Joe Ausanio, pitcher, from Pittsburgh Pirates, 1992

PURCHASED (1 player)

Archie Corbin, pitcher, from Milwaukee Brewers, 1993

Turning Pro

SIGNED OR DRAFTED OUT OF COLLEGE (20)		SIGNED OR DRAFTED OUT OF HIGH SCHOOL (21)	
Joe Ausanio	Tim Barker	Shane Andrews	Miguel Batista
Miah Bradbury	Mike Daniel	Mario Brito	Archie Corbin
Rick DeHart	Rob Fitzpatrick	Reid Cornelius	Rafael Diaz
Heath Haynes	Rod Henderson	Joey Eischen	Cliff Floyd
Marc Griffin	Brian Looney	Mike Hardge	Tyrone Horne
Chris Martin	Curtis Pride	Chris Johnson	Ron Krause
Lance Rice	Kirk Rueter	Oreste Marrero	Glenn Murray
Matt Rundels	Mitch Simons	Yorkis Perez	Ed Puig
Mike Thomas	Derrick White	Edgar Tovar	Ugueth Urbina
Randy Wilstead	Darrin Winston	Gabe White	Rondell White
			Tyrone Woods

The Right Fit

Outside of Cincinnati and a few outposts in the minor leagues, the news back in 1992 was relegated to a single line of tiny type in the transactions section of the morning newpaper's sports section.

Cincinnati Reds fire minor league field coordinator Jim Tracy.

The move was announced by Jim Bowden, the barely 30-something front office staffer whom the Reds named as their new general manager on Oct. 16, 1992.

Bowden, in what seemed like nanoseconds, immediately began to tear down and rebuild the Reds in his image, which given his impetuous nature made Tracy — not to mention anyone else not previously associated with Bowden — the perfect candidate to be replaced.

Not that Tracy understood at the time.

Who could?

After three seasons managing the Reds' Class AA affiliate in Chattanooga, the 36-year-old Tracy was tasked with running Cincinnati's underproducing farm system in 1992.

In one season with Tracy as their field coordinator, the Reds' minor league affiliates went from a combined .491 winning percentage in 1991 to .570 in 1992 with half of the organization's six teams reaching the playoffs.

The Reds' farm system quickly jumped out of the abyss and into one of the game's top 10, as ranked then by *Baseball America.*

Tracy's performance was worthy of a raise.

Instead, he was fired from his $45,000 a season job.

Back home in Sarasota, Florida, with his wife, Deb, and their three sons, Tracy pondered his situation and their future.

To hell with Bowden, he thought.

He knew his resume was too good, too deep, to be out of the game. He also knew he would not be out of the game for long, so he prepared to start making phone calls.

Only his phone rang first. The day was Friday, less than 72 hours after Bowden fired him.

"The ink wasn't even dry yet on my release papers," Tracy said 25 years later.

Deb answered the phone. The man on the other end of the line introduced himself: *"Dan Duquette of the Montreal Expos."*

Deb quickly passed the phone to her husband, who then listened as Duquette talked of how the Expos had been following his work with the Reds' minor leaguers.

"What was very flattering was that he told me that they had been following what I had been doing up to that point and time in my career," Tracy remembered, "and wondered what it was that I would like to do with my next job."

This went on for awhile. Not that Duquette was known for his loquaciousness, but Tracy was. Always had been.

Finally, Duquette the suitor popped the question: Know much about Harrisburg?

Never been there, Tracy told Duquette, although his father grew up a couple of hours away in South Philly and that he still had cousins living there. Did that help?

Duquette actually cared less about geography and more about personality, about the character of the man he was planning to send to Harrisburg for his Class AA team. He knew the Senators were going to be good, and he wanted the right person to manage them.

"During the course of the conversation he did tell me that they had several prospects they were planning on keeping together, and wanted to try to push the majority of them into Double-A at the start of the '93 season," Tracy said.

"I had no idea whatsoever who any of them were and if they had any talent or not," Tracy said years later. "Do you think I was in for a little bit of a surprise?"

Just a bit.

Duquette talked some more and finally made Tracy an offer. Fifty grand to manage in Double-A, more than twice what Tracy had earned in 1987 at his first managerial stop in Class A Peoria.

Duquette told Tracy to take the weekend to ponder his offer.

Tracy did not need that much time. He received other calls over the weekend from teams looking for a roving hitting instructor, but Tracy wanted to manage again. The decision was an easy one.

Just a few days after Bowden unceremoniously fired him, Tracy accepted Duquette's offer. Word of the hiring leaked out a couple of weeks before Tracy turned 37 on New Year's Eve.

Two months later — and a month before the Senators were to open their 1993 spring training camp — Tracy traveled to Harrisburg in mid-February to greet the fans, meet the media and answer the same questions he already had answered at his previous stops in Peoria, Illinois, and Chattanooga, Tennessee.

Mark Mattern, the team's broadcaster and PR director, paused when initially hearing of Tracy's hiring.

"When I was first told that our new manager was going to be Jim Tracy, my thought went to pitcher Jim Tracy, who was with the Senators in 1989 and 1990," Mattern said 25 years after first meeting the other Jim Tracy. "Of course, that was not the right guy."

WITH GM TODD VANDER WOUDE LOOKING ON, JIM TRACY SAID HELLO TO HARRISBURG ON FEB. 15, 1993

Jim Tracy — the new manager, not the old pitcher — took a morning flight out of Florida on Feb. 15, 1993, made a quick tour of downtown Harrisburg and the Erector set of a ballpark that would be his home from April to September, dined in the late afternoon at a popular local watering hole called Zembie's and then flew home that night to Sarasota.

In between, Tracy talked with everyone he was meeting for the first time and made them feel as if Tracy had known each of them for years. That was just his personality.

He also fidgeted with a starched collar and bright, patterned tie that were not part of his usual business attire and proceeded to stumble over the name "Montreal Expos" the first time he mentioned his new employer in public.

An hour later, the well-tanned Tracy looked perfectly at ease for a team photographer as he shed his sports coat, tie and shirt to put on a Senators jersey.

Then Tracy provided a glimpse into what was to come.

"I've managed adequate clubs. I've managed bad clubs. I've made them all competitive," he said at the time.

"Now, I have a good club and, hey, you're not going to beat me. That's what I'm striving for."

Tracy talked for 90 minutes that day to the fans and assembled media. Ever the conversationalist, Tracy made those 90 minutes feel like nine as he talked about his brief playing career as an outfielder in the majors with the Chicago Cubs in 1980 and '81, and about his five seasons managing in the minors both for the Cubs and Reds.

He also talked about his desire to take a team to the postseason for the first time as a manager.

Never having reached the playoffs gnawed at Tracy, despite his success in cultivating the careers of aspiring major leaguers for two different organizations.

Tracy worried how his career record of 338-369 would be received by a Harrisburg fan base that had grown accustomed to watching playoff teams.

> *"I've managed adequate clubs. I've managed bad clubs. I've made them all competitive. Now, I have a good club and, hey, you're not going to beat me."*
>
> *Jim Tracy on Feb. 15, 1993*

Four of the first six teams in the Senators' modern era had reached the playoffs with three of those teams going to finals. The first of those teams, the Class of '87, won the Eastern League title, a championship that six years later still resonated with the Senators' fans who were awaiting the arrival of the Class of '93.

Tracy knew fans tended to miss the point of the minor leagues, knowing they tended to judge the success or failure of a team and its manager by wins and losses rather than how many players were developed for the majors. That, of course, always had been the sole purpose of the minors. Developing players for the majors was the only goal. Wins were a luxury. Nice if you have them, but not necessary to achieve your goals.

Tracy also knew that Harrisburg's fans, if they had not already heard, soon would find out that none of his first five teams reached the playoffs.

"Through it all, there's still something hanging over my head with people thinking, 'How good of a manger is this guy?' " Tracy said of never reaching the playoffs, despite his resume.

"I think they're aware of my communications skills, my rapport with players," Tracy said, " … but I'd like to get to the dance just once."

Seven months later, he would get his chance.

SPRING TRAINING

Of Mold And Men

LANTANA, Fla. — No one looked forward to the trip here.

Really, who would? Not when you have been rousted early in the morning from your comfy room at the Courtyard Marriott in West Palm Beach to be taken on a 20-minute ride south on the always congested I-95 to Santaluces Community High School.

Once there, you were greeted at the parking lot by a lone, plump, white-shirted sentry sitting in a golf cart.

Beyond the gate were four ballfields to the left and a rundown building with an equally rundown locker room to the right.

Somewhere in between there were more than 150 professional baseball players. All minor leaguers. Their talents varied, as talents do with minor leaguers. Their dreams, though, all were the same.

Everyone here wanted to play in the major leagues.

Most, of course, would not. Long before their dreams would be extinguished, though, the hopefuls moved from station to station on the backfields of the high school, out of sight of the lone rent-a-cop protecting the parking lot.

No one ever seemed quite sure exactly what he was protecting because, in reality, this place was a dump. Barely passable for high school fields, and most definitely no place to train aspiring major leaguers.

Yet this was where the Montreal Expos, a team with some of Major League Baseball's best prospects, sent their future stars to be cultivated in a Petri dish of dust and mold.

Among the players were the Senators' Class of '93. They were comprised of the Expos' top prospects, yet treated like chattel.

The only shade on the backfields for the players came in an undersized, one-customer-at-a-time bathroom built into the base of a ratty-looking observation tower overlooking the four fields.

Players began showing up around 8 in the morning, dressing in a dimly lit locker room built for the high school's football team, working out on the fields until noon, breaking for lunch and then playing a game at 1 p.m. against another minor league team before making their way back to the Courtyard late in the afternoon.

"Coming over from the New York Mets, I was spoiled," outfielder Curtis Pride remembered 25 years later of his first Lantana camp in 1993. "I go to Lantana and I get one small cup of soup and one small Dixie cup of Gatorade for lunch. That was it."

36

Twenty minutes to the north, the Expos' major leaguers shared a complex in West Palm Beach with the Atlanta Braves at aging Municipal Stadium, which despite its flaws still was a significant upgrade over the backfields of Lantana.

Mind you, old Municipal Stadium was a dump, too. Just a nicer dump with a clearer path to the major leagues.

SOMETIMES, AS SENATORS HOPEFUL MATT CONNOLLY FOUND OUT, LUNCH IN LANTANA INCLUDED AN APPLE

This was 1993, and the amenities now commonplace both for major leaguers and minor leaguers in spring training did not yet exist throughout the game.

Some places, like the one Pride left behind with the Mets in St. Lucie, were nice both for the major and minor leaguers.

Lantana? Dante's Inferno had a better rating from AAA.

"It was a high school field, and it was bad," Pride remembered. "The clubhouse was small. The bleachers were in the sun. No shade. … Now, you have beautiful, million-dollar complexes."

A quarter-century later, Lantana remained seared into the brains of those who suffered there for three weeks of spring training in 1993.

"Lantana was awful," Senators manager Jim Tracy said 25 years after first seeing the place.

"As I look back at my entire playing, coaching and managerial career, I don't ever recall being in a facility that was as bad as that one. The mold growing on the walls in the minor league staff's locker room may have been the tip of the iceberg for me."

For Tracy, there was so much more to remember about Lantana, and none of it was destined for the local Chamber of Commerce's tourist brochures.

"The minor league fields were no day at the beach, either," Tracy said. "What a dustbowl it was. I remember what the Q-Tips that I would use after a shower in the afternoon looked like when I was done. It was a pretty rough place."

This was the place, though, where Tracy would form his team.

In mid-March, in the embryonic stages of camp, Tracy knew most of the players on his roster on a given day either would open the season in Class A or be released.

HEATH HAYNES TOILING IN LANTANA

The core of the Senators' Class of '93 still was in major league camp at West Palm Beach with the Expos, who eventually would reassign those players to Harrisburg.

While waiting for those players to arrive from big league camp, Tracy spent the early days of training camp getting to know the Class A players who eventually might find their way to the 'Burg.

"What I didn't realize at the time," Tracy recalled 25 years later, "was how many of them that I had early on would eventually show up in Harrisburg as a result of all the promotions that took place during the course of the '93 season.

"Getting to know them early on, as I look back on it, was a huge help when they became the second wave of guys to show up to the club during the second half of that season."

Eventually, the Expos began to reassign players from their camp in West Palm Beach, starting with third baseman Shane Andrews.

Outfielders Glenn Murray and Tyrone Woods followed, as did infielders Chris Martin and Oreste Marrero, and pitchers Joey Eischen, Heath Haynes and Gabe White.

Eventually, Montreal's top two prospects — left fielder and reluctant first baseman Cliff Floyd, and center fielder Rondell White — made the trip down I-95 from West Palm to Lantana.

"From about midway in camp down to the latter stages of the spring," Tracy recalled, "each and every day brought another face with a very interesting pedigree and, along with it, quite a bit of ability."

The most intriguing prospect was Floyd, whom the Expos had selected with the 14th overall pick in the 1991 amateur draft. At only 20 years old, Floyd already was one of the best prospects in baseball, a left handed-hitting behemoth whom some of the older scouts had been comparing to a young Willie McCovey.

Tracy also remembered that Floyd was impressive enough in big league camp to have a chance to open the '93 season in the majors, but that was before Montreal manager Felipe Alou wanted Floyd to learn to play first base.

Alou already had plenty of All-Stars in the outfield with his son, Moises, in left field, Marquis Grissom in center and Larry Walker in right. What he did not have was a first baseman who could hit like Cliff Floyd.

Tracy was to be Floyd's teacher at Class AA Harrisburg.

"He had never even worn a first baseman's mitt before," Tracy said of Floyd. "I can still see him coming over that hill to our lovely Lantana playing fields after having been sent down from big league camp about a week before they were going to break for the season.

"He was dragging along with him a first baseman's mitt that he had never seen before and looking like someone had stolen his dog," Tracy said. "When I first laid eyes on him, I thought, 'Oh, my God, what a specimen this guy is.' "

Floyd was the final piece of the Senators' roster that spring.

"When I looked around at the players that were now all together on our field at the complex that morning," Tracy said years later, "I realized that the team that was going to come out of all of this was going to have a chance to be pretty good."

39

A Sloth By Any Other Name

HARRISBURG — Baseball is no different than any other sport in that the names thoughtfully given out by parents often are replaced by inane nicknames handed out by players, managers and coaches because that is how they best remember a teammate.

Also helps when you have players with the same name, as the 1993 Senators did with a pair of Tyrones, three Mikes, a couple of guys named Chris and three players with the surname of White.

Some of the nicknames were obvious, like Marty for infielder Chris Martin, Lancer for catcher Lance Rice, D-White for first baseman Derrick White and Uggy for pitcher Ugueth Urbina.

Others in the Class of '93 did not have fun nicknames, because either nothing stuck or, in the cases of catcher Miah Bradbury and infielder Ron Krause, they were not around long enough to get one.

Many of the rest had nicknames that, to this day, were still used by manager Jim Tracy, who himself was known as "Shooter."

Here are some of the best of the rest:

Third baseman Shane Andrews	Mongo
Catcher Rob Fitzpatrick	40-Man
First baseman-left fielder Cliff Floyd	Sleepy
Pitcher Heath Haynes	Heater
Pitcher Rod Henderson	Hot Rod
Left fielder Tyrone Horne	Mushmouth
Pitching coach Chuck Kniffin	Mule
First baseman Oreste Marrero	Full Metal Jacket
Outfielder Glenn Murray	G-Wiz
Pitcher Ed Puig	Benny
Pitcher Kirk Rueter	Woody
Infielder Mitch Simons	Whitey
Center fielder Rondell White	Rock
First baseman Randy Wilstead	Sloth

"When you talk to Randy Wilstead," Tracy said 25 years after last seeing his former first baseman, "please tell him I called him 'Sloth' as a term of endearment … but he just wasn't very fast."

No need to apologize, Shooter. Over time, the Sloth, a natural-born hitter, learned to embrace his God-given lack of speed.

"I'm so slow," Wilstead said a quarter-century after first meeting the Shooter, "that I couldn't run out of sight in a week."

THURSDAY, APRIL 1
Water? What Water?

HARRISBURG — Puddles up to 40 feet across covered half of the dirt portion of the infield with standing water in 30 percent of the outfield. Geese were everywhere on the field, having a great time doing whatever geese like to do.

This was what Mayor Stephen Reed saw as he surveyed the mess created by the annual spring flooding of City Island.

Opening Day was eight days away. Reed was undeterred.

"Things are still a 'go,' " he said.

Reed was optimistic here, if nothing else because he was a politician, and politicians tended to say those kinds of things.

Senators general manager Todd Vander Woude also was optimistic, but that was because Vander Woude genuinely was a nice guy who always could find sunlight through raindrops.

"We really didn't worry about it," Vander Woude remembered 25 years later. "The feeling was that the water was in deep center and the outfield, so the infield was spared, along with the pitcher's mound. Also, I believe the weather forecast was for highs in the 70s, so nature would help dry also."

FRIDAY, APRIL 2

How's the Weather?

WEST PALM BEACH, Fla. — On a day when Rondell White launched Blase Sparma's fourth pitch of the game into another county and Shane Andrews drove in two more runs, Jim Tracy spent most his postgame chat talking little about the Senators' 6-4 victory over Greenville in another mindless spring training game.

Instead, the Senators' manager talked about the phone calls he spent most of the day making and of the messages he was waiting to have answered.

Tracy was not pleased with the reports he was receiving from 1,100 miles away, the stories that his team full of the Montreal Expos' best and brightest prospects was only a couple of days away from flying to Harrisburg and opening the season in a swamp of a stadium.

For a couple of days, word had been arriving from Harrisburg with news of nature's annual overwatering of City Island.

Outfield flooded. Infield threatened. Geese everywhere.

"Our main concern is the opener is a week away," Tracy said then. "With as much work as we've done in spring training, we can ill afford to ignore the situation, go in there with pitchers ready to go and then back them up for four or five days."

Senators team president Scott Carter said "there is no consideration" of moving the season-opening series against the Albany Yankees to upstate New York.

As for the players, most seemed oblivious to the news that parts of their summer home were under two feet of water.

"Should I tell them?" infielder Chris Martin asked. "Nah."

Martin, prepping for his third season in Harrisburg, was unfazed by the reports of geese taking over water-logged City Island.

"It's something you can't control," Martin said. "It's basically just the outfield. … Now, if it gets to the infield, then I may go up a few days early and help clean it up."

42

Updating the Resume

WEST PALM BEACH, Fla. — He originally signed a two-year contract to extend his playing career in the Montreal Expos' already deep farm system.

That was back in the fall of 1991, when Greg Fulton was approaching his 29th birthday — an age where minor leaguers already had morphed from being a prospect into being a journeyman.

GREG FULTON

The Expos gave Fulton that two-year deal knowing quite well he possibly would be done as a player before the contract expired. Alas, possibility met reality on this day as Fulton was told his playing days were over and, if he wanted, a coaching career was about to begin.

Fulton, who played for Harrisburg in 1991 and '92, came to spring training hoping to win a roster spot at Class AAA Ottawa. Instead, he listened to the Expos' sales pitch to make him a coach for Senators manager Jim Tracy.

"I'd welcome that gladly," Tracy said. "We're talking about a quality guy who is highly thought of in the organization."

Fulton, naturally, preferred to keep playing. He had been playing professionally since 1985, starting a meandering journey that over eight seasons took him to 11 teams in seven leagues.

"It's going to be tough not playing," Fulton said, "but it's better to do this now than later."

Still, there may yet be some time on the field for Fulton.

"We told him not to get fat and lazy," said Expos minor league director Kent Qualls, "and to be ready to play, just in case."

As Fulton was joining Harrisburg's staff, the 1993 Senators had their first promotion to the major leagues. Well, sort of.

Will Schnell, City Island's Sod God, left the Senators to become the assistant head groundskeeper for the NFL's Cleveland Browns.

His parting gift: Working OT to dry out soggy RiverSide Stadium before the April 9 season opener.

"I'm calling it now," said longtime Senators infielder Chris Martin. "In two or three days that place will be fine. I have faith in that crew up there."

SUNDAY, APRIL 4
Ready, Set, Go

RONDELL WHITE   **CLIFF FLOYD**   **GLENN MURRAY**   **CURTIS PRIDE**

LANTANA, Fla. — They already were considered among the Montreal Expos' best prospects. Rondell White, Cliff Floyd and Glenn Murray all were going to play in the major leagues.

Just in case, though, the three Harrisburg outfielders may have had another career in sports.

Track. Specifically, the 4x100 relay.

They were that fast. Each was timed in the 60-yard dash during the Expos' organizational camp day — where no games were played, just a little extra recess time for players who had spent most of the last month broiling under Florida's relentless sun.

White was timed at 6.4 seconds, and he was the slowest with Floyd timed at 6.36 seconds and Murray — still recovering from an offseason gunshot wound to his left leg — following at 6.37.

No one was faster than Curtis Pride, one of the Senators' backup outfielders who had a camp-best time of 6.35 seconds.

"I ran with a group of three or four guys," Pride remembered with a smile a couple of decades later. "And, I beat them all."

Watching all of this at the time was pitcher Joey Eischen.

"If you put the ball in the air with this team," Eischen said, "it's either going to hit some leather or it's going over the fence."

Some 1,100 miles north, Harrisburg Mayor Stephen Reed reported standing water had been removed from RiverSide Stadium's outfield and that maintenance crews had started aerating the base paths to expedite the drying process.

No such drying was needed for the clubhouses, though. Have to love those submarine-style, waterproof doors.

MONDAY, APRIL 5
Setting the Roster

LANTANA, Fla. — Long weeks now were measured in mere hours. And a couple of questions still remained after three weeks of minor league spring training. Here, in humidity-dripping Lantana, the Montreal Expos sent their future to develop on the dreary backfields of Santaluces Community High School. Now, with the end of camp so near, the Senators' roster mostly was set.

There were questions regarding the health of second baseman Ron Krause and middle infielder Chris Martin.

Krause was bothered by a strained right quadriceps. Martin was aching from Matt Connolly's fastball that he took between his shoulder blades during an intracamp game against AAA Ottawa.

And what to do with relief pitchers Chris Johnson and Darrin Winston? Especially after the Expos today reassigned relievers Mario Brito and Yorkis Perez from Ottawa to Harrisburg.

The arrival of Brito and Perez gave the Senators 12 pitchers, but only 11 of them were going to leave camp with the team.

"It could come down to the last day," Herm Starrette, the Expos' minor league field coordinator, said in the morning. "Hell, one year I didn't sign my contract until the sixth inning of a game, and then I pitched in the eighth."

By the end of the night, though, the Expos finally set the Senators' 23-man roster to start the 1993 season.

In for the pitching staff were starters Miguel Batista, Reid Cornelius, Joey Eischen, Kirk Rueter and Gabe White, as well as relievers Rafael Diaz, Heath Haynes, Archie Corbin, Brito, Johnson and Perez. Out was Winston, who missed the '92 season after elbow surgery. He would be left behind in the netherworld that was extended spring training.

Also in were catchers Miah Bradbury and Rob Fitzpatrick; infielders Shane Andrews, Oreste Marrero, Edgar Tovar, Krause and Martin; and outfielders Cliff Floyd, Glenn Murray, Curtis Pride, Rondell White and Tyrone Woods.

"I'm tickled to death to go to war with these guys," manager Jim Tracy said then. "We're ready to go now."

Alas, Tracy had to wait another day before he and his players finally could escape the hellhole that was Lantana.

TUESDAY, APRIL 6

The Waiting Game

LANTANA, Fla. — His roster was set the night before. All Senators manager Jim Tracy wanted to do on this day was keep his players out of the trainer's room.

"You don't want anybody getting hurt in the last hour," Tracy said then. "That's my main concern right now."

A secondary concern, of course, was what Tracy would find the next day, when the Senators would arrive in Harrisburg to get their first look at a home field that days earlier was under water.

The folks in Harrisburg assured Tracy that the standing water in the outfield no longer was a problem. Nor were the geese still inhabiting the outfield where Cliff Floyd, Rondell White and Glenn Murray — three of the Expos' top prospects — were going to play.

"That must be some drainage system they have there," Tracy said on the eve of leaving spring training.

New head groundskeeper Ed Kautz Jr. and his predecessor, the NFL-bound Will Schnell, had been steadily reclaiming the field from the flood waters and the geese that came with the recent rains.

"They've been starting at 8 in the morning and working until dark," said Senators general manager Todd Vander Woude.

Besides, Harrisburg Mayor Stephen Reed only days earlier told anyone carrying a microphone, TV camera or notepad that RiverSide Stadium would be ready for Opening Night on April 9.

Back then, 15 years before his political career ended in disgrace, Reed seemingly could will anything he wanted into reality.

And he wanted RiverSide Stadium ready on time for the opener.

"My first thought was that the mayor was crazy," Senators broadcaster Mark Mattern remembered a quarter-century later. "There would be no way we would be ready to play."

But.

"Mayor Reed had a pretty good track record of getting things done," Mattern said.

Reed brought in the city's fire department to help clean the island, augmenting the tireless work of the Senators' staff.

"We had a great group in that front office," Mattern said. "As we had done so many other times, we worked as hard and as long as we needed to pull it off. With the city's help, of course."

Checking Out Home

HARRISBURG — Their flight from West Palm Beach landed just a couple of hours earlier, and the Senators already had traded their sunblock lotion for jackets and sweatshirts.

They needed the sunblock during spring training. The jackets and sweatshirts were musts now, considering the season opener was just 48 hours away and Pennsylvania in April can be a cold, damp place more suited for football than baseball.

The field at RiverSide Stadium reflected the weather — cold and damp, but looking much better than it had only a few days earlier when March's blizzard turned into April's flooding.

"Considering everything we heard, this place looks great," said prized pitcher Gabe White, who was lined up to start Friday's season opener against the Albany Yankees.

Not everyone agreed with White.

"Thought this field was supposed to be in good shape," outfielder Glenn Murray said in a half-mumble, half-growl.

"Just look at this."

Murray then pointed to his mud-splattered pants that moments before had been bright white.

"All I did," Murray said, now in a full growl, "was walk on the field."

Hey, Murray was told, don't complain. A week ago, you would have needed scuba gear to take your spot in the outfield.

Senators manager Jim Tracy looked at the field and decided to take no chances. His pared-down workout consisted of bunt drills, pitchers throwing off the bullpen mounds and some light running — more mud for Murray! — in the outfield.

Besides, the lights were on, a regular occurrence during the season but something not done during spring training in Lantana.

"The main thing." Tracy said, "was to get them out here under the lights."

The final approval came from infielder and team weather geek Chris Martin, who played the previous two seasons in Harrisburg and knew best of the island's annual spring flooding.

"Considering what I was hearing, and being a Weather Channel watcher," Martin said, "I assumed the field would be a lot worse."

47

THURSDAY, APRIL 8

Who's On First?

HARRISBURG — Manager Jim Tracy had seen the field the
night before. He had walked out to left field, where his spikes
softly sank into the turf that only a few days before had been under
water.

He was not happy.

He had less than 48 hours before the Senators' season opener to
make a decision, or rather have the Montreal Expos —
Harrisburg's major league affiliate — make the decision for him.

The decision was on 20-year-old Cliff Floyd, considered the top
prospect on a stacked Harrisburg team already filled with the
Expos' best and brightest prospects.

To the Expos, all of those prospects were special. Floyd,
though, was a tad more special, not just in Montreal's stunningly
deep pool of talent but a tad more special in all of baseball.

Floyd reminded some of a young Willie McCovey, the Hall of
Famer who when he was 20 years old was just as tall and powerful.
Like Floyd, he was a left-handed hitter who crushed baseballs.

Unlike Floyd, McCovey was a first baseman and not an
outfielder, as Floyd mostly had been since the Expos selected him
with the 14th overall pick of the 1991 amateur draft.

While Floyd played first base in 72 of his first 191 games as a
pro, the Expos wanted to relocate him there full-time. Made sense,
too, considering the Expos already had a dynamic outfield in the
majors with Moises Alou, Marquis Grissom and Larry Walker.

They also had Rondell White stashed in Harrisburg and he was
expected one day to replace Grissom as the Expos' center fielder.

As for Floyd, he could not match the corner outfield defense
played by Alou and Walker, and since the Expos had a need at first
base, well, that made moving Floyd there inevitable.

The task of converting Floyd into a viable first basement was
given to Tracy, who spent half of seven seasons in the minors as a
first baseman with the other half in the outfield.

The transition for Floyd from the outfield to first base was
expected to be a gradual one. At least that was the plan.

And then Tracy stepped onto the field at RiverSide Stadium,
which had been underwater just days before.

THURSDAY, APRIL 8

Tracy had been told the field's drainage system, a fairly good system at that, was located in right field.

Floyd, however, was supposed to be the Senators' starting left fielder on Opening Night, which now was only a day away.

"My immediate concern was Cliff Floyd," Tracy remembered a quarter-century later, "and what it was (the Expos) wanted me to do with him from a defensive standpoint."

So, Tracy reached for the phone to call Montreal. He knew his options were limited. He could use Floyd as the designated hitter in the season opener against Albany — the Class AA affiliate of the New York Yankees and always used the DH.

WHO'S ON FIRST? CLIFF FLOYD

The Senators, though, only used the DH in games against American League affiliates like Albany. Since the Expos were a National League team that did not use the DH, Tracy did not want to use Floyd in a position he would not play in the majors.

"DH was not going to be an option," Tracy said. "Did they want me to put him out in an outfield that was completely saturated, and was going to be that way for a while?"

Tracy lamented not having more time to work with Floyd.

"We had had very little time together working at first base (in spring training)," Tracy said, "and I didn't really want to just dive into that because I really felt with the right amount of time prior to actually doing it that I could make him a pretty damn good big league first baseman, if that is what they wanted me to do with him."

First, Tracy had to find out if RiverSide Stadium would be ready for the opener. He needed to talk with Todd Vander Woude, the team's general manager.

"Woody assured me that the field was going to be wet in the outfield, but playable for Opening Night," Tracy said, "so we had to figure out what we were going to do with Cliff."

49

FRIDAY, APRIL 9
So It Begins ...

HARRISBURG — The batting order was set, in many ways predetermined by a prospect's status in the organization.

Rondell White batted first to take advantage of his speed, power and ability to get on base.

Chris Martin hit second in the order, because of his experience and ability to bunt.

Cliff Floyd batted third, because, every team's best hitter hit third and Floyd was the brightest of all the prospects to the start the Senators' 1993 season.

Floyd was followed in the order by Glenn Murray and Shane Andrews, because those two could turn fastballs into home runs.

And so went the top of Jim Tracy's batting order for Opening Night.

Where to play them, well, that was another question.

White was supposed to be the center fielder, Martin the shortstop, Floyd the left fielder with Murray in right field and Andrews at third base.

That changed as soon as Tracy arrived in the early afternoon at RiverSide Stadium and walked out to left field, Floyd's position was in a spot that still was soaked from the recent flooding that left portions of the stadium's outfield under water.

A quarter-century later, Tracy clearly remembered what he saw on his Tour de Flood and thought of how to deal with Floyd, whom everyone on the team affectionately called "Sleepy."

"That hole I saw in left field on the afternoon of Opening Night," Tracy said, "convinced me that Sleepy was going to start playing first base a whole helluva lot sooner than what our original thinking was."

Tracy kept his batting order the same, at least through the top five spots, but he switched the positions in the field.

With left field still more marsh than turf, Tracy moved White to Floyd's expected spot in left, shifted Martin to second base with Ron Krause still hobbling and slid Murray from right to center with Andrews staying at his natural position, third base.

As for Floyd, the erstwhile left fielder now was a first baseman.

50

FRIDAY, APRIL 9

GABE WHITE   **BRIEN TAYLOR**

So ended, at least for now, the drama of where to play the Montreal Expos' top prospect. Next up was Game 1 of 140, this one against the Albany Yankees.

Just as Harrisburg was to Montreal, Albany was the prized Class AA affiliate for the New York Yankees, filled with prospects. Just like the Senators.

None was brighter than left-hander Brien Taylor, whom the pundits considered the best pitching prospect in the game.

While Floyd was the 14th overall pick of the 1991 amateur draft, Taylor was No. 1. Taken by the Yankees, a reward for being the American League's worst team in 1990.

Taylor was paid a signing bonus of $1.55 million, a record at the time for amateurs. He was coming off a 1992 season in which he struck out 187 batters in 161 innings in the pitcher-friendly, Class A Florida State League. He had a fastball that approached 100 mph and hype that touted a limitless future that surely one day would take him to the Hall of Fame.

First, he had to get out of the Class AA Eastern League and, on this night, past the Harrisburg Senators.

Taylor was just 21 years old and making his Albany Yankees debut as their Opening Night starter.

So was Gabe White. Like Taylor, left-handed. Also, like Taylor, just 21. He was one of Montreal's first-round picks in the 1990 draft, and their No. 1 pitching prospect at the time.

51

FRIDAY, APRIL 9

At 7:11 p.m., White and Taylor began exchanging fastballs, and changeups designed to make batters look foolish. This went on for six innings on a typically cool April night in Harrisburg in front of a capacity crowd of 5,671 — the second largest since pro baseball returned to City Island in 1987.

White left after six innings with eight strikeouts, but trailed 2-0. Taylor should have left after six, too, having allowed just three singles and a Shane Andrews double over those innings.

Instead, Taylor lasted three batters into the seventh. That was enough for the Senators to tie the score on Andrews' leadoff walk and Rob Fitzpatrick's two-run homer to right-center. The homer came on a fastball that was Taylor's 90th and final pitch.

Two innings later, at 9:41 to be exact, the light-hitting Edgar Tovar ended the game with a two-out, opposite-field single to right off reliever Darren Hodges that scored Andrews from second base for a 3-2 victory. The win went to reliever Heath Haynes, who struck out all three batters he faced in the ninth.

Floyd and White were a combined 1-for-8 with Floyd getting that hit on a two-out, opposite-field single to left in the first.

Turned out the headlines belonged to Fitzpatrick, the gritty catcher who was an afterthought in the lineup, and Tovar, the shortstop who never was given much of a thought at all.

Fitzpatrick and Tovar combined for three of the five hits off Taylor and four of the six that the Senators totaled for the game.

Fitzpatrick later talked of again facing Taylor as he had done in 1992 in the Class A Florida State League. While he was just a .252 lifetime hitter, Fitzpatrick knew how to approach Taylor and that was to look fastball first, fight off everything else.

"I knew a little bit more about him than some of the other guys," said Fitzpatrick who also had a single to center off Taylor in the second inning.

As a catcher, he was comfortable in playing the game of think-along-with-the-pitcher.

"I don't want to say I'm a guess hitter," he said. "I'm more of an educated guesser."

EASTERN LEAGUE STANDINGS on April 9			
	Record	Pct.	GB
Reading	2-0	1.000	—
SENATORS	1-0	1.000	1/2
Bowie	1-0	1.000	1/2
Canton	1-0	1.000	1/2
Albany	0-1	.000	1 1/2
London	0-1	.000	1 1/2
New Britain	0-1	.000	1 1/2
Binghamton	0-2	.000	2

Eischen Must Wait

HARRISBURG — Today was to be the great reveal of the new Joey Eischen, the emotionally charged pitcher who in 1992 was as likely to punch out a clubhouse wall with a fist as he was to punch out a batter with a strikeout.

JOEY EISCHEN

At 22, the left-hander from West Corvina, California, was ready to show his new, more matured self in his first start of the season. Alas, he will have to wait another day as this game against the Albany Yankees was rained out, as if the already saturated turf on City Island needed more water.

Eischen's start was pushed back a day.

"He has very good stuff," Senators manager Jim Tracy said in the days leading up to Eischen's Class AA debut, "but he has to continue working very hard at learning how to pitch and how to control his emotions in the face of adversity."

Eischen was coming off a 1992 season in which he was 9-8 with a 3.08 earned run average in 26 starts at Class A West Palm Beach. He had 167 strikeouts in just under 170 innings. He also had 83 walks and a one-sided encounter with a clubhouse wall. Turned out the wall was no match for a kick and a shove from Eischen.

"It was sort of accidental, sort of not," Eischen said with a smile. "I didn't mean to make the hole as big as I did."

Or as big of an impression on the Expos that his maturity needed more tweaking than his changeup. Up to now, neither had been fully developed. That was part of the reason why the Texas Rangers shipped Eischen — their third-round pick in the 1989 amateur draft — to Montreal in the middle of the '91 season as part of the trade for pitcher Oil Can Boyd.

"What Trace was mentioning is true," Eischen said. "In the past, I'd wear my emotions on my sleeve. I have to control that."

EASTERN LEAGUE STANDINGS on April 10			
	Record	Pct.	GB
Bowie	2-0	1.000	—
Canton	2-0	1.000	—
Reading	2-0	1.000	—
SENATORS	1-0	1.000	1/2
Albany	0-1	.000	1 1/2
Binghamton	0-2	.000	2
London	0-2	.000	2
New Britain	0-2	.000	2

So Much For 140-0

HARRISBURG — The whimsical thought of a perfect 140-0 season ended early.

Like four batters into the game early

A leadoff walk to Andy Fox, a single to left by Robert Eenhoorn and Lyle Mouton's one-out homer to straightaway center gave the Albany Yankees a 3-0 lead before pitcher Joey Eischen wriggled out of the first inning.

ROB FITZPATRICK

Two more runs followed in the fourth to chase Eischen from the game and leave the Senators in a 5-1 hole on their way to a 9-6 loss before an afternoon crowd of 2,193 on City Island.

Eischen's final line before leaving with one out in the fourth: five earned runs on seven hits, four walks and a wild pitch. The Senators trimmed Albany's lead to 6-5 after seven before Albany scored three in the ninth off Chris Johnson and Yorkis Perez.

The game took 3 hours, 26 minutes to play and that meandering pace came after a 56-minute delay at the outset of the scheduled 2 p.m. start. By the time the game ended, the two pitching staffs combined for eight pitching changes and 378 total pitches.

Even the Senators' initial rally was a tedious one as they cut Albany's lead to 6-3 in the sixth with a pair of one-out, bases-loaded walks to pinch-hitters Tyrone Woods and Chris Martin.

Rob Fitzpatrick brought the Senators to within a run at 6-5 in the seventh with a two-run homer to left-center off reliever Darren Hodges. The homer was Fitzpatrick's second in as many games and gave him four hits in six at-bats of the rain-shortened series.

Albany pushed its lead to 9-5 in the ninth with another three-run homer from Joe DeBerry to left-center off Perez.

"We kept our heads up," Fitzpatrick said. "We realized we can battle back. We put ourselves in a position to win, and that's all you can ask for."

EASTERN LEAGUE STANDINGS on April 11			
	Record	Pct.	GB
Bowie	3-0	1.000	—
Canton	3-0	1.000	—
Reading	2-0	1.000	1/2
SENATORS	1-1	.500	1 1/2
Albany	1-1	.500	1 1/2
Binghamton	0-2	.000	2 1/2
London	0-3	.000	3
New Britain	0-3	.000	3

That's More Like It

HARRISBURG — This was not going to go well from the start for the New Britain Red Sox. They were, after all, a collection of journeymen who were no match for a team loaded with some of the best prospects in baseball.

RONDELL WHITE

On this night, too, New Britain was starting Tim Smith, who was coming off a 1992 season in which he led all of baseball with 20 losses, including five against a Harrisburg team not nearly as potent as its successors in '93.

Not hard to imagine what was going to happen in this game on City Island — 2-0 Harrisburg after the first inning; 4-0 after the third, thanks to Cliff Floyd's first homer in Class AA; 11-0 after the fourth and 15-1 after the sixth.

Final: 18-1, much to the delight of the 1,355 fans on City Island.

By the time the game ended, the Senators had 23 hits, a walk and two batters hit in just 53 plate appearances. Glenn Murray and Rondell White combined for eight of the 23 hits, the third-highest total for the Senators since they returned to the EL in 1987.

New Britain? One run on four hits, two of which came in starter Reid Cornelius's sixth and final inning. By then, the Senators had an 11-0 lead. Mario Brito replaced Cornelius with two outs in the sixth, retiring all four batters he faced before Archie Corbin worked the final two innings. Corbin's first appearance of the season had a shaky start with a double and a walk, but a fast finish as he struck out five of the final six batters in the game.

"You're going to have games like this during the course of a season," said manager Jim Tracy. "It's possible — although I don't think it's possible with this pitching staff — that we could be on the other end of this."

Hmm ... not likely.

EASTERN LEAGUE STANDINGS on April 12			
	Record	Pct.	GB
Canton	4-0	1.000	—
Bowie	3-0	1.000	1/2
SENATORS	2-1	.667	1 1/2
Reading	2-1	.667	1 1/2
Albany	1-2	.333	2 1/2
London	1-3	.250	3
Binghamton	0-2	.000	3
New Britain	0-4	.000	4

TUESDAY, APRIL 13
Better Late Than ...

HARRISBURG — Go figure. A night after the Eastern
League's best offense annihilated the league's worst pitching staff,
this happened. No 18 runs. No 23 hits. No rout. No easy story.

Geez, we had been spoiled already.

Instead, the Senators were stymied by New Britain right-hander
Frankie Rodriguez, one of the Boston Red Sox's top prospects who
scattered four singles over seven innings on City Island. Then, of
course, the eighth came along and, with it, the Senators' offense
awoke and New Britain went back to being, well, bad.

With Rodriguez out of the game, the Senators — trailing 2-0 —
took turns smacking around three relievers for a 3-2 victory before
a crowd of 1,554 on City Island.

First, Curtis Pride led off the bottom of the eighth by rocketing
the seventh pitch he saw from reliever Kevin Uhrhan over the wall
in right. Uhrhan then retired Chris Martin and Rondell White
before New Britain summoned Todd Fischer to face Cliff Floyd.

Lefty on lefty. Right move. Wrong result for New Britain as
Floyd smoked Fischer's 2-2 curveball over the wall in right to tie
the score at 2. The homer was Floyd's second in as many games.

Out went Fischer and, soon enough, out went the Red Sox's
chances for a win. Zack Dzafic, New Britain's third reliever of the
inning, promptly used his first four pitches to walk Rob Fitzpatrick,
who promptly stunned all with a delayed steal of second on the
next pitch before scoring on Glenn Murray's single to left.

The 3-2 lead was preserved by Yorkis Perez, who worked a
perfect ninth after two shutout innings by Mario Brito (1-0). Kirk
Rueter, in his Class AA debut, allowed two runs in six innings.

On the night after totaling 23 hits, the Senators managed seven
in this game. Just enough.

"Usually goes that
way," said Floyd, who
had three of the hits.
"You get a lot of runs and
hits the night before and
then come out and get
nothing the next night."

EASTERN LEAGUE STANDINGS on April 13			
	Record	Pct.	GB
Canton	5-0	1.000	—
SENATORS	3-1	.750	1 1/2
Bowie	3-2	.600	2
Binghamton	2-2	.500	2 1/2
Reading	2-2	.500	2 1/2
London	2-3	.400	3
Albany	1-3	.250	3 1/2
New Britain	0-5	.000	5

Pavlov's Senators

HARRISBURG — Pavlov in the 1890s had his salivating dogs. Seemed each time old Ivan showed up with a bell, his dogs thought they were going to be fed.

GLENN MURRAY

Pavlov's experiment still was around a century later. Only the dogs here were the Senators with the stimuli being New Britain's bullpen. Chomp.

For the second straight night, the Senators devoured the Red Sox's pen, scoring six runs in the eighth inning to rally for a 7-2 victory before a crowd of 3,243 on City Island.

The victory was the third straight for the Senators, who swept the winless and, so far, utterly hopeless Red Sox.

The six-run outburst came against New Britain starter Ed Riley and beleaguered reliever Zack Dzalic, who in facing the Senators for a second straight game gave up five runs on six hits and a walk.

"It's like, 'Let's go,' " leadoff hitter Rondell White said of the late rally. "Like, 'Let's turn it up another notch.' "

The notch turned out to be a choke hold as the Senators sent 12 batters to the plate in the eighth. White drove home the first run with a single, tying the score at 2. Three batters later, Glenn Murray singled to left for two more runs and a 4-2 lead.

Murray's game-winning hit was nearly identical to his one from 24 hours earlier, a single to left field off the sinkerball-happy Dzalic with each single giving the Senators the lead.

Murray also accounted for Harrisburg's first run with a solo homer off Riley to lead off the fifth. His second homer of the season provided a 1-0 lead for starter Gabe White, who tired after six no-hit innings. Rafael Diaz (1-0) gave up two runs in two innings, but stayed in long enough for the rally.

"I don't know what it is with that team," Murray said, "but when those guys come in from the bullpen, we're on them."

EASTERN LEAGUE STANDINGS on April 14			
	Record	Pct.	GB
Canton	6-0	1.000	—
SENATORS	4-1	.800	1 1/2
Bowie	4-2	.667	2
Reading	3-2	.600	2 1/2
Albany	2-2	.500	3
Binghamton	2-3	.400	3 1/2
London	2-4	.400	4
New Britain	0-6	.000	6

57

THURSDAY, APRIL 15
From Starter to Goner

HARRISBURG — Coming out of spring training, the plan was to use Chris Johnson out of the bullpen with an occasional start.

Johnson, a starter for nearly all of his time with the Senators in 1991 and '92, had little choice with prospects Gabe White, Joey Eischen, Reid Cornelius, Kirk Rueter and Miguel Batista already in the rotation for '93. Johnson also knew he needed to throw more than fastballs and sliders to last as a starter.

"If I had a good change or curveball, I might want to be a starter," Johnson said, "but my stuff is more for relief."

CHRIS JOHNSON

Only not for the Senators. Johnson, 24, became the season's first roster casualty as the Expos — less than two years after picking up Johnson from Milwaukee — sent him to the Chicago Cubs as the player to be named later from an earlier trade for outfielder Scott Bryant. Johnson appeared in one game this season, allowing two runs over just 1 1/3 innings in the previous Sunday's 9-6 loss to Albany.

Johnson still found his way into the Senators' record book. At 6-foot-8, he was the tallest player in modern-franchise history, a height not surpassed until 6-10 pitcher Chris Young joined the Senators in 2003.

FRIDAY, APRIL 16

COLONIE, N.Y. — Left-hander Darrin Winston arrived today from extended spring training in Florida to replace Chris Johnson in the bullpen. No need, though, to get into uniform just yet, because it's April, it's Albany and, of course, it's raining. No game tonight at Heritage Park. Might play tomorrow. Not likely.

SATURDAY, APRIL 17

COLONIE, N.Y. — Rain. Rinse. Repeat.
Doubleheader tomorrow. Maybe.

Finally, Some Games

COLONIE, N.Y. — A scheduled day off followed by two rainouts. No shock then that the Senators were a tad slow in starting their doubleheader here against the Albany Yankees.

OK, real slow in Game 1 as Miguel Batista made his season debut one to quickly forget as he managed to record only five outs as the Yankees raced to a 7-1 lead en route to winning the opener 8-5 before a crowd of 1,409 at Heritage Park.

The Senators won the second game 6-0.

In all fairness to Batista (0-1), the Senators were quite New Britainesque in the first game by committing five errors after making just four of them in the season's first five games.

Curtis Pride hit his second homer of the season, a solo shot in the third off Albany starter Mark Carper. Carper also gave up Oreste Marrero's first homer — a three-run drive — in the fifth inning that cut Albany's once healthy lead to 7-5.

"We did a helluva job, as we've done for seven games, fighting our way back into it," manager Jim Tracy said.

"You get down 7-1 in a seven-inning game, it's very easy at times to shut it down. We kept battling"

Normalcy returned in the second game as Reid Cornelius (2-0) allowed a single to Kevin Jordan with one out in the second and nothing else as he struck out eight in six innings. Archie Corbin pitched a perfect seventh and final inning of the 6-0 shutout.

Shane Andrews' RBI single in the second gave the Senators the only run they needed to beat Rafael Quirico.

Rob Fitzpatrick, the regular catcher-turned-DH in the second game, and regular backup catcher Miah Bradbury broke open the game in the fifth as Fitzpatrick followed Murray's RBI double with a two-run homer and Bradbury added a solo homer for a 5-0 lead.

"Cornelius just got ahead of us," Albany manager Mike Hart said.

"He just stayed ahead of us the whole game, and that's the essence of good pitching."

EASTERN LEAGUE STANDINGS on April 18			
	Record	Pct.	GB
Canton	9-0	1.000	—
Reading	6-2	.750	2 1/2
SENATORS	5-2	.714	3
Bowie	5-4	.555	4
London	4-5	.444	5
Albany	2-5	.286	6
Binghamton	2-6	.250	6 1/2
New Britain	0-9	.000	9

Staying In The Zone

NEW BRITAIN, Conn. — Senators manager Jim Tracy and Gomer Hodge, the Expos' minor league hitting instructor, never had trouble starting a conversation. They began with hitting, followed by more hitting and, finally, even more hitting.

They shared those conversations with Tracy's hitters, already the Eastern League's best offense. Not quite fair to the rest of the league, like giving honors students an open book test. Every day.

"I preach to all of our players to stay within the strike zone," Tracy said.

Among those listening was catcher Rob Fitzpatrick, the owner of a pedestrian .252 batting average over his first three pro seasons who through the first seven games this season was hitting .400 with 10 hits and three homers in 25 at-bats.

He added to those totals in this game, picking up two more hits and another home run in an 11-5 victory over the New Britain Red Sox before a smattering of 839 fans at Beehive Field.

Fitzpatrick's team-high fourth homer gave the Senators at least one home run in each of their first eight games.

"We worked with Fitty in the middle to the end of spring training," Tracy said. "We got him to keep his hands out a little farther away from his body. Fitty has been disciplined at swinging at pitches inside the zone, and he is getting good pitches to hit."

Everyone was getting good pitches to hit from the dreadful Sox.

The Senators piled up 12 hits in only 37 at-bats with Fitzpatrick, Shane Andrews and Oreste Marrero combining for seven hits.

Joey Eischen (1-1) picked up the victory while dodging three runs on six hits and four walks over five laborious innings.

Heath Haynes worked two more perfect innings — the sixth and seventh. He retired all 12 batters he had faced so far this season.

"You have to feel for them with losing their first 10 games," Tracy said of the luckless Red Sox.

"But," Tracy said, "you can't let them up."

EASTERN LEAGUE STANDINGS on April 19			
	Record	Pct.	GB
Canton	9 - 1	.900	—
SENATORS	6 - 2	.750	2
Reading	6 - 3	.667	2 1/2
Bowie	6 - 4	.600	3
London	5 - 5	.500	4
Albany	3 - 5	.375	5
Binghamton	2 - 7	.222	6 1/2
New Britain	0 - 10	.000	9

TUESDAY, APRIL 20
The Beat Goes On

NEW BRITAIN, Conn. — The pounding continued here. Eight more runs. Eleven more hits. Another victory for the Senators over the winless and (insert your own adjective here for lousy) New Britain Red Sox.

This one ended 8-4 before 1,079 fans at Beehive Field as the Senators beat the Red Sox for the fifth time in as many games and they did so without needing another outstanding start by Gabe White, the Montreal Expos' top pitching prospect.

White (2-0) entered the game with seven straight hitless, scoreless innings, a streak that quickly ended on Boo Moore's two-run, two-out double in the first inning.

Solo homers by Rob Fitzpatrick — who else? — in the second inning and Glenn Murray in the fourth tied the score at 2 before the Red Sox took a 3-2 lead in the bottom of the fourth.

Like that was going to last.

Chris Martin's two-out RBI single tied the score in the fifth inning before an RBI single by Shane Andrews and back-to-back doubles by Miah Bradbury and Tyrone Woods in the sixth gave the Senators a 6-3 lead.

White pitched through the sixth, allowing three runs on nine hits and leaving with a three-run lead.

New Britain scored a so-what run off reliever Yorkis Perez in the seventh before Andrews hit a solo homer — his first of the season — in the eighth and Martin had his second RBI single for the Senators' final run in the ninth.

Martin's hit was the Senators' last of the game, giving them 23 over the last 24 hours against the Red Sox, who were outscored 19-9 in their last two losses against the Senators and 47-14 in five games against them so far this season.

The solo homers by Fitzpatrick, Murray and Andrews pushed the Senators' total to 15 in the season's first nine games.

EASTERN LEAGUE STANDINGS on April 20			
	Record	Pct.	GB
Canton	10 - 1	.909	—
SENATORS	7 - 2	.778	2
Reading	7 - 3	.700	2 1/2
Bowie	7 - 4	.636	3
London	5 - 6	.455	5
Albany	3 - 6	.333	6
Binghamton	2 - 8	.200	7 1/2
New Britain	0 - 11	.000	10

Playing Little Ball

NEW BRITAIN, Conn. — For the first time in 10 games, the Senators did not hit a home run. Didn't matter, either. Not so long as the New Britain Red Sox were on the schedule.

So, instead of again pile driving the Red Sox into the turf, the Senators bolted to a 4-0 lead by the third inning and then held on for a 4-3 victory before fewer than 700 fans at Beehive Field.

They took a 2-0 lead on RBI singles by Chris Martin in the first inning and Edgar Tovar in the second. Two more runs came in the third when Martin scored on the front end of a double steal and Cliff Floyd followed with an RBI single to score Rondell White, who moments earlier had been on the back end of that double steal.

White preceded the double steal with a single to center, a desperately needed hit that snapped his 0-for-17 skid.

The beneficiary of the Senators' early offense was starter Kirk Rueter (1-0), who allowed only one earned run on five hits through seven innings. Seven strikeouts. No walks. Nicely done.

Rueter's earned-run average dropped to 1.93 after three starts, second among the starters only to Reid Cornelius' 0.77 ERA after his first two starts.

Rueter then had to sit through an arduous final two innings as the Red Sox scored an unearned run off the previously impervious Heath Haynes in the eighth before putting two runners on base in the ninth against Archie Corbin. Corbin, though, ended the game by striking out Scott Bethea on a 3-2 pitch to clinch the Senators' second three-game sweep of the Red Sox in two weeks.

In those six games, the Senators outscored New Britain 51-17. Since the start of the 1992 season, they had won 23 of 26 games against the Boston's beleaguered Class AA team.

Half of New Britain's losses so far had come against the Senators. The other half had been against league-leading Canton. Sometimes, life just isn't fair.

EASTERN LEAGUE STANDINGS on April 21			
	Record	Pct.	GB
Canton	10 - 2	.833	—
SENATORS	8 - 2	.800	1
Bowie	8 - 3	.727	1 1/2
Reading	7 - 4	.636	2 1/2
London	5 - 7	.417	5
Albany	4 - 6	.400	5
Binghamton	2 - 8	.200	7
New Britain	0 - 12	.000	10

THURSDAY, APRIL 22

HARRISBURG — Day off. Time to get caught up on laundry.

FRIDAY, APRIL 23

Working Overtime

HARRISBURG — Sometimes, you do little right and still win. That happens to good teams, and the Senators were quite good in winning eight of their first 10 games. OK, six of those wins were over New Britain, but who knew the Red Sox would be so awful?

Finally, a good team showed up on the schedule with the Bowie Baysox, who wasted the early chances they had in this game before losing 2-1 in 10 innings before 2,309 fans on City Island.

The Senators scored the winning run on a two-out throwing error by shortstop Tim Holland. The rally started on Shane Andrews' single to left and Miah Bradbury's sacrifice bunt off Jim Dedrick, who then stuck out pinch-hitter Curtis Pride before intentionally walking pinch-hitter Ron Krause with two outs.

Rondell White then bounced a ball to Holland, whose high throw pulled first baseman T.R. Lewis off the bag as Andrews rounded third base on his way to the plate with the winning run.

The Senators' victory came after relievers Rafael Diaz, Mario Brito and Heath Haynes (2-0) combined for six innings of two-hit, scoreless relief for the previously reliable Reid Cornelius, who struggled through 87 pitches in only four innings.

Not that the Senators' offense did much against Bowie starter Rick Krivda, one of the Baltimore Orioles' top pitching prospects who in seven innings allowed just five hits while striking out six.

One of those five hits was a solo homer to right in the fourth inning by Cliff Floyd, who entered the game with just four hits in 19 at-bats off left-handers like Krivda. Floyd had three hits off Krivda to hike his early batting average against lefties from .214 to .318.

"We dodged some bullets tonight," manager Jim Tracy said.

"No doubt about it."

EASTERN LEAGUE STANDINGS on April 23			
	Record	Pct.	GB
Canton	11 - 2	.846	—
SENATORS	9 - 2	.818	1
Bowie	9 - 4	.692	2
Reading	7 - 5	.583	3 1/2
London	5 - 7	.417	5 1/2
Albany	4 - 6	.400	5 1/2
Binghamton	2 - 10	.167	8 1/2
New Britain	1 - 12	.077	10

63

SATURDAY, APRIL 24
Back In The Game

HARRISBURG — For the season's first two weeks, the Senators showed a swagger unlike any other Harrisburg team since pro baseball returned to City Island in 1987.

DARRIN WINSTON

Cocky? No. Confident. Oh, yeah. The attitude permeated their clubhouse full of alpha males.

Except for one. Reliever Darrin Winston. At 26, the soft-spoken Winston was one of the oldest players on the league's youngest team.

He also had not thrown a pitch in anger since undergoing elbow surgery in September 1991. While so many of his new teammates were constantly moving up on the Montreal Expos' burgeoning list of prospects, Winston simply was hoping the surgeons knew what they were doing 18 months earlier in rebuilding his left elbow.

"I've been waiting for this chance for a year and a half," Winston said.

The chance finally came in this game, a 5-3 victory over Bowie before a crowd of 2,592 on City Island.

After replacing starter Miguel Batista (1-1) to start the sixth, Winston allowed just one hit while striking out four in two innings.

"It's a pleasure just to be out here again," Winston said. "It's been an uphill battle. I'm in a proving process all over again. ... Now, I have to keep producing."

He was the latest to produce out of the bullpen, where six relievers so far had combined for a skinny 1.23 ERA in 40 innings.

"We know we have a lot of depth there," Cliff Floyd said. "We feel confident when they're in there," he said. "We don't feel that we have to help them out, thinking, 'Oh, we better do something, because they're going to get hit hard.' "

More like they hardly get hit. So far anyway.

EASTERN LEAGUE STANDINGS on April 24			
	Record	Pct.	GB
Canton	11 - 2	.846	—
SENATORS	10 - 2	.833	1/2
Bowie	9 - 5	.643	2 1/2
Reading	7 - 5	.583	3 1/2
Albany	6 - 6	.500	4 1/2
London	5 - 9	.357	6 1/2
Binghamton	3 - 10	.231	8
New Britain	1 - 13	.000	10 1/2

Crash Course In Loss

HARRISBURG — Gabe White's day started at 6 a.m., when a motorist rammed into White's parked car outside his home.

GABE WHITE

The back end of White's Ford Probe, the one just brought here from Florida, was totaled. The rest of his day wasn't much better.

White, the prized left-hander, and three relief pitchers were victims of their teammates' shoddy defense in losing 6-5 to the Bowie Baysox in 10 innings before 4,041 fans on City Island.

"No big deal," White said. "There are many more days ahead."

Good, because this one was forgettable as the Senators' defense totaled five errors and a passed ball that led to five unearned runs while their offense botched a suicide squeeze. The rare ineptitude cost the Senators their six-game winning streak.

"I'll go on the record with this," manager Jim Tracy said, "that this group won't play like this too many times."

The only earned run Bowie scored came in the 10th inning, when Gregg Zaun's sacrifice fly off Archie Corbin (0-1) chased home Stanton Cameron. Bowie's Rafael Chaves pitched a perfect 10th inning to save the victory for Tom Taylor, who allowed four runs in the eighth as the Senators rallied to briefly take a 5-4 lead.

The Senators might have had more runs in the eighth had Shane Andrews not been caught at home when Rob Fitzpatrick missed Tracy's sign for a squeeze bunt. Andrews' out was the second of the eighth. Fitzpatrick followed with a strikeout to end the inning.

Bowie, which had four unearned runs off White, tied the score in the ninth on another unearned run. While White dropped his ERA to 1.90, his thoughts were elsewhere.

"The car was on my mind. I wasn't sharp," he said. "At least I didn't get anybody hurt, and we showed we can come back."

EASTERN LEAGUE STANDINGS on April 25			
	Record	Pct.	GB
Canton	12 - 2	.857	—
SENATORS	10 - 3	.769	1 1/2
Bowie	10 - 5	.667	2 1/2
Albany	7 - 6	.538	4 1/2
Reading	7 - 6	.538	4 1/2
London	5 - 11	.313	8
Binghamton	3 - 11	.214	9
New Britain	3 - 13	.188	10

Working The Off Day

HARRISBURG — A three-town, nine-game road trip was about to start, so the Senators enjoyed a rare off day today.

Most of them anyway. Rondell White did not rest. No time for that, not in the midst of a dreadful 4-for-34 slump.

A day earlier, White looked as if he might be emerging from that skid as he drilled a 1-1 pitch from Bowie's Jason Satre over the wall in left-center in his first at-bat of Sunday's 6-5 loss to the Baysox. Alas, four hitless at-bats followed. So here was one of baseball's best prospects — on a scheduled day off for the team — back at RiverSide Stadium to hit off a batting tee.

"Sometimes," he said, "I just say, 'Hey, guys, what's wrong with me with me?' But I've learned you can't really get down on yourself. I know I'll come around. Last year, I started slowly and tried to laugh it off. I was just smiling and laughing."

Last year, White batted .316 in 111 games for Class A West Palm Beach. This year, he was hitting .218 in 13 games.

"We're doing everything but talking baseball with him," first baseman Cliff Floyd said. "We're trying to take his mind off of it."

"I've been going to the movies, getting out of the house," White said. "If you sit around the house, you just end up thinking about it more."

Hasn't worked, which is why White was back on City Island to refine his swing before leaving on a road trip to Canton, Reading and Bowie. Nine games in nine days with White expected to play every one of those games in center field.

"I'm trying to be so quick on the ball inside and trying to turn on it," White said. "I'm missing on pitches I should hit."

"Rondell just has to realize that he has to hit the ball in the field and not up into the trees," manager Jim Tracy said. "The main thing he can ill afford to do is spin off the baseball. If he does that, then he becomes very susceptible at the plate."

EASTERN LEAGUE STANDINGS on April 26			
	Record	Pct.	GB
Canton	12 - 2	.857	—
SENATORS	10 - 3	.769	1 1/2
Bowie	10 - 5	.667	2 1/2
Albany	7 - 6	.538	4 1/2
Reading	7 - 6	.538	4 1/2
London	5 - 11	.313	8
Binghamton	3 - 11	.214	9
New Britain	3 - 13	.188	10

Slow Start, Fast Finish

CANTON, Ohio — They had combined to play 27 games and, between them, Canton and Harrisburg had won 22 of those games.

Now, for the first time in the still-young Eastern League season, the two met here at dimly-lit, monochromatic Thurman Munson Memorial Stadium.

"That ballpark was gloomy," Senators outfielder Curtis Pride remembered a quarter-century later.

The dreary ballpark, named for one of grittiest catchers ever to play the game, housed the Cleveland Indians' top prospects.

Manny Ramirez. David Bell. Brian Giles. Paul Shuey.

Canton was loaded.

So were the Senators, of course, with Montreal's best and brightest.

Canton was not a team you wanted to give an early lead, which was exactly what Senators starter Joey Eischen did in a game the Senators eventually won 6-4 before a crowd of 1,955.

Eischen allowed four of Canton's first five batters to reach base and found himself trailing 3-0 before he finally escaped the inning.

Somehow, manager Jim Tracy found the compassion to stick with Eischen (2-1). Eischen quickly found his command as he held Canton to one run on four more hits while striking out seven before leaving with one out in the seventh and the Senators leading 6-4.

While Eischen was recovering, the Senators cobbled together single runs in the second, fifth and sixth innings before taking the lead with a three-run rally in the seventh. Those last three runs came on singles by Rondell White and Glenn Murray that bracketed an RBI groundout by Cliff Floyd.

From there, Heath Haynes and Archie Corbin worked the final three innings, allowing just one hit while striking out six, including Bell and Jose Hernandez to end the game.

Turned out this was the last night the Senators spent out of first place.

EASTERN LEAGUE STANDINGS on April 27			
	Record	Pct.	GB
Canton	12 - 3	.800	—
SENATORS	11 - 3	.786	1/2
Bowie	11 - 6	.647	2
Reading	8 - 7	.533	4
Albany	7 - 7	.500	4 1/2
London	6 - 11	.353	7
Binghamton	4 - 11	.267	8
New Britain	3 - 14	.176	10

Rising To The Top

CANTON, Ohio — No team outside of Harrisburg had a better offense in the Eastern League than the Canton Indians. They had Cleveland's top prospect in right fielder Manny Ramirez, who would become a perennial All-Star in the American League. For now, Ramirez was the most dangerous hitter in a lineup full of dangerous hitters destined for the majors.

TIM BARKER

Not that any of that mattered to Kirk Rueter, who entered this game with a 1.93 ERA that dropped to 1.23 by the time he left. In between, the left-hander scattered six hits over eight shutout innings in a 9-1 victory before 2,095 here. The victory moved the Senators into first place.

Once again, the offense came from everywhere, starting in the first inning with a pair of RBI singles by newly arrived Tim Barker and Shane Andrews. Two more runs came in the fourth on solo homers by Cliff Floyd and Glenn Murray off top pitching prospect Paul Shuey.

The 4-0 lead was plenty for the metronome-like Rueter (2-0), who recorded 16 of his 24 outs on groundballs with 13 of those grounders going to either Barker at shortstop or Andrews at third.

EDGAR TOVAR

As for Barker, who 48 hours ago was en route from Class AAA Ottawa to Harrisburg, the onetime Dodgers prospect finished with two of the Senators' 11 hits.

Over two games with the Senators, Barker had five hits — all singles — in 10 at-bats. Barker, acquired four months earlier from Los Angeles in a deal for All-Star third baseman Tim Wallach, replaced Edgar Tovar on the roster. Tovar, the Opening Night shortstop, was hitting .262 in 12 games. That was not bad.

Sadly, his four errors in just 12 games were.

EASTERN LEAGUE STANDINGS on April 28			
	Record	Pct.	GB
SENATORS	12 - 3	.800	—
Canton	12 - 4	.750	1/2
Bowie	12 - 6	.667	1 1/2
Albany	8 - 7	.533	4
Reading	8 - 8	.500	4 1/2
London	7 - 11	.389	6 1/2
Binghamton	4 - 12	.250	8 1/2
New Britain	3 - 15	.167	10 1/2

Not For Prime Time

READING, Pa. — Every so often, the Reading Phillies had their games televised back to Philadelphia by SportsChannel.

"To be honest," said Reading first baseman Ron Lockett, "that, and playing at home, gets you a little more pumped."

Exploiting Harrisburg's suddenly shaky defense did not hurt, either. With two more errors, giving them 11 in the last five games, the Senators lost 7-3 before a crowd of 2,437 at old Municipal Stadium. Who knew how many were watching in Philadelphia?

The errors by third baseman Shane Andrews and starter Reid Cornelius (2-1) led to Reading's first five runs with Lockett driving in two of them on a single that capped a three-run fifth inning for a 5-3 lead. Lockett accounted for the final two runs with a homer in the eighth off Rafael Diaz.

"If you replay this game," manger Jim Tracy said, "you're going to find several mistakes that set up big innings for them."

No one from Harrisburg wanted to see a replay of this game.

Three Reading pitchers held the Senators to six hits, but only two after the fourth inning. Didn't help the Senators that top prospect Cliff Floyd sat out with a sore right hand.

Also, for the first time this season, Harrisburg — in playing a National League affiliate like Reading — did not have a designated hitter to bolster the Eastern League's best offense.

Ron Krause, playing in only his seventh game while splitting time at second base with Chris Martin, had three of the Senators' six hits as he raised his batting average from .300 to .375.

"We gave them too many outs," Tracy said. "We gave them three runs (in the fifth) after two outs and nobody on base. You can't win too many games like that."

Not that the Senators had played many games like this so far, although lately their defensive woes had been covered up by their explosive offense.

Just not in this game.

EASTERN LEAGUE STANDINGS on April 29			
	Record	Pct.	GB
SENATORS	12 - 4	.750	—
Canton	12 - 5	.706	1/2
Bowie	13 - 6	.684	1/2
Reading	9 - 8	.529	3 1/2
Albany	8 - 8	.500	4
London	8 - 11	.421	5 1/2
Binghamton	4 - 13	.235	8 1/2
New Britain	4 - 15	.211	9 1/2

Promotion? No, Thanks

READING, Pa. — Curtis Pride, pinch-hitting for Tyrone Woods, launched one of Toby Borland's side-armed fastballs over the wall in right field, a two-out, two-run homer in the ninth inning that lifted the Senators over the Reading Phillies 4-3.

Turned out the news from the game became secondary to the sidebar.

While Pride was talking after the game about the importance of waiting on a particular pitch, catcher Miah Bradbury was holed up three miles away in his hotel room at the Wellesley Inn.

A few hours earlier, Pride and Bradbury were teammates, but that was before manager Jim Tracy told the 25-year-old Bradbury he was being promoted to the Expos' Class AAA team in Ottawa.

Seems Ottawa's top catcher — former Senator Tim Laker — was hurt. Instead of packing his gear for Ottawa, though, Bradbury told Tracy he was packing up. Quitting. Going home to San Diego. Four years in the minors, he said, was enough. See ya.

Tracy was stunned because, well, nobody ever turned down a promotion that moved you one step away from the majors, especially a player who was batting .313 in nine games as Rob Fitzpatrick's backup.

"I was so excited to call Miah in," Tracy remembered a quarter-century later, "because it was always a gratifying feeling when you managed in the minors leagues to call one of your players in and see their reaction when you let them know that they were advancing to the next level.

"In comes Miah and when I informed him that he was headed for Ottawa, he looked right at me and informed me that he was going home instead," Tracy said. "I was shocked and tried to steer him in the other direction, but to no avail. I really didn't get a good response from him, but reading between the lines, I can only assume that he had lost interest in being a backup catcher, which is what he would have done if he would have decided to go there."

Tracy quickly called Kent Qualls, the Expos' director of minor league operations. Qualls told Bradbury to go back to the hotel and wait there.

FRIDAY, APRIL 30

"We're going to give him a day or two to get his thoughts together," Qualls said at the time.

Did not matter if Qualls gave Bradbury a day or two or 22. He was not returning, a decision that years later still perplexed Tracy.

"What I tried to explain to him," Tracy recalled, "and what I had observed over my 18 years as a manager in the minor leagues and big leagues, was that there had been more than a few guys that were backup catchers in the minor leagues, find their way to the big leagues and end up making a nice career for themselves due to the injury factor and demand at the position.

"He was not going to change his mind."

Not everyone at the time was shocked by Bradbury's decision.

"Miah's an older player (for Double-A)," relief pitcher Heath Haynes said. "He's used to playing every day. Here, he was the No. 2 catcher. Some people can't handle that."

"I wasn't really all that surprised," said infielder Chris Martin, who played against Bradbury in college and lockered next to him for the first month of the season. "He told me a couple of weeks ago that he was going back to school for his master's (degree) in June, no matter what."

That would have been handy information for the Expos to know, but Martin kept that nugget to himself.

"When a guy gets to go to play Triple-A ball and he doesn't want to go, you have to wonder what the hell is going on," said Herm Starrette, the Expos' minor league field coordinator. "We had no indication."

With Bradbury gone, the Expos activated Senators coach Greg Fulton as Fitzpatrick's emergency backup.

Fulton, in his first season as a coach, was released in spring training by the Expos, who had no roster spot for him at Class AAA Ottawa but wanted to keep him in the organization as an old head for the young, prospect-packed team on its way to Harrisburg.

The Expos also told Fulton to keep in shape.

Just in case.

How prophetic of them.

EASTERN LEAGUE STANDINGS on April 30			
	Record	Pct.	GB
SENATORS	13- 4	.765	—
Bowie	14- 6	.700	1/2
Canton	12- 6	.667	1 1/2
Albany	9- 8	.529	4
Reading	9- 9	.500	4 1/2
London	8-12	.400	6 1/2
Binghamton	5-13	.278	8 1/2
New Britain	4-16	.200	10 1/2

SATURDAY, MAY 1

Getting An Opportunity

READING, Pa. — Coming out of spring training, backup outfielder Tyrone Woods knew his best chances to contribute to the Senators would come against left-handed pitching.

TYRONE WOODS

Which made perfect sense, given Woods' right-handedness and his penchant for hitting balls harder and farther than most players in the Class AA Eastern League.

One problem: He had just two hits in 18 at-bats against lefties in the first 17 games.

With Cliff Floyd having moved from left field to first base, manager Jim Tracy hoped to platoon Woods and Curtis Pride in the outfield. But Pride was hitting, Woods was not. No matter as Tracy gave Woods another chance here in a game against a Reading left-hander named Mike Farmer. Nice move.

All Woods did was homer in each of his first two at-bats against Farmer to start a 7-2 victory before a crowd of 5,330. Floyd and Glenn Murray also homered, but their homers no longer were news. That Woods finally started to hit, well, that was news.

"Over the last couple of days, I've been working on hitting down on the ball," Woods said. "They keep telling me just to hit the ball hard and the home runs will happen on their own."

Woods nearly had a third homer in the eighth, but his drive to center against left-hander Scott Wiegandt went off the wall for a double. Woods' homers accounted for the first multi-homer game this season by a Senator.

"Just been trying to keep up with the other guys," Woods said with a smile. Tracy also smiled.

"He hadn't been getting too many hits against anybody to this point," Tracy said.

"But the players know I'm not going to quit on them. They knew they're going to keep getting opportunities."

EASTERN LEAGUE STANDINGS on May 1			
	Record	Pct.	GB
SENATORS	14 - 4	.778	—
Canton	13 - 6	.684	1 1/2
Bowie	14 - 7	.667	1 1/2
Albany	10 - 8	.556	4
Reading	9 - 10	.474	5 1/2
London	8 - 13	.381	7 1/2
Binghamton	6 - 13	.316	8 1/2
New Britain	4 - 17	.190	11 1/2

Playing Catch Up

READING, Pa. — When Greg Fulton went from being a player to a coach late in spring training he was told to be ready, just in case.

Those three words — *just in case* — were ones nobody with the Senators wanted to hear.

Until today's game, when they were forced to hear them, when the scenario arrived at the most inopportune time.

With catcher Rob Fitzpatrick ejected after his first at-bat — for littering the field with paper cups after striking out — and his erstwhile backup, Miah Bradbury, now in the third day of his abrupt retirement, the Senators

GREG FULTON

were forced to use Fulton to catch the last eight innings of what eventually was a 7-5 victory over the Reading Phillies.

"I was battling the whole time," said Fulton, who only 48 hours earlier was activated when Bradbury opted to retire rather than accept a promotion to Class AAA Ottawa.

That was strange enough.

Fulton behind the plate was even stranger, especially when he was tasked with catching the hard-throwing, often-erratic Joey Eischen.

Fulton, as uncomfortable as he was behind the plate, was the poster child for a game that lacked any sense of rhythm, a game that included 11 stolen bases, five wild pitches, 29 strikeouts, a passed ball by Fulton and 5,906 pairs of glazed-over eyes at Reading's old Municipal Stadium.

ROB FITZPATRICK

Oh, add to the total one dented chest, which relief pitcher Heath Haynes received when he was nailed with Fulton's throw to second base on Ron Lockett's seventh-inning stolen base.

Haynes survived into the ninth inning, but not before ducking and covering on the mound when Fulton looked to throw out the next Phillie trying to steal second.

73

SUNDAY, MAY 2

"I took it one pitch at a time, one batter at a time and one-half inning at a time," said the 30-year-old Fulton, who retired at the end of spring training after playing eight years in the minors.

Fulton last caught in a game on June 2, 1991, when he handled the eighth and ninth innings of the Senators' 11-0 rout of Williamsport on City Island.

Those innings were his fifth and sixth behind the plate in a pro career that totaled 821 games.

"I added a couple of more to that total," Fulton said.

"To be put in a position like that," manager Jim Tracy said when asked of Fulton's day, "that was one helluva effort."

As Tracy spoke, Fulton slowly packed his equipment bag for the bus ride to Bowie, the final leg of a nine-game road trip.

"He'll be asleep on the bus before the first full revolution of the tires," Tracy said.

Fulton's day included six Reading steals in as many attempts, a passed ball, three strikeouts in which he recorded the out with a throw to first base and three more strikeouts in which he tagged out the batter.

"I was a little concerned, too, about him almost decapitating Haynes," Tracy said with a smile.

Hideous stats aside, Fulton's effort provided a morale boost.

"I just told Fulty, 'Let's have some fun,' " said Eischen (3-1), who overcame his usual shaky first inning to strike out a season-high 11 batters before leaving in the sixth with a 3-2 lead.

"Punchouts take a lot of effort," Eischen said, "and we worked well together."

Among Fulton's greatest supporters was Fitzpatrick, who in the midst of a 1-for-25 slump was banished to the clubhouse by umpire Brad Geaslin for tossing a couple of hundred water cups onto the field after his strikeout in the top of the second.

"I sat here listening to the game on the radio," Fitzpatrick said later in the clubhouse.

"I felt awful, putting the team in this situation. He picked me up, as well as the whole team."

EASTERN LEAGUE STANDINGS on May 2			
	Record	Pct.	GB
SENATORS	15 - 4	.789	—
Bowie	15 - 7	.682	1 1/2
Canton	13 - 7	.650	2 1/2
Albany	10 - 9	.526	5
Reading	9 - 11	.450	6 1/2
London	8 - 14	.364	8 1/2
Binghamton	7 - 13	.350	8 1/2
New Britain	5 - 17	.227	11 1/2

Fume Then, Laugh Now

Jim Tracy laughs now about that long-ago Sunday afternoon in Reading, where he specifically told catcher Rob Fitzapatrick that he could not get ejected from the game, only to have the Senators' starting catcher — their only catcher that day — turn around and promptly get himself ejected.

JIM TRACY

In the top of the second #$%!* inning.

What followed was eight harrowing innings for coach-turned-emergency catcher Greg Fulton, who allowed six steals in six attempts and drilled reliever Heath Haynes in the chest with one of his throws to second base.

Even though the Senators won 7-5, Tracy was not amused that Fitzpatrick put the team — and Fulton — in that situation.

A quarter-century later, Tracy remembered the couple of hundred water cups that Fitzpatrick tossed onto the field after being called out on strikes in the second inning.

Tracy also remembered his pregame words to Fitzpatrick, his in-game worries for Fulton and his suddenly urgent anticipation of the arrival of new backup catcher Lance Rice.

"I told Fitty that no matter what happens as far as his situation is concerned that he was not to utter a word to an umpire regardless of the situation," Tracy said years later.

"He was completely aware of what we were dealing with at the time, with Fulty of all people being the only guy who could replace him temporarily until Lance Rice arrived. I really can't remember the circumstances that took place to get him ejected, but I had him informed as he came toward our dugout to find someplace in the clubhouse where I couldn't find him and, hopefully, as a result, he would survive at least until the game was over.

"When he got ejected, I muttered a lot of different words that would not be suitable for this book.

LOOKING BACK

"My major concern was two-fold.

"One, getting Fulty hurt badly because I believe it was Joey Eischen that was our starting pitcher that day and he was a very difficult guy to catch especially with that wicked curveball he possessed. There were a lot of breaking balls that were going to have to be blocked.

"Two, messing Joey up having to throw to a guy who, no disrespect meant, was a borderline emergency catcher at best.

"Oh my God, reliving it right after the game ended … thinking about it again …

JOEY EISCHEN

because of the fact that we won the game and Joey came out of it unscathed, we laughed our asses off about it and had a lot of fun as a club at the expense of Fulty and Fitty.

"But rest assured, what Fulty did that day left an unbelievable positive mark as far as how every guy in a Harrisburg uniform,

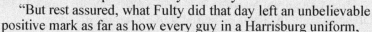

"When (Fitzpatrick) got ejected I muttered a lot of different words that would not be suitable for this book."

Manager Jim Tracy

including myself, perceived him as a person and a player. His completely unselfish nature was on center stage that day.

"Here is what I remember about those last eight innings that afternoon: Fulty was nervous as hell about what it

was that he was facing. I tried to lighten the air with regard to the situation, although I was still incensed with Fitty and what had just happened with his ejection.

"I told Fulty not to put too much pressure on himself and just try to catch every other pitch and knock the rest of them down!

"There was no one in the starting rotation more difficult to catch than Joey Eischen due to the fact that at times he would start spraying his fastball and with that nasty breaking ball that he possessed … Suffice to say, Fulty had his hands full and was going to get a helluva workout in his return to active duty.

LOOKING BACK

"Joey was special on this day also in that he didn't pout about the fact that Fitty had been kicked out. He just made up his mind that he was going to pitch his game as if it was one of his starts with a regular, front-line catcher.

HEATH HAYNES

"Greg Fulton was unbelievable in his effort to pull this off. He never backed off and, when he was done, he looked like a California grape in our clubhouse from all the bruising on his arms and the rest of his body blocking Joey's nasty two-strike breaking balls and the ones that ended up that way, even though the intent was to just throw a 'get-me-over' breaking ball early in the count.

"Framing pitches was not in the equation at all; catching as many as he could was. The courageous part of Fulty on this day was his unwillingness to back off at any time. Runners in scoring position, runners on third base with hitters in breaking-ball counts knowing full well he may have to block the pitch. He would still call for the breaking ball and knock them down in front of him as if he were Patrick Roy protecting his goal in the NHL.

"His attempts to throw to second base were awfully rough, including the one that hit Heater right in the chest. It was the maddest I ever saw Heath Haynes get. … Once we knew Heater was OK, there was some serious chuckles in our dugout after that heave from Fulty.

"From that point forward in the game, I just told him to let them steal for the benefit of the staff and the rest of our season. The beauty of the situation was after the game — we had a ball in that clubhouse and on the bus that afternoon with Fulty and the rest of the club.

"We all wore Fitty out for putting us in that situation, but because of what had transpired, Greg Fulton could do no wrong with any player on that club for the rest of the season. He had more than earned his respect from every player on that club."

And a well-deserved nap.

From Start to Finish

BALTIMORE — Jim Tracy had made a commitment to Kirk Rueter, who had scattered four hits through the game's first eight innings.

KIRK RUETER

Rueter could allow one runner, but no more, in the ninth inning of a game the Senators led by two runs.

Tracy wanted to give Rueter a chance to finish what he started. He was not, however, going to let Rueter put himself in position to lose the game. He worked too hard for that.

Tracy had Archie Corbin ready in the bullpen. Had the soft-throwing Rueter struggled in the ninth, Tracy was ready to go with the hard-throwing Corbin.

No need for Corbin, though, as Rueter dodged a one-hit single to right by T.R. Lewis by retiring both Stanton Cameron and Brent Miller on fly balls to left fielder Curtis Pride and end the 2-0 shutout before a crowd of 1,133 at Memorial Stadium

Rueter's complete game was the Senators' first of the season.

The Senators gave Rueter all of the runs he needed in the first inning, scoring on a throwing error by Bowie catcher Gregg Zaun and Shane Andrews' two-out single to left. During the rally, Cliff Floyd singled to right, extending his hitting streak to 10 games.

"The kid pitched a fabulous game. He gives himself the chance to succeed," said Tracy, who was ready to take out Rueter had either Cameron or Miller reached base after Lewis.

"I wouldn't let him lose the game," Tracy said. "He pitched too well to let that happen."

In the end, Rueter (3-0) had scattered five hits and one walk, striking out only three over his 111 pitches.

The shutout dropped his already spectacular ERA from 1.23 to 0.87.

"I was happy to finish," Rueter said. "They knew I was getting tired."

EASTERN LEAGUE STANDINGS on May 3			
	Record	Pct.	GB
SENATORS	16 - 4	.800	—
Bowie	15 - 8	.652	2 1/2
Canton	13 - 8	.619	3 1/2
Albany	11 - 9	.550	5
Reading	10 - 11	.476	6 1/2
Binghamton	7 - 13	.350	9
London	8 - 15	.348	9 1/2
New Britain	5 - 17	.227	12

TUESDAY, MAY 4

Firemen Melt Down

BALTIMORE — There always were slight hiccups during the course of the marathon that was any baseball season.

MARIO BRITO

Then, at times, you had that wall-rattling belch. Like the kind Uncle Oskar had after eating too much kielbasa when everyone at the table tried not to stare. So went the Senators' bullpen in this game, coughing up four runs in the bottom of the ninth to lose 7-6 to Bowie before a crowd of 1,170 at Memorial Stadium.

The four runs came off relievers Archie Corbin and Mario Brito (1-1), who combined to give up those runs on two hits and four walks. The game ended on an error by catcher Rob Fitzpatrick, whose throw to finish off a would-be, inning-ending double play was low to first baseman Cliff Floyd and caromed away as Jim Wawruck scored the winning run.

Quite a New Britain-like performance from a team that had won 16 of its first 20 games.

"We didn't get it done," manager Jim Tracy said. "The bullpen didn't come through. We didn't throw strikes and pitched ourselves into trouble."

Keep in mind, Corbin entered the game with a 0.83 ERA, having allowed just one earned run in 9-plus innings. Brito was not far behind with a 2.45 ERA in his first 11 innings.

Their rare hiccup made a footnote of another solid start by Reid Cornelius, who allowed two earned runs in six innings, and Yorkis Perez, who worked two scoreless innings in the seventh and eighth.

Center fielder Rondell White, in the talons of a 6-for-61 slump, launched a three-run homer in the eighth inning off Kevin Ryan to give the Senators a seemingly safe 6-3 lead.

Well, seemingly safe anyway.

EASTERN LEAGUE STANDINGS on May 4			
	Record	Pct.	GB
SENATORS	16 - 5	.762	—
Bowie	16 - 8	.667	1 1/2
Canton	14 - 8	.636	2 1/2
Albany	12 - 9	.571	4
Reading	10 - 12	.455	6 1/2
Binghamton	8 - 13	.381	8
London	8 - 16	.333	9 1/2
New Britain	5 - 18	.217	12

WEDNESDAY, MAY 5

Ottawa-Bound, Sort Of

BALTIMORE — Gabe White, the Expos' top pitching prospect, was supposed to start tonight, but that was before the Senators' game against the Bowie Baysox was rained out.

Turned out White was not going to start the next game for the Senators, either. Or the game after that.

Instead, White was told moments after the rainout became official that he was going to Class AAA Ottawa.

The news came from manager Jim Tracy and initially was not received well by White. The left-hander simply did not hear the entire message as Tracy told White that he was going to Ottawa only long enough to start next Monday's exhibition game there between the Expos and their Class AAA affiliate.

"When Tracy said I was going to Ottawa, I thought, 'Oh ...,' " White said. "I love this team. I love being around the guys, and when I leave I want it to be for the big leagues."

In Ottawa, White (1-0, 2.03 ERA) was scheduled to pitch for the Expos, who like every other team in the majors avoided using their own pitchers for inconsequential, in-season exhibition games.

Reliever Heath Haynes (2-0, 1.86 ERA) also was told he would join White in pitching for the Expos with both returning afterward to the Senators.

"It's just a great chance to show what I can do in a no-lose situation," White said, "I'm just going to go up and throw like I did (for the Expos) in spring training. I think I'll be fine."

THURSDAY, MAY 6

Manager Jim Tracy planned a few drills for today's scheduled off day. The day also gave newly acquired catcher Lance Rice a chance to introduce himself to his teammates.

Rice, 26, a onetime Los Angeles Dodgers prospect, was signed to replace Miah Bradley, who abruptly retired a week ago and forced Tracy to use coach Greg Fulton to back up Rob Fitzpatrick.

The happiest person to see Rice was the 30-year-old Fulton, who still was recovering from catching eight innings after Fitzpatrick was ejected during last Sunday's 7-5 win in Reading.

80

Pitching, Not Throwing

HARRISBURG — Miguel Batista had been told more than once to stop nibbling, to stop trying to be perfect with every pitch.

Pitch, he was told, *don't throw.*

Batista listened in this game, holding Reading to three singles in eight shutout innings of a 6-1 victory before a crowd of 4,106 on City Island.

MIGUEL BATISTA

The win was the third straight for Batista (3-1), who left in the ninth with the bases loaded and no one out. Yorkis Perez then gave up an RBI single to Sam Taylor before striking out Ron Lockett, Jeff Jackson and Pat Brady to end the game.

"I didn't have my fastball, but I had my brains on my shoulder," Batista said. "I was pitching, not throwing."

Batista, with some help from Perez, had the Senators in and out of this game in only 2 hours and 13 minutes, quite the Rueter-like effort from a pitcher who was as plodding as he was talented.

"His tempo was as good as I've ever seen," manager Jim Tracy said. "He wasn't walking behind the mound. He wasn't stepping off or picking up the rosin bag. He was ready to go and his eight fielders were ready to go."

No one more so than second baseman Chris Martin, who made a pair of outstanding plays in the eighth. After Brady led off the inning with a walk, Martin went hard to his right to stop John Escobar's grounder up the middle and flipped the ball to Tim Barker for the force at second. Martin then started an inning-ending double play off a hard grounder to his left by Ed Rosado.

Most appreciative of Martin's glovework work, of course, was Batista, who lowered his earned-run average from 4.26 to 3.05.

"When you challenge the hitters," Batista said, "you're going to get plays like that."

EASTERN LEAGUE STANDINGS on May 7			
	Record	Pct.	GB
SENATORS	17 - 5	.773	—
Canton	16 - 8	.667	2
Bowie	16 - 9	.636	2 1/2
Albany	13 - 9	.591	4
Reading	10 - 14	.417	8
London	9 - 16	.360	9 1/2
Binghamton	8 - 15	.348	9 1/2
New Britain	6 - 19	.240	12 1/2

SATURDAY, MAY 8
A Bad 24 Hours

HARRISBURG — Three more errors led to four unearned runs and a 6-0 deficit before the seventh-inning stretch arrived. At the same time, Reading's Ron Allen shut out the Eastern League's highest-scoring team until the Senators finally cobbled together a run on four singles in the seventh inning.

In the end, Allen and the Phillies beat the Senators 6-2 before a crowd of 3,574 on City Island with Allen driving in half of the runs with a bases-loaded triple in the seventh off reliever Rafael Diaz.

The Phillies' five-run rally in the seventh off Joey Eischen (3-2) and Diaz was fueled by errors on shortstop Tim Barker, third baseman Shane Andrews and second baseman Ron Krause.

"We were flat today," manager Jim Tracy said, "but give Mr. Allen credit. He mixed his pitches. He mixed his speeds. He kept us off stride. ... We really opened things up for them. When you're down 6-0, there's not a whole lot of trickery out there."

SUNDAY, MAY 9

HARRISBURG — Well, at least they did not make any errors. Alas for the Senators, though, there was no help from the bullpen, either, as Reading scored three runs in the eighth off Yorkis Perez to rally for a 6-4 victory before a Mother's Day crowd of 3,839.

The loss was the Senators' second in less than 24 hours to the Phillies. Just as they did Saturday night with Joey Eischen, they wasted a fine start by Kirk Rueter, who left in the seventh up 4-3.

Phillies closer Toby Borland, replacing Robert Gaddy with one out and two runners on in the ninth, needed only three pitches to end the game as Rondell White lined his 0-2 slider into a double play to second baseman John Escobar with the ever-dangerous Cliff Floyd on deck.

"I don't know how he hit that ball. I didn't want to look," Borland said.

"I'm glad it ended the way it did, because I did not want to face Floyd."

Really, who would?

EASTERN LEAGUE STANDINGS on May 9			
	Record	Pct.	GB
SENATORS	17 - 7	.708	—
Canton	17 - 9	.654	1
Bowie	17 - 10	.630	1 1/2
Albany	14 - 10	.583	3
Reading	12 - 14	.462	6
London	10 - 17	.370	8 1/2
Binghamton	9 - 15	.360	8 1/2
New Britain	7 - 20	.259	11 1/2

Martin's Late Night

HARRISBURG — Chris Martin was not supposed to be in this game. With second baseman Ron Krause batting .351 and shortstop Tim Barker doing even better at .375, Martin found himself — and his .218 batting average — on the bench as the Senators started a four-game series against second-place Canton.

Martin was going to sit until he understood what manager Jim Tracy was trying to teach him in spring training, lessons about swinging to put the ball in play rather than trying to launch balls into the trees on City Island. The Senators already had plenty of other players who could do that. So, Martin watched.

Until the ninth inning, when Tracy used Martin as a pinch-hitter for designated hitter Oreste Marrero. Martin promptly doubled to start a two-run rally that tied the score at 7 to force extra innings.

Martin again singled with two outs in the 10th before ending the game in the 12th with a one-out double that scored Shane Andrews from first base for an 8-7 victory before 1,614 fans on City Island.

"I've been trying to stay on top of everything," Martin said. "I'm off to a slow start, but what else is new?"

Martin finished with three of the Senators' 16 hits, the first of which was Curtis Pride's homer to right to lead off the bottom of the first. Krause also homered, his first in Class AA, with one out in the fourth to give the Senators a 5-4 lead. Canton then scored runs in the seventh, eighth and ninth innings to take a 7-5 lead before Martin, hitting for Marrero, led off the bottom of the ninth with a double to jump-start a two-run rally to tie the score at 7.

"A tremendous performance," Tracy said of Martin, who lifted his batting average 41 points to .259. "It goes back to discussions we had with Chris two weeks into spring training. We had some real heart-to-hearts."

Mostly on approach.

"Chris isn't going to succeed hitting fly balls," Tracy said. "He has to get on top of the ball, and tonight he hung three ropes out there."

EASTERN LEAGUE STANDINGS on May 10			
	Record	Pct.	GB
SENATORS	18 - 7	.720	—
Canton	17 - 10	.630	2
Bowie	17 - 11	.607	2 1/2
Albany	15 - 10	.600	3
Reading	13 - 14	.481	6
London	11 - 17	.393	8 1/2
Binghamton	9 - 17	.346	9 1/2
New Britain	7 - 21	.250	12 1/2

TUESDAY, MAY 11
The Rock Was Hot

HARRISBURG — There had been opportunities for the start of a turnaround for Rondell White. A hard hit ball here. A home run there. Nothing sustainable, though, as those infrequent hits were followed by more strikeouts and listless flyouts.

One of the game's brightest hitting prospects mostly had stumbled through the Senators' first 25 games, batting just .172 with 20 strikeouts and only four walks in 103 plate appearances. He had not had a multi-hit game since April 14.

RONDELL WHITE

"He was struggling so much," outfielder Curtis Pride remembered a quarter-century later of a player the Senators called "Rock."

"I thought he was going to quit," Pride said.

Coming into this game, White's slump had reached its nadir with only nine hits in his last 78 at-bats. So, naturally, manager Jim Tracy made White his leadoff hitter against Canton.

While the Senators lost 10-7 before 1,972 fans on City Island, White was a winner, going 5-for-5 with four singles that bracketed a solo homer with two outs in the fifth.

"If there is a positive to come out of tonight, it was Rondell's game," Tracy said. "If you wanted to mold a baseball player, it is all in Rondell's locker over there."

There, by his locker in the clubhouse corner with an occasional drip of water from the AC above him, White analyzed a swing that led to the Senators' first five-hit game since 1987.

"I was keeping my front leg straight instead of bending it," he said. "It seems the lower I can get, the better I hit."

Finally.

EASTERN LEAGUE STANDINGS on May 11			
	Record	Pct.	GB
SENATORS	18 - 8	.692	—
Canton	18 - 10	.643	1
Albany	16 - 10	.615	2
Bowie	17 - 12	.586	2 1/2
Reading	14 - 14	.500	5
London	12 - 17	.414	7 1/2
Binghamton	9 - 18	.333	9 1/2
New Britain	7 - 22	.241	12 1/2

A Good Night's Sleep

HARRISBURG — Amazing how a couple of hits can change an attitude from maudlin to magnificent. In Rondell White's case, five hits just 24 hours earlier brought his attitude to something even better than magnificent.

So imagine what three more hits did for him?

White, just a day removed from ending an 9-for-78 slump, had a single, double and triple, and teamed with Curtis Pride, who had a single, double and homer, for half of the Senators' 12 hits in an 8-3 victory over Canton before a crowd of 1,383 at RiverSide Stadium.

"It's gone," White said with a smile of what he hoped to be a soon-forgotten slump.

"Every time I go to bed now, I feel like I'm going to get a hit," White said. "Before, I felt the other way, that I wasn't going to get a hit."

"He has a pretty good feel for what he's doing up there," said manager Jim Tracy. "You can tell by the crispness of his swing, by his aggressiveness."

White and Pride each had as many hits as Canton had against Senators starter Miguel Batista.

Batista (4-1) allowed two singles and a double by Manny Ramirez, the Cleveland Indians' top prospect, before leaving after six innings with an 8-1 lead. Actually, Batista, who threw 115 pitches, was more than willing to leave after walking seven and working behind in the count to 17 of the 26 batters he faced.

"I had made a lot of pitches," Batista said. "I was having a mechanical problem."

He said he also had an obligation to his teammates to pitch well.

"When you have a team like we have, you know you have the responsibility to pitch well," Batista said. "We lost last night. When I got here today, I knew I had to win."

EASTERN LEAGUE STANDINGS on May 12			
	Record	Pct.	GB
SENATORS	19 - 8	.704	—
Canton	18 - 11	.621	2
Albany	16 - 11	.593	3
Bowie	17 - 12	.586	3
Reading	14 - 14	.500	5 1/2
London	13 - 17	.433	7 1/2
Binghamton	9 - 19	.321	10 1/2
New Britain	8 - 22	.267	12 1/2

THURSDAY, MAY 13

Ready, Willing, Able

HARRISBURG — On a team of A-list prospects, Oreste Marrero sometimes was perceived, and unfairly so, as an afterthought.

ORESTE MARRERO

Understandable, considering much of the Senators' prized talent still was in high school when Marrero began his pro career in 1987 along the outposts of the Class A Pioneer League.

Back then, Marrero waited for his chance to play. He still did. Confined to a role as a part-time designated hitter and sometimes first baseman, Marrero did in the series finale against Canton what he always did best: deliver a big-time hit.

This hit turned out to be a solo homer in the sixth inning that snapped a 4-4 tie and carried the Senators over Canton 5-4 before a crowd of 2,862 at RiverSide Stadium.

Marrero's homer — a shot to right field off a 2-2 fastball from Paul Shuey — gave the Senators their third victory in the four-game series against the second-place Indians.

"I'm always ready to go," said Marrero, who was traded to the Expos in the offseason after six years in the Milwaukee Brewers' system. "It doesn't matter if it's to be the DH, or to play first base or the outfield."

In this game, Marrero, as usual, was filling the role of DH, where he had been used 15 times and batted .364 in that role.

"If there is one guy who comes prepared to play every day, this guy is the best example on this team," manager Jim Tracy said. "I'd like to find more spots for him."

So would with the 23-year-old Marrero, who continued to be stuck behind top prospect Cliff Floyd at first base and younger, faster prospects in the outfield.

"Right now, he said, "I have to concentrate on being a DH."

EASTERN LEAGUE STANDINGS on May 13			
	Record	Pct.	GB
SENATORS	20 - 8	.714	—
Canton	18 - 12	.600	3
Bowie	18 - 12	.600	3
Albany	16 - 12	.571	4
Reading	14 - 15	.483	6 1/2
London	14 - 17	.452	7 1/2
Binghamton	9 - 20	.321	11 1/2
New Britain	9 - 22	.290	12 1/2

THURSDAY, MAY 13

Marrero's homer snapped a 4-4 tie in a game that earlier was careening wildly out of control.

Canton had taken a 2-0 lead off Joey Eischen in the second, thanks to a two-run homer from Mike Sarbaugh — the pride of nearby Mt. Joy, Pa. Shuey, Cleveland's top choice in the 1992 amateur draft, promptly lost that lead in the bottom of the second when Shane Andrews drilled a two-run homer to left-center.

The teams again traded a couple of runs in the third inning, but not nearly in as dramatic style. Canton's runs came on a — ho-hum — RBI double by David Bell and a follow-up, run-scoring single by Herbert Perry. The Senators' runs were not nearly as aesthetically pleasing as those that came on infield hits by Rondell White and Glenn Murray, and a flare to right field by Andrews.

Not that White cared. Two more singles gave him 11 hits in 17 at-bats in the series to jump his batting average 72 points to .239.

Catcher Rob Fitzpatrick, mired in a 7-for-57 slump, rested for the first time in nine games. Apparently, he completed his penance for getting ejected May 2 in Reading and forcing coach-turned-player Greg Fulton to catch the final eight innings of that game.

Dusted off was Lance Rice, who was signed after Fitzpatrick's regular backup, Miah Bradbury, abruptly retired on April 30, creating the scenario in which Fulton was activated in case of the very emergency that Fitzpatrick subsequently caused on May 2.

Rice went 0-for-4, but no one seemed to mind.

As White continued to soar and Fitzpatrick continued to slide, Eischen (4-2) continued in his role of the mythical bird Phoenix, again crashing and burning early in the game only to rise again.

Eischen, owner of a gawd-awful 6.17 ERA through the first four innings of his starts and 2.70 thereafter, allowed four runs in two-plus innings before settling down and lasting seven innings.

"I was just pitching stupid," Eischen said. "I was throwing too many fastballs and Canton let me know about it."

So did the restless crowd of just under 3,000.

"We absolutely had to have some innings out of Eischen," Tracy said, knowing his bullpen worked 13 innings in the last three games. "I know a lot of people up in the crowd were moaning when he gave up four runs and wanted me to go the bullpen, but, hell, the bullpen was in the clubhouse with ice on their arms."

The Rumor Du Jour

LONDON, Ont. — The season was less than 30 games old when the Senators had their first major distraction involving a top prospect.

Seemed center fielder Rondell White might be headed to the Dodgers, so reported the *Los Angeles Times*. Seemed the Expos were looking for starting pitching and the Dodgers, the Times reported, were happy to provide some in return for White.

Well, at least that was the rumor of the day.

The reality of the night found White picking up another hit and a walk in a 6-4 win over London in 10 innings before just 815 fans at Labatt Memorial Park.

YORKIS PEREZ

The reality also found another of the game's premier prospects, first baseman Cliff Floyd, launching two homers, including the game-winner in the 10th. After Mike Lumley walked White with two outs, Floyd greeted another reliever, Mike Guilfoyle, by driving the first pitch to him over the wall in right to snap a 4-4 tie.

Yorkis Perez (2-1) pitched the final two innings after Kirk Rueter and Heath Haynes allowed just two unearned runs on seven hits in eight innings. Rueter and Haynes combined for 11 strikeouts with Perez adding four more against the six batters he faced.

Floyd also homered off Lumley with one out in the eighth to tie the score at 4. Floyd, held to three hits in 19 at-bats over the four previous games, finished with three hits and his first multi-homer game in Class AA. His homers off Lumley and Guilfoyle tied him with Glenn Murray for the team lead at seven.

Meanwhile, Ron Krause started his third straight game at short for Tim Barker, owner of a nine-game hitting streak before being sidelined by an ingrown toenail.

Remember, kids, always trim carefully.

EASTERN LEAGUE STANDINGS on May 14			
	Record	Pct.	GB
SENATORS	21 - 8	.724	—
Bowie	19 - 12	.613	3
Albany	17 - 12	.586	4
Canton	18 - 13	.581	4
Reading	14 - 16	.467	7 1/2
London	14 - 18	.438	8 1/2
Binghamton	10 - 20	.333	11 1/2
New Britain	9 - 23	.281	13 1/2

SATURDAY, MAY 15

Another Cliffhanger

LONDON, Ont. — Tie score. Final inning. Cliff Floyd hitting.

CLIFF FLOYD

Once again, this was the scenario for the London Tigers. And, again, their nightmare as Floyd homered for the third time in 24 hours — and the second time in the final inning — to decide a game.

This one was a two-run homer off relief pitcher Jim Henry in the top of the ninth to snap a 5-5 tie in an afternoon game won by the Senators 7-6 at Labatt Memorial Park.

Just as he did a night earlier in the 10th inning, Rondell White started the rally with a double to lead off the ninth. Floyd was next, and manager Jim Tracy pulled him aside to tell him to hit the ball toward the right side of the infield and move White to third.

"I told Floyd the important thing was getting the runner to third base," Tracy said. "I told him only to swing at a pitch from the middle to the inside half of the plate, so he could pull it to the right side. … I never said he had to keep it in the park."

Hard not to keep the ball from going out of hitter-friendly Labatt, especially when a slider from the left-handed Henry broke over the plate. Floyd quickly lined the pitch over the wall in right.

"I don't go out looking for home runs," Floyd said. "That's when I have a hard time. I was just looking for a good pitch, and this is a good park to hit in."

Floyd had company. Glenn Murray hit a three-run homer and sore-toed Tim Barker, playing for the first time in four games, had a solo homer, his first since joining the Senators in late April.

"There's some light air here," Tracy wryly said. "I do know Floyd's last two homers and Murray's all would have been out of any park in the Eastern League."

EASTERN LEAGUE STANDINGS on May 15			
	Record	Pct.	GB
SENATORS	22 - 8	.733	—
Bowie	20 - 12	.625	3
Albany	18 - 12	.600	4
Canton	18 - 14	.563	5
Reading	14 - 17	.452	8 1/2
London	14 - 19	.424	9 1/2
Binghamton	11 - 20	.355	11 1/2
New Britain	9 - 24	.273	14 1/2

SUNDAY, MAY 16

Diaz's Day

LONDON, Ont. — Gabe White started five of the Senators' first 17 games, and had not pitched for them since.

RAFAEL DIAZ

In part because he was summoned by the Montreal Expos to pitch four innings in their exhibition game May 10 at Class AAA Ottawa.

In part, unfortunately, because White had pain in his prized left arm after working those four innings in that meaningless exhibition game.

Enter Rafael Diaz from the bullpen to fill in for White on days when the latter was supposed to start for the Senators. Like today.

With White out again, Diaz (2-1) scattered five hits and four walks over six shutout innings as the Senators beat London 14-3 to complete a three-game sweep at Labatt Memorial Park.

The six scoreless innings dropped Diaz's ERA from 4.12 to 3.20. Darrin Winston allowed three runs in two innings before Archie Corbin dodged a two-walk ninth to finish off London.

Unlike the series' first two games, won by the Senators in their final at-bat, the Tigers were no match in this game as the Senators pounded five pitchers for 16 hits. The feast was the Senators' largest since totaling 23 hits in an 18-1 victory over New Britain on April 12 on City Island.

Tim Barker, Glenn Murray and Rondell White each had three hits. Murray and Curtis Pride also homered twice, while Barker, owner of an 11-game hitting streak, homered for the second straight game as the Senators finished the week winning six of seven games from Canton and London.

For the week, the Senators hit .295 as a team with 18 homers while averaging 7.9 runs per game.

Not too bad.

EASTERN LEAGUE STANDINGS on May 16			
	Record	Pct.	GB
SENATORS	23 - 8	.742	—
Bowie	20 - 12	.625	3 1/2
Albany	18 - 13	.581	5
Canton	19 - 14	.576	5
Reading	15 - 17	.469	8 1/2
London	14 - 20	.412	10 1/2
Binghamton	11 - 21	.344	12 1/2
New Britain	9 - 24	.273	15

Bad Day For A Visit

HARRISBURG — The start of a seven-game homestand brought some visitors from out of town.

The parents of manager Jim Tracy were here. So were Nardi Contreras, Gomer Hodge and Bobby Mitchell, the roving instructors who essentially were godfathers to the Expos' minor leaguers.

"Time to look at the prospects," Tyrone Woods said, "not the suspects."

Woods was a gifted hitter, but one who considered himself to be a "suspect" and, perhaps, rightfully so being a backup outfielder on a team loaded with outfield prospects.

Turned out the Senators played more like suspects than prospects in this game, losing 9-4 to the lowly Binghamton Mets after blowing a 4-2 lead in front of 1,989 fans on City Island.

With three of the Expos' most important coordinators looking on, the Senators managed just eight hits while their bullpen gave up seven unearned runs in the eighth inning, thanks to three errors.

The highlights:

— A leadoff homer in the bottom of the first from Rondell White, who finished with three of the Senators' eight hits after earlier in the day being named the Eastern League's player of the week for his 18-for-32 run against Canton and London.

— Another strong start from Miguel Batista, who allowed two runs on five hits before leaving after six innings with a 2-1 lead.

— An infield single in the ninth by Tim Barker to extend his hitting streak to a league-leading 12 games.

And, finally ... well ... did we mention Jim Tracy's parents had a wonderful time on their cruise before arriving here to see this mess of a finish?

"I've seen this happen before," Jim Tracy of the late collapse. "I know we're 23-9, but that isn't the point. When we break down, everything just snowballs. It's happened three times now."

EASTERN LEAGUE STANDINGS on May 17			
	Record	Pct.	GB
SENATORS	23 - 9	.719	—
Bowie	20 - 12	.625	3
Albany	18 - 13	.581	4 1/2
Canton	19 - 14	.576	4 1/2
Reading	15 - 17	.469	8
London	14 - 20	.412	10
Binghamton	12 - 21	.364	11 1/2
New Britain	9 - 24	.273	14 1/2

Woods Hot, Krause Not

HARRISBURG — A day after joking, OK carping, about being considered more of a suspect than a prospect, Tyrone Woods had a chance to show he was more of the latter.

Pinch-hitting for Curtis Pride in the sixth inning, Woods launched a two-out, three-run homer to help the Senators beat the Binghamton Mets 7-4 before 1,133 fans on City Island.

Woods' homer off reliever Todd Douma gave the Senators a 7-0 lead. The homer to left field — his third of the season — came at a most

RON KRAUSE

opportune time as Montreal general manager Dan Duquette and minor league field coordinator Herm Starrette arrived earlier in the day on City Island to join an already large contingent of Expos talent evaluators in town to watch their prized Class AA team.

"That doesn't bother you," Woods said of performing in front of those who shaped his career. "You just want to have a good at-bat. I wanted to hit the ball hard, and he threw it in my wheelhouse."

At least with so many Expos officials in town, the paperwork went smoother for infielder Ron Krause, who was batting .288 in 17 games when he announced he was retiring. Krause, 22, joined backup catcher Miah Bradbury as the second Senator in less than three weeks to abruptly quit.

"His reason wasn't much more than he just didn't enjoy playing the game anymore," manager Jim Tracy said.

Still enjoying the game, despite pitching with a nasty blister, was Joey Eischen (5-2), who threw five scoreless innings. His start provided a much needed boost, given that 24 hours ago the Senators lost 9-4 to the downtrodden Mets.

"This game showed once again losing doesn't sit well with these kids," Tracy said.

EASTERN LEAGUE STANDINGS on May 18			
	Record	Pct.	GB
SENATORS	24 - 9	.727	—
Bowie	21 - 12	.636	3
Canton	20 - 14	.588	4 1/2
Albany	18 - 14	.563	5 1/2
Reading	16 - 17	.485	8
London	14 - 21	.400	11
Binghamton	12 - 22	.353	12 1/2
New Britain	9 - 25	.265	15 1/2

Quick Work For Kirk

HARRISBURG — The pace staggered even Cliff Floyd, who admitted he lost track of how many home runs the Senators had hit so far.

Floyd also said he occasionally lost track of some details in games pitched by Kirk Rueter. You know, like the number of outs in an inning.

Floyd only knew something good was coming when the fast-working Rueter pitched.

Like in this game as Floyd drove in two runs with a homer and a single while Rueter pitched eight shutout inning in a 4-3 victory over the

KIRK RUETER

Binghamton Mets before a crowd of 2,989 on City Island.

The game took just 1 hour, 59 minutes to complete — and that included a messy ninth when Yorkis Perez gave up three runs.

"Sometimes when he pitches," Floyd said of Rueter, "you forget how many outs there are or how many runs you have. We know that if he does his job, we'll win."

Floyd started the latest victory for Rueter (4-0) in the fourth when he drove Pete Walker's first-pitch curveball over the wall in right. The homer was Floyd's ninth of the season and the Senators' 50th, putting them on pace to hit 206.

"Can't even think about home runs," he said. "They just come."

"I've never come close to being on a team like this," Rueter said. "It's a feeling that if (the pitchers) keep them in the game, they'll get going."

Rueter could have kept going, too, needing only 82 pitches over eight innings to lower his ERA to an Eastern League-best 1.39.

Rueter left in the ninth so Montreal Expos general manager Dan Duquette and a cadre of top evaluators could see Perez pitch an inning.

"They wanted to see Yorkis pitch," Rueter said. "That's alright. I just wanted to get the win."

EASTERN LEAGUE STANDINGS on May 19			
	Record	Pct.	GB
SENATORS	25 - 9	.735	—
Bowie	21 - 13	.618	4
Canton	21 - 14	.600	4 1/2
Albany	19 - 14	.576	5 1/2
Reading	17 - 17	.500	8
London	14 - 22	.389	12
Binghamton	12 - 23	.343	13 1/2
New Britain	9 - 26	.257	16 1/2

Off And Running

HARRISBURG — Mike Hardge learned more from what he did not do in his Senators debut a couple of nights ago than from what he did right in that game against Binghamton.

After trotting down the first-base line on a foul ball, Hardge received some friendly advice from his new teammates.

Run. Run hard. Run faster. Repeat.

Hardge remembered that in this game as he ran himself into a three-run, inside-the-park home run to ignite a 7-2 victory over the London Tigers before 1,560 fans at RiverSide Stadium.

MIKE HARDGE

"They were breaking me in," said Hardge, whose seventh-inning homer was one of his three hits — his first hits — since being promoted from Class A West Palm Beach when infielder Ron Krause retired earlier this week.

Hardge's homer, which gave the Senators a 5-1 lead in the seventh, was sandwiched between four London errors, a suicide squeeze by Tim Barker in the third and a pair of game-clinching RBI singles by Glenn Murray and Rob Fitzpatrick in the eighth.

"This is a good team here," Hardge said. "You don't want to be embarrassed out there."

Which was what he did just a night earlier, only to be reminded that the league's most talented team did not win by talent alone.

"Fitzpatrick told me that as long as I run out everything, I'll be OK here," said Hardge, who also received the same message from first baseman Cliff Floyd and coach Greg Fulton.

Hardge started at second base for the second straight game, taking over for Krause and taking away playing time from Chris Martin.

And he was more than OK as the Senators won for the ninth time in their last 11 games.

EASTERN LEAGUE STANDINGS on May 20			
	Record	Pct.	GB
SENATORS	26 - 9	.743	—
Bowie	21 - 13	.618	4 1/2
Canton	21 - 15	.583	5 1/2
Albany	19 - 14	.576	6
Reading	18 - 17	.514	8
London	14 - 23	.378	13
Binghamton	13 - 23	.361	13 1/2
New Britain	9 - 27	.250	17 1/2

THURSDAY, MAY 20

Hardge jump-started the Senators' offense in the third inning with a one-out single to center. He moved to second when pitcher Felipe Lira sailed the first of his two errors on pickoff throws past first baseman Mike Rendina.

Curtis Pride followed with a single to right, but Hardge stopped at third base after a slow start off second. Hardge, though, did not stay long at third as he easily scored when Lira again threw past Rendina trying to pick off Pride, who ended up on third.

Barker — owner of an Eastern League-best, 15-game hitting streak — then squeezed home Pride for a 2-1 lead.

Gabe White (2-0), pitching for the first time since hurting his left shoulder on May 10, carried that one-run lead through five innings before he was replaced by Rafael Diaz.

White, out since pitching four innings for the Expos in their exhibition game at Class AAA Ottawa, was on an 80-pitch, five-inning limit. Whichever came first.

White finished with 78 pitches, allowing just one unearned run on a single and two walks. He struck out five before Diaz and Yorkis Perez split the final four innings.

In between, Hardge personally finished off the Tigers in the bottom of the seventh in a rally that started with Tyrone Woods reaching first on an error by third baseman Jim Adler and Fitzpatrick walking.

Hardge then drilled Lira's 0-1 pitch to the wall in right-center to score Woods and Fitzpatrick.

Hardge was motoring along right behind them as manager Jim Tracy, coaching at third, never hesitated sending Hardge home as outfielders Danny Bautista and Rudy Pemberton had trouble picking up the ball.

"I was kind of shocked he sent me," Hardge said, "but I didn't know where the ball was. He told me to run as hard as I can until they tell me to stop, and he never told me to stop."

Tracy said he had no intention of stopping Hardge, especially not with a chance to so quickly reinforce Wednesday's lesson.

"We made it perfectly clear to him [Wednesday] that he didn't give the same effort that 22 other guys give this club," Tracy said.

"Tonight," Tracy said, "the inside-the-park home run was a chance to reiterate how important it is to run out everything."

Murray's Fast Start

HARRISBURG — April and May had been Glenn Murray's months. Strong starts in each of the last two seasons made Murray nearly invincible in Class A.

Alas, sputtering finishes made him mortal, but then again that gave him something to work on for 1993.

For now, the month was May and Murray remained hot as his sixth-inning grand slam broke open a 7-0 victory over the London Tigers before a crowd of 4,513 on City Island.

GLENN MURRAY

The win was the Senators' fifth in five games against London and 10th in 12 overall.

The homer was Murray's league-high 11th.

"These are my two months," said Murray, whose .591 slugging percentage almost mirrored his pace from 1992 before finishing then at .384. "I don't know what it is. I guess I'm so full of energy now. Hopefully, I can keep it going for the whole year."

Murray's slam came off Ken Carlyle, who found himself facing Murray with none out in the sixth after the Senators loaded the bases on leadoff walks to Rondell White and Cliff Floyd, and an error on Shane Andrews' grounder to shortstop Jim Givens.

Carlyle missed on his first pitch to Murray and then hung a slider that Murray did not miss, lining it over the left-field wall.

With that, the Senators' lead grew to 7-0 from the 3-0 lead built on Curtis Pride's RBI groundout in the third and on Pride's two-run homer in the fifth.

"Glenn Murray has been a project since Day One," manager Jim Tracy said. "It's a matter of making him understand there has to be a transfer of weight from has backside to the front."

Then Tracy gave a more distilled analysis, saying with a smile that "you can't hit a ball much harder than he did there."

EASTERN LEAGUE STANDINGS on May 21			
	Record	Pct.	GB
SENATORS	27 - 9	.750	—
Bowie	21 - 14	.600	5 1/2
Canton	22 - 15	.595	5 1/2
Albany	20 - 14	.588	6
Reading	18 - 18	.500	9
London	14 - 24	.368	14
Binghamton	13 - 24	.351	14 1/2
New Britain	10 - 27	.270	17 1/2

FRIDAY, MAY 21

An inning before Murray's slam, Pride turned a two-out, hit-and-run play into a two-run homer off Carlyle for a 3-0 lead.

REID CORNELIUS

"He was throwing me inside fastballs in my first two at-bats," Pride said. "I knew he would try to come back inside with another one."

Carlyle did, and it cost him.

With Mike Hardge running on the pitch, Pride launched Carlyle's first-pitch fastball over the right-field wall for his ninth homer of the season and fourth in five games against London.

"It's always an effective hit-and-run when it leaves the ballpark," Tracy said. "I like to see my hitters swinging. I don't want them feathering their swings and trying to hit the ball the other way."

As it was, the Senators managed only six hits with two of them coming on a pair of singles by designated hitter Oreste Marrero.

Another hit came from Rob Fitzpatrick, the catcher who has started all but five of the Senators' first 36 games but likely will not play for a while after spraining his left ankle in the fifth inning.

> "He had stuff tonight that would have beaten a big-league club."
>
> *Jim Tracy on Reid Cornelius*

None of the Senators' six hits, though, came from Tim Barker, who was hitless for the first time in 16 games, and Rondell White, who went 0-for-3 to lose an 11-game hitting streak during which he had 26 hits in 49 at-bats.

Pride's hit-and-run homer and Murray's slam were more than enough for Reid Cornelius, who had been winless since April 18.

Cornelius (3-1) allowed only two hits while striking out a season-high 10 batters in seven innings.

Heath Haynes worked the last two innings, striking out three in his best performance in nearly four weeks.

The only hits Cornelius allowed were leadoff singles to Shannon Penn in the fourth inning and Evan Pratte in the seventh.

"This was his best start, by far, since Day One," Tracy said of Cornelius. "He had stuff tonight that would have beaten a big-league club."

97

Tigers By The Tail

HARRISBURG — By now, the first two games played between the Senators and London were, if nothing else, moral victories for the Tigers.

Those two games now seemed like eons ago for the Tigers, who only the weekend before took the Senators into extra innings once and were tied in the ninth in the other game before losing both.

Since then, the Tigers were trounced in four games, including this one that ended 11-2 in front of a crowd of 5,216 on City Island.

This rout, in which the Senators had four doubles and two home runs among their 14 hits, was their sixth victory in six games against London and pushed their winning percentage to .757 — the best of any team, majors or minors.

"We talked about that in a little five-minute meeting," manager Jim Tracy said of the Senators' record. "It means nothing unless you go out there and play baseball. Once you build a reputation, everybody wants to beat you."

London never came close to doing that as Miguel Batista (5-1) dodged three singles and six walks before leaving after six innings with a 10-2 lead. Just as he did six days ago in a 14-3 victory at London,

Curtis Pride led off the game against Steve Wolf with a homer as he drove the right-hander's first pitch of the night over the wall in left-center for a 1-0 lead.

"I was looking fastball," said Pride, who also had two singles and a double to raise his batting average against London to .462.

"I was looking to be aggressive and take the ball the other way."

The opposite-field homer was Pride's 10th of the season and fifth against the Tigers, who were outscored 39-7 in their last four losses to the Senators.

"We did absolutely everything right tonight," Tracy said. "Absolutely everything."

EASTERN LEAGUE STANDINGS on May 22			
	Record	Pct.	GB
SENATORS	28 - 9	.757	—
Canton	23 - 15	.605	5 1/2
Albany	21 - 14	.600	6
Bowie	21 - 15	.583	6 1/2
Reading	18 - 19	.486	10
London	14 - 25	.359	15
Binghamton	13 - 25	.342	15 1/2
New Britain	11 - 27	.289	17 1/2

SUNDAY, MAY 23
The Beatdown

HARRISBURG — This was coming. The frustration was easy to see. Over the last week, the disappointment morphed into anger, which grew into an uncontrollable rage.

The London Tigers had become the Senators' personal piñata, having lost to them in all six of their previous games.

The last four games had been particularly ugly from London's perspective as the Tigers were outscored 39-7 in those losses. Certainly not helping London's mood was waking up this morning to see the latest game story in the local newspaper with the six-column headline that screamed:

MIKE HARDGE

"Senators continue hobby of beating up on London"

The real beatdown, though, came in the seventh inning of this game, another Senators victory, of course. This one ended 9-1 before a crowd of 3,243 on City Island.

The victory was not all that surprising, given the Senators' success against London.

How the game ended, well, that took a little more to figure out as the Senators played the final two innings with regular third baseman Shane Andrews, who was supposed to have the day off, playing shortstop, Cliff Floyd moving from first base to right field, backup outfielder Tyrone Woods holding down third base and Mike Daniel, the new backup catcher, manning first base.

MIKE DANIEL

This was not what the Senators planned for this game, but then again not many expected a bench-clearing brawl — OK, maybe the players did — in the bottom of the seventh.

The melee led to the ejections of second baseman Mike Hardge and right fielder Glenn Murray.

EASTERN LEAGUE STANDINGS on May 23			
	Record	Pct.	GB
SENATORS	29 - 9	.763	—
Canton	23 - 16	.590	6 1/2
Albany	21 - 15	.583	7
Bowie	21 - 16	.568	7 1/2
Reading	19 - 19	.500	10
Binghamton	14 - 25	.359	15 1/2
London	14 - 26	.350	16
New Britain	12 - 27	.308	17 1/2

99

SUNDAY, MAY 23

Suddenly, manager Jim Tracy was forced to become a tad more creative than usual in deploying his defense. He really had no choice since umpires Brad Geaslin, Doug Eddings and Eric Cooper ejected Hardge and Murray for their roles in a brawl that started when London's Brian Warren buzzed a fastball by Hardge's head after giving up long homers to Floyd and Oreste Marrero.

No matter. Daniel easily fielded the only grounder to him to start the eighth, while Woods made a fine stop on Mike Rendina's grounder to end the inning. By then, the game was all but over.

Warren had been tasked with keeping London close when he replaced starter Jose Lima with one out in the seventh, the Tigers trailing 4-1 and Floyd coming to bat with one out and two on.

Floyd, who already hit a solo homer off Lima in the fourth, turned Warren's first-pitch slider to him into a three-run homer and a 7-1 lead. Marrero followed Murray's popout to second baseman Shannon Penn with another homer to right.

"I was in the dugout and I saw the guys starting to move to the top step," equipment manager Steve Purvis remembered a quarter-century later. "You could tell something was about to happen."

Something did as Warren aimed his next pitch at Hardge's head.

Warren missed hitting Hardge. The Senators, though, did not miss much in the ensuing 12-minute brawl.

Pitcher Joey Eischen (6-2), the Senators' starter who already was out of the game, manhandled two Tigers by home plate, while Murray and Curtis Pride tag-teamed London manager Tom Runnells, blindsiding him along the first-base line.

As this was going on, relief pitcher Rafael Diaz tangled with a couple of Tigers near shortstop, while Woods had a couple of more pinned against the backstop. Pride remembered last seeing Marrero chasing London infielder Kirk Mendenhall into left field.

And Floyd? He just stood outside the Senators' dugout. Alone. Nobody from London was foolish enough to mess with him.

"I'll never forget that," Pride said 25 years later of his role in the brawl, "but I'm just embarrassed by that now."

Three years after the brawl, Pride briefly played for Detroit's Class AAA affiliate in Toledo, where his manager was, of course, the same Tom Runnells he had tackled on the island.

"He didn't know who hit him until years later," Pride recalled with a smile.

100

SUNDAY, MAY 23

"I asked him in spring training (in 1996) if he remembered that fight that we had between Harrisburg and London. He said, 'Yeah, I remember that.' Then I asked him if he knew who had knocked him down. He said, 'You know, I never found out who did it.' I told him I did it and he said, 'Oh, you son of a bitch.' "

CURTIS PRIDE

Hardge had similar words for Warren on this day in 1993. He already was wondering just where Warren was going to throw his next pitch after Marrero's long homer. Maybe at his feet or his knees. Perhaps the ribs. Hardge was ready for any spot.

Except upstairs.

"I was expecting something," Hardge said. "Something tight and inside, but not at my head."

When the pitch sailed past his head, Hardge started toward the mound. He never reached Warren, though, as Murray rushed onto the field and pushed Warren to the ground. Hardge had to settle for another pitcher, Ben Blomdahl.

"The way I analyze it," Tracy said that day before pausing, "... we got to beat them five times this weekend, not four."

The brawl began percolating a week ago in London, where Tim Barker was brushed back after Pride homered in the eighth inning of the Senators' 14-3 victory. Then, less than 48 hours before this soiree, Reid Cornelius hit two batters with pitches in a 7-0 victory. A day later, Murray and Hardge were drilled in an 11-2 win.

"They have a lot of hitters who like to stand on top of the plate," Runnells said of the Senators. "We're not trying to hurt anybody, but we're not going to sit there and pitch batting practice."

"Hey," Floyd said, "we're just going about our business. We can't help it that we hit balls a long way. If they can't pitch to us, then let them walk us."

Among the faces in the crowd watching the beatdown was Bill Madlock, the four-time National League batting champion who was at RiverSide Stadium for a postgame charity softball game.

"I don't know what those London boys were thinking," Madlock said after the game.

"Those guys are just babies compared to Harrisburg."

SUNDAY, MAY 23

As Madlock gave his post-fight analysis, Tracy held a closed-door meeting in the clubhouse.

"Tracy was pumped," Pride remembered. "He was like, 'All right, boys, but we have to keep our cool now.' "

The players also were comparing notes.

"They were joking around," Purvis said, "and telling war stories about who they took care of."

As for Tracy, he was gratified.

"I closed the doors," Tracy recalled a quarter-century later, "and I told them how God-damned proud of them I was in how they handled themselves. We didn't create this melee.

"I lauded their professionalism. I looked at every one of them in that room and I said to them, 'Do you know how good you are? This doesn't happen to mediocre teams.' "

Tracy already knew his players wanted to brawl at London, where the Tigers — under similar ass-kicking circumstances — previously buzzed Tim Barker's head with a fastball.

At the time, Tracy told his players to be patient, to wait for the right moment. Like next weekend, when the teams would be back in Harrisburg, where Tracy told his coaches, Chuck Kniffin and Greg Fulton, that a reckoning was coming.

And delivered by Hardge, once he got back on his feet after ducking Warren's head-high fastball.

"I never encouraged my players to fight, ever," Tracy said years later. "We're not going to strike the first blow. That's not the way I managed teams. But, in my mind, if someone takes a potshot at us, we will respond.

"So Mike Hardge took a moment (after Warren's pitch), looked down at me in the third base coach's box and we made eye contact. And, I said, right out loud, 'What the hell are you waiting on?' "

Without needing to hear another word from Tracy, Hardge charged the mound.

Twelve minutes later, the most lopsided baseball fight in the history of City Island — a history that dated to 1890 — was over.

In that time, the Tigers went in mere moments from being frustrated over the course of six-plus games to being humiliated.

"They picked on the wrong outfit," Tracy said. "I had some stallions in my dugout."

MONDAY, MAY 24
A Minute With Rice

HARRISBURG — Lance Rice had been with the Senators for a couple of weeks, doing little more than sitting in the bullpen and waiting to warm up the next relief pitcher.

LANCE RICE

Occasionally, he would start a game to give a day off to regular catcher Rob Fitzpatrick, who started 19 of 20 games after backup Miah Bradbury abruptly retired on April 30.

Rice thought about asking manager Jim Tracy for more playing time, but being selfish simply was not part of Rice's DNA.

"Jim gave me some time to get my legs under me," Rice remembered a quarter-century later.

"I really should have pushed to play more, but that was not my style. My role had become the veteran backup guy. I tried to do that as best as possible."

Rice actually welcomed this regularly scheduled off day.

Closer back then to 27 than 26, Rice was one of the oldest players on the Eastern League's youngest team.

He also was coming off catching 22 innings in less than 48 hours as he unexpectedly found himself behind the plate after Fitzpatrick sprained his left ankle in the fifth inning of Friday's 7-0 victory over London.

In those two-plus games, Rice caught three future major leaguers in Reid Cornelius, Miguel Batista and Joey Eischen — a couple of nibblers in Cornelius and Batista, and the hard-throwing but sometimes erratic Eischen, the latest "Wild Thing" in baseball.

Until now, Rice mostly had seen the Senators' staff from afar in spring training as a minor leaguer with Los Angeles. That was before the Dodgers released him at the end of camp in '93.

"I knew the Expos had some talent (in Harrisburg)," Rice said.

"The team carried so much confidence. This helped the pitchers, too," he said. "They knew we would score some runs. We didn't have to be so careful with everything."

103

Kirk's Final Frontier

BINGHAMTON, N.Y. — Timing was everything for Kirk Rueter through the season's first six weeks. No pitcher on the Senators' vaunted staff had matched his consistency. No starter in the Eastern League had a better earned-run average.

KIRK RUETER

All of which made this start so, well, Rueteresque as the left-hander scattered nine hits and two walks over eight innings of an 8-1 victory here over the Binghamton Mets before a crowd of 2,173 at Municipal Stadium.

In running his record to 5-0, Rueter lowered his ERA to 1.36. Just for fun, he worked out of four jams, thanks to two double plays that he started and a season-high seven strikeouts. Five of those strikeouts came with runners in scoring position.

The Senators gave Rueter all the runs he needed, and more, with a four-run first inning off Pete Walker. In return, Rueter made sure the game ended in less than 2 hours and 30 minutes — once again guaranteeing his teammates an early night on the town, although Binghamton hardly was the garden spot of pro baseball.

Of the 11 pitchers who started games for the Senators in 1993, no one came within 22 minutes of matching the 2:18 that Rueter averaged during his nine starts.

Turned out that this start was Rueter's last with the Senators.

His next came at Class AAA Ottawa with 336 starts to follow in the majors, where on occasion Rueter worked so fast the home plate umpire had to tell him to slow down with his warmup pitches so teams could finish their between-innings commercial breaks.

"There aren't too many guys who use that kind of brush to paint the plate," said manager Jim Tracy.

"And, this kid uses one of those brushes with the very thin bristles."

EASTERN LEAGUE STANDINGS on May 25			
	Record	Pct.	GB
SENATORS	30 - 9	.769	—
Bowie	22 - 16	.579	7 1/2
Albany	21 - 16	.568	8
Canton	23 - 18	.561	8
Reading	19 - 20	.487	11
London	16 - 26	.381	15 1/2
Binghamton	14 - 26	.350	16 1/2
New Britain	13 - 27	.325	17 1/2

LOOKING BACK

POSTGAME PLANS ALWAYS WERE MADE AROUND KIRK RUETER

Making Dinner Plans

Downtown Harrisburg in the summer of '93 had a few late-night eateries and more than enough places to grab a beer.

The Senators had some starting pitchers who could get you to those places well before closing time. Ugueth Urbina was one of those pitchers. Brian Looney was another.

Kirk Rueter, though, well, he was Captain Kirk at warp speed.

No Senators starter worked faster than Rueter, who quickly put together a 5-0 record on his way to becoming the first Senator from the Class of '93 to reach Class AAA Ottawa and then the first from that class to reach the majors.

Rueter always made sure his teammates had ample time to indulge themselves after the game.

"The guy saved my marriage," manager Jim Tracy recalled a quarter-century later. "I set my dinner plans by him. When he pitched, the games would be over before it got dark. I could take my wife to dinner or to the movies on the nights he pitched."

The Senators all knew to plan early with Rueter, whose starts averaged a mere 2 hours and 18 minutes from start to finish.

Urbina's times of game were next, albeit a distant second, at 2:41, followed by Looney at 2:42 with Gabe White, Rick DeHart and Rafael Diaz having their starts clocked at 2:43.

Routinely crushing late-night dinner plans were Miguel Batista, who fidgeted his way to 2:52, and Joey Eischen, whose wildness led to his starts averaging a mind-numbing 3:07.

Everyone needed to pack a snack when those two started.

Taking Pride In A Win

BINGHAMTON, N.Y. — Through 40 games, the Senators not only had the best record in the Class AA Eastern League, but the best in all of professional baseball. Many of those first 31 victories were easy, either thanks to shutdown pitching or an offense that could bludgeon any other team's pitching staff.

This game, well, not so easy. Yes, the Senators beat the Binghamton Mets 5-3 here, but they had to work for this one. Actually, they won the old-fashioned way, manufacturing runs in the eighth and ninth innings to win their eighth straight game.

After falling behind early 2-0, the Senators rallied for a 3-2 lead on Tyrone Woods' solo homer in the fifth and Cliff Floyd's two-run homer in the sixth. The homer was Floyd's league-high 13th.

The pesky Mets tied the score in the seventh before Curtis Pride's legs helped the Senators regain the lead, 4-3, in the eighth.

A night after losing his 10-game hitting streak by striking out as a pinch-hitter, Pride opened the eighth inning with a pinch-hit single to right. He then stole second, moved to third on Rondell White's groundout to first baseman Frank Jacobs and scored on Mike Hardge's sacrifice fly to center fielder Ricky Otero.

Pride took less time to get around the bases than you needed to read the previous paragraph.

Just a year earlier, Pride was playing here, completing his seventh and final season in the New York Mets' system. Back then, in 1992, he batted just .227 in 118 games for Binghamton with 110 strikeouts and only 12 stole bases in 22 attempts. The steal in this game was Pride's 17th in 18 attempts for the Senators. The single gave him a .347 batting average.

"That was just a bad, bad year," Pride said years later of his dismal 1992 season, when he also broke up with his girlfriend and found himself being taunted for his deafness. "I really thought about quitting."

He was glad he didn't.

EASTERN LEAGUE STANDINGS on May 26			
	Record	Pct.	GB
SENATORS	31 - 9	.775	—
Bowie	23 - 16	.590	7 1/2
Canton	23 - 18	.561	8 1/2
Albany	21 - 17	.553	9
Reading	20 - 20	.500	11
London	16 - 26	.381	16
Binghamton	14 - 27	.341	17 1/2
New Britain	13 - 28	.317	18 1/2

LOOKING BACK
A Work In Progress

CURTIS PRIDE FINALLY HAD HIS CAREER POINTED IN RIGHT DIRECTION

HARRISBURG — Carmen Fusco first heard of Curtis Pride in the spring of 1986, just before baseball's annual amateur player draft. Fusco, then a scout with the New York Mets, was told only of a talented high school shortstop from Silver Spring, Maryland.

"There were no reports on him. Nothing," Fusco said. "I just heard that I should come see this kid play."

So Fusco went to Silver Spring with no scouting reports, no preconceived notions and no expectations.

There, Fusco found a player who could run faster than most and hit a baseball harder than most.

He also found a player who was 95-percent deaf.

"In the scouting business, you can justify anything," Fusco said. "I easily could have said this guy isn't going to make it because he's deaf. But this kid had one helluva mental makeup. You add in physical abilities, and it spells prospect."

The Mets, on Fusco's recommendation, used their 10th-round pick in the 1986 draft to select Pride.

LOOKING BACK

They decided by the fall of '92 that Pride, after seven seasons mostly in the low minor leagues, no longer was a prospect.

The Montreal Expos thought otherwise.

They quickly signed Pride, pro baseball's only deaf player, and sent him to Class AA Harrisburg to be a bench player. Only Pride's inspired play continued to force manager Jim Tracy to use him more and more in the outfield.

At the age of 24, Pride once again was a prospect.

"He's well on his way right now," Tracy said.

Pride was on that track, in part, because of Tracy, who changed Pride's mechanics during spring training and turned a career .247 hitter into the EL's most feared leadoff batter.

"People are amazed," Pride said then, "but I've worked hard. I get great satisfaction proving other people wrong. When people say, 'You can't do that,' I say, 'Oh, I can prove you wrong.' "

The 5-foot-11, 195-pound Pride often delivered the proof in tape-measure home runs.

Pride, who had the rare combination of power and speed from the leadoff spot, had 10 homers through his first 35 games with and 17 stolen bases in 18 attempts. He was batting .347.

"You don't do that by accident," Tracy said.

Pride's time of 6.35 seconds in the 60-yard dash during spring training was the fastest of any of the Expos' minor leaguers.

"When you have a guy who has some ability and who wants to work," Tracy said, "there's no telling what you can do."

That would be quite a lot in this case, considering in 1992 Pride totaled just 10 homers and 12 stolen bases while batting .227 in 118 games for Binghamton.

"Curtis is as strong as a bull," said B-Mets pitching coach Randy Niemann. "He's always had the power; he just hasn't always made contact."

Just as he did with Binghamton during the 1992 Eastern League season, Pride struggled in his first six seasons with the Mets' Class A teams. Four of those years were split between playing in the short-season Appalachian League and attending the College of William & Mary.

"His numbers before really didn't tell you a whole lot," Tracy said.

LOOKING BACK

"But once I saw him for a few days ...," Tracy said, "the way he ran, the way he played the outfield that's when I started asking myself, 'Hey, how can this guy hit .210? I'm going to figure out the answer to that.' That's the fun part of my job."

Pride's work habits made Tracy's job that much easier.

"Makeup and work ethic, if you have some ability, are very important," Tracy said. "That's something that separates Curtis Pride from a lot of guys."

Pride was separated from most since birth after the Rubella his mother contracted during her pregnancy left him deaf.

"I've had a lot of people doubt my abilities because of my deafness," said Pride, who wore a hearing aid while playing.

"I've been trying all my life to show people I'm an educated person," he said. "I can speak well. I can lip read well. I can communicate with other people."

His parents questioned his desire to leave special-education classes in the seventh grade to join the mainstream student body.

"They said I'd be the only deaf person in the whole school," Pride said, "but they gave me a try, to see how well I could perform. A lot of people doubted me, but I'm a confident, independent person."

Pride responded with a 3.6 GPA at Silver Spring's John F. Kennedy High School, where he also was an All-America soccer player and highly recruited point guard in basketball.

"Soccer was my best sport," Pride said, "but there was no future in playing it."

At first, the baseball scouts had doubts about Pride because of his hearing deficiency. Later, they questioned his dedication as a player because of his commitment to college.

Pride responded by excelling academically at William & Mary, where he earned a degree in finance while also playing Division I college basketball in the winter.

"I don't want people to treat me different because I'm deaf," Pride said. "I want to be treated the same way as other people."

"He was a little bit different from a physical standpoint," said Steve Swisher, the onetime Chicago Cubs All-Star catcher who in 1992 managed Pride at Binghamton.

"But, I'll tell you, I've had a lot of guys who can hear out of both ears who don't have as much desire as Curtis Pride."

A Taylor-Made Win

HARRISBURG — Brien Taylor, the top pitching prospect in the minor leagues, could not help but notice how the Senators were playing.

Actually, all of baseball had noticed the Senators, whose record was better than any team on any level in the game.

"I don't care if you're playing a first-place team or a last-place team," Taylor said. "If you're going to get hit, you're going to get hit."

Taylor got hit — a lot — in this game as the Senators tagged Albany's prized left-hander for four doubles and four runs in the first two innings of an 8-1 victory before 2,533 fans on City Island.

The win was a franchise-record ninth straight for the Senators, whose only real concern for the day was making sure pitcher Kirk Rueter made his flight to Class AAA Ottawa, where he was promoted earlier in the day.

> *"It's so easy pitching for this team. This team scores early and they score late, and they score in bunches."*
> *Pitcher Reid Cornelius*

The expected pitching showdown in this game between Taylor, the top pick in the 1991 amateur draft, and the Senators' Reid Cornelius never materialized.

"It was just one of those nights," said Taylor, who in this game was victimized for seven runs, five steals — his pickoff move was atrocious — three errors by his own defense, a balk and a wild pitch before leaving with one out in the fifth inning.

At that point, the Senators led 7-1 and the Yankees had done nothing against Cornelius (4-1) after taking a 1-0 lead in the first on Robert Eenhoorn's RBI groundout. After that, Cornelius held Albany to three singles — all with two outs — before leaving after six innings.

"It's so easy pitching for this team," Cornelius said. "This team scores early and they score late, and they score in bunches."

EASTERN LEAGUE STANDINGS on May 27	Record	Pct.	GB
SENATORS	32 - 9	.780	—
Bowie	24 - 16	.600	7 1/2
Canton	23 - 19	.548	9 1/2
Albany	21 - 18	.538	10
Reading	20 - 20	.500	11 1/2
London	16 - 27	.372	17
Binghamton	14 - 27	.341	18
New Britain	14 - 28	.333	18 1/2

Night Of The Pen Men

HARRISBURG — There were times when the starters struggled and the relievers thrived.

This was one of them.

Thanks to seven-plus innings of one-run relief, the Senators were able to sweep the Albany Yankees 5-2 and 7-5 in a doubleheader before a crowd of 5,533 at RiverSide Stadium.

The victories extended the Senators' franchise-record winning streak to 11 games.

PEREZ

Picking up the victories were left-handers Yorkis Perez (3-2), who recorded the final 11 outs in the opener, and Darren Winston (1-0), who worked three innings of one-run relief in the second game before Mario Brito finished with his third save.

"We don't ever, ever get dismayed when we're down," said Glenn Murray, whose two-run single highlighted a four-run rally in the third inning of the first game. "With this offense, we know we can break out at any time."

WINSTON

The Senators hit four more homers, giving them 65 in just 43 games. Rondell White hit one in the first game, a solo drive off Brian Faw that accounted for Senators' fifth and final run in that win.

Cliff Floyd, Tyrone Woods and Shane Andrews all homered in the second game off Darren Hodges with Floyd hitting a two-run homer to right in the third inning, Woods a three-run shot to right in the fourth and Andrews a solo homer to center in the sixth.

BRITO

"I knew there was something different about this team from about the fourth or fifth day of the season," manager Jim Tracy said.

"Hey, 43 games into the season, this team knows it's for real."

EASTERN LEAGUE STANDINGS on May 28			
	Record	Pct.	GB
SENATORS	34 - 9	.780	—
Bowie	24 - 17	.585	9
Canton	23 - 20	.535	11
Albany	21 - 20	.512	12
Reading	21 - 20	.512	12
London	17 - 27	.386	17 1/2
New Britain	15 - 28	.349	19
Binghamton	14 - 28	.333	19 1/2

SATURDAY, MAY 29
"A Little Payback"

HARRISBURG — With each outing, Joey Eischen distanced himself a little more from the disaster of his first start.

Nearly seven weeks had passed since Albany routed Eischen in his Senators debut. Since then, Eischen has been nearly unstoppable.

Like in this game.

Backed by four more homers, including two by Cliff Floyd, Eischen cruised to an 8-2 victory against the Yankees before a crowd of 5,607 on City Island. The victory pushed the Senators' team-record winning streak to 12 games.

Eischen (7-2), the Eastern League's first seven-game winner, won seven of eight decisions since he was drilled by Albany for five runs in 3 1/3 innings in his Class AA debut

JOEY EISCHEN

on April 11. In this game, Eischen allowed just one earned run before leaving with two outs in the eighth inning.

Eischen also left knowing he made good on a pregame promise to pitching coach Chuck Kniffin.

"I told Chuck before the game that I had a little payback coming against this team," he said. "They did a pretty good job on me the first time."

His offense took care of Albany this time with Floyd hitting two solo homers, while Rondell White launched a solo homer and Glenn Murray added a two-run homer during a five-run seventh.

Eischen also had plenty of help on defense with second baseman Mike Hardge ranging hard to each side to take away hits from Jason Robertson to start the game and Mike Hankins in the fourth.

"Hardge made some plays," Eischen said, shaking his head, "that would show up on ESPN highlights."

EASTERN LEAGUE STANDINGS on May 29			
	Record	Pct.	GB
SENATORS	35 - 9	.795	—
Bowie	25 - 17	.595	9
Canton	23 - 21	.523	12
Reading	22 - 21	.512	12 1/2
Albany	21 - 21	.500	13
London	17 - 28	.378	18 1/2
New Britain	16 - 28	.364	19
Binghamton	15 - 29	.341	20

DeHart DeFlated

HARRISBURG — Rick DeHart arrived three days ago, taking the place of a fellow left-handed pitcher, the unbeatable Kirk Rueter.

RICK DeHART

On his way out of the clubhouse for batting practice that day, manager Jim Tracy stopped by DeHart's locker to welcome him to the team. The usual small talk before Tracy casually added on his way out the door, "By the way, I hate pitchers."

Tracy was smiling, but DeHart never saw it. Instead, the Senators' newest arrival from Class A looked puzzled, wondering if his new manager truly hated pitchers.

DeHart quickly was told that Tracy was teasing. Now, he was replacing the Class AAA-bound Rueter in the rotation of the best team in the minors, a team with a franchise-record, 12-game winning streak. He had watched from the bench as the Senators beat Albany in the first three games of the series on City Island.

He started this game, the series finale, and ended up being chased after just two innings in a game Albany eventually won 8-2.

In all, DeHart faced 13 batters with eight of them reaching on six hits, a walk and a hit batter. The biggest of the six hits was Rich Barnwell's first-inning grand slam that gave Albany a fast 4-0 lead.

Barnwell added a solo homer off reliever Darren Winston to start the third, giving him more RBIs in the game than the Senators had hits off Albany starter Mark Carper and reliever Rich Polak.

"We've been shoving it to them the last two or three nights," DeHart said. "They were ready today. Unfortunately, I was the one out there."

Tracy, who truly did not hate any of his pitchers, understood.

"That's a tough situation for this kid," he said. "Here he is starting for a team that's 35-9, that's won 12 games in a row. ... That's a lot of pressure."

EASTERN LEAGUE STANDINGS on May 30			
	Record	Pct.	GB
SENATORS	35- 10	.778	—
Bowie	25 - 18	.581	9
Reading	23 - 21	.523	11 1/2
Albany	22 - 21	.512	12
Canton	23 - 22	.511	12
London	18 - 28	.391	17 1/2
New Britain	17 - 28	.378	18
Binghamton	15 - 30	.333	20

MONDAY, MAY 31

Business As Usual

HARRISBURG — Tuesday's newspaper would carry a familiar headline.

Senators Rip Sox.

Beating the New Britain Red Sox, though, hardly was news. Now, getting bored with winning, well, that was news with the Senators.

So, in the afterglow of beating New Britain 8-0 in this game before a crowd of 1,647 on City Island, the Senators took time to look back 30 hours and dissect a loss to Albany that snapped their franchise-record, 12-game winning streak.

TYRONE WOODS

"I don't want to say it's a good thing we lost," Glenn Murray said, "but we've been doing a lot of winning. Sometimes that gets boring. We just took it for granted that we were going to win."

Tyrone Woods was more succinct.

"Complacent," Woods said. "We were getting lackadaisical."

To avoid a second straight loss, manager Jim Tracy deployed his "money" lineup of four former first-round picks, three second-rounders, a fifth-rounder and a seventh-rounder.

The time had returned, he said, to decimate somebody and the woefully undermanned Red Sox again filled that role, losing to the Senators for the seventh time in as many games.

On the night after the day in which they managed only four hits in that streak-busting loss to Albany, every Senator in the lineup had at least one hit against the Red Sox.

In all, they had 12 hits, including three doubles and another homer. They also stole three bases, all coming during a six-run rally in the fifth inning off Gary Painter. Painter actually beat himself by walking five of the first seven batters he faced in the fifth to fall behind 5-0.

"It seems like after we get beat, we come back the next day with more intensity," Tracy said.

"And this team is an intense bunch."

EASTERN LEAGUE STANDINGS on May 31			
	Record	Pct.	GB
SENATORS	36- 10	.783	—
Bowie	25 - 18	.581	9 1/2
Albany	23 - 21	.523	12
Reading	23 - 22	.511	12 1/2
Canton	23 - 23	.500	13
London	19 - 28	.404	17 1/2
New Britain	17 - 29	.370	19
Binghamton	15 - 30	.333	20 1/2

114

MONDAY, MAY 31

Woods followed Painter's fifth walk of the fifth inning — this one to Murray — with an RBI single to left for a 6-0 lead.

Rob Fitzpatrick, playing for only the second time since spraining his left ankle on May 21 against London, then singled to center for the Senators' final two runs of the inning.

Starter Gabe White (3-0) actually received all the runs he needed in the bottom of the fourth, which Rondell White started by lining Painter's 2-0 pitch deep over the wall in left-center.

ARCHIE CORBIN

The homer was the Senators' 70th in only 46 games.

Of those 70 homers, 46 came off the bats of Murray, White, Cliff Floyd and Curtis Pride. By themselves, the quartet had more homers than the totals of any of the league's seven other teams.

Just in case White's homer was not enough, the Senators added a second run in the bottom of the fourth as Floyd followed White's homer with a double off the base of the wall in center and scored two batters later on Murray's double to left-center.

The other White — Gabe — allowed only three singles and double over the first seven innings. He also struck out seven batters before leaving after the seventh, having lowered his earned-run average to 1.65.

"The big thing from the performance we got out of Gabe was getting our bullpen recharged," Tracy said. "We went through the bullpen pretty good this weekend."

Oh, yeah, big time. Against Albany, Tracy was forced to use his bullpen in 16 of the 32 innings played during the three-day, four-game series.

Archie Corbin, three days removed from starting the second game of Friday's doubleheader against Albany, worked the final two innings in this game. He struck out three, including Boo Miller looking to end the game, to finish the Senators' fourth shutout of the season.

As much as the bullpen needed the break, Corbin needed the mental boost, given his ERA in May had been 9.28.

"I'm feeling more relaxed out there," Corbin said. "I need to get a lot more of these in."

115

Martin's Moment

HARRISBURG — Chris Martin had a $10 fine hanging over his head for every fly ball he hit in his first at-bat of a game.

CHRIS MARTIN

That was the penalty assigned by manager Jim Tracy, who constantly had been reminding Martin that he needed to hit line drives to the gap, not make easy outs in the air.

Martin only once hit ball hard in this game, and that ball was hit into the air.

No fine, though, for Martin as the ball he hit turned into his first home run of the season, a shot to left field to lead off the bottom of the 10th and lift the Senators over New Britain 4-3 before a crowd of 1,955 on City Island. Martin's homer off a first-pitch fastball from Zack Dzafic gave the Senators their 20th victory in 23 games.

"I'm just trying to hit line drives," Martin said.

Instead, Martin hit the Senators' league-leading 71st home run.

Martin's homer made a memory of the ninth inning in which the Sox tied the score at 3 on Mike Hardge's throwing error at second.

"I was trying to be aggressive," Hardge said. "The throw sailed. I guess it made the game that much more exciting."

Martin had been waiting for this moment after starting for the Senators over much of the previous two seasons.

Slowed by a back injury late in spring training, Martin saw his playing time limited initially by the presence of Ron Krause at second and Edgar Tovar at short, and later by Hardge and Tim Barker. With Barker out with a toe injury, Martin had his chance.

"It was on a serious clothesline," Tracy said of Martin's homer. "This one wasn't in the air for long.

"And," Tracy said with a smile, "if he hits one in the air the first time up tomorrow night, it'll cost him $10. He knows that."

EASTERN LEAGUE STANDINGS on June 1			
	Record	Pct.	GB
SENATORS	37- 10	.787	—
Bowie	27 - 18	.600	9
Albany	23 - 22	.511	13
Canton	24 - 23	.511	13
Reading	23 - 23	.500	13 1/2
London	20 - 28	.417	17 1/2
New Britain	17 - 30	.362	20
Binghamton	15 - 32	.319	22

116

Had To Happen Sometime

HARRISBURG — Blind squirrel. Acorn.

Eventually, they had to meet.

They did here with the mostly moribund New Britain Red Sox morphing into the squirrel, beating the Senators 8-2 on soggy City Island in front of a crowd of 1,853.

The victory for the Red Sox was their first in nine games this season against the Senators, who despite the loss still owned the best record in professional baseball.

Until this game, the Red Sox had been outscored 63-20 in their eight losses to the Senators. This game, though, belonged to them after a five-run second inning off Miguel Batista (5-2), who in the inning allowed three hits, three walks and a wild pitch.

He never reached the third inning.

"I was behind on my fastball," Batista said, holding up his hand to show his two-finger grip. "I was working to come over the ball on my curve, but my fingers were too far back on my fastball."

Batista's short night forced the Senators' bullpen to pick up the final seven innings with Archie Corbin doing most of the work, throwing four no-hit innings before tiring in the seventh.

"We're using Archie to fill a different role for us," manager Jim Tracy said. "Instead of looking for an inning, we're prolonging his outings. We want to allow him to get himself into some kind of sync, and his last three outings have been much better."

In sync was Frankie Rodriguez, Boston's top pitching prospect who held the Senators to three hits over seven innings. The only run he allowed was Curtis Pride's solo homer in the fifth.

By then, though, New Britain already had a five-run lead.

Tracy being Tracy, of course, found something positive to say about an otherwise gloomy night.

"We won six of eight games over the last seven days," he said. "If we can win six of every eight, I'll take that."

EASTERN LEAGUE STANDINGS on June 2			
	Record	Pct.	GB
SENATORS	37- 11	.771	—
Bowie	27 - 19	.587	9
Canton	25 - 23	.521	12
Albany	23 - 23	.500	13
Reading	23 - 24	.489	13 1/2
London	21 - 28	.429	16 1/2
New Britain	18 - 30	.375	19
Binghamton	16 - 32	.333	21

THURSDAY, JUNE 3
Aiming At History

HARRISBURG — Another off day on the schedule allowed for some rest, a little work and lots of speculation.

The Senators had just played 10 games in nine days, winning eight of them as they remained the hottest team in all of pro baseball.

Among those in need of a rest was third baseman Shane Andrews, who had played in each of the Senators' first 48 games.

Same, too, for first baseman Cliff Floyd, center fielder Rondell White and right fielder Glenn Murray, each of whom had missed only one of those 48 games.

Not everyone rested, though.

While nearly everyone else did whatever they wanted, pitching coach Chuck Kniffin worked with reliever Rafael Diaz, specifically to see if Diaz's sore right shoulder had healed

CLIFF FLOYD

enough for him to throw for the first time since May 20.

Of course, no day with the Senators, whether they were playing or not, was complete without wondering just how many games they might win before the season ended.

Even after losing 8-2 to New Britain a day earlier, the Senators still were on pace to win 108 of their 140 scheduled games, a stunning total that easily would break the Eastern League record of 101 victories set by the 1953 Reading Indians in a 154-game schedule.

"Can't help but think about it," Floyd said. "Everybody talks about it every day, so let's go for it. Why not?"

At 37-11, the Senators entered the off day with the best record in pro baseball and on pace to win the Eastern League race by 26 games.

"This is a helluva pace, isn't it?" manager Jim Tracy rhetorically asked at the time.

The Senators also were on pace to hit a league-record 210 home runs with Floyd, Murray and Curtis Pride projected to hit 88 of them.

THURSDAY, JUNE 3

"We have an attitude that we're good," Floyd said, "but we're also going to go out there and prove we're good."

"It's within reach," shortstop Tim Barker said of 100-plus victories. "We have to have a lot of luck. But you're going to have injuries and you're going to have people moving on."

That already happened once with Kirk Rueter, the Eastern League's best pitcher, recently being promoted from

KIRK RUETER

the Senators to the Expos' Class AAA team in Ottawa.

Others would follow, of course, because that was the nature of the minors. Players excelled at one level and moved to the next.

Even with Rueter's departure, the Senators still had the league's best power hitter in Floyd, the best shortstop in Barker, the best third baseman in Andrews, the best leadoff hitter in Pride and the best starting pitching staff.

All this, too, without a mention of White, arguably the most gifted hitter both in the Eastern League and the Expos' system.

"This is what we were hoping for coming out of spring training," said Kent Qualls, the Expos' minor league operations director, "but you're never really sure going into the season."

Nearly 50 games into the season, though, others were sure.

"You can't really say they have any flaws," said Brien Taylor, the Albany Yankees' pitcher and one of baseball's most hyped prospects — if not the most hyped prospect — this season.

In his last start against the Senators, Taylor was clipped for seven runs on seven hits before leaving in the fifth inning of an 8-1 loss on City Island.

Just as certain was Reading Phillies closer Toby Borland, who had been frustrating Eastern League batters since 1990.

"Harrisburg is the best team I've ever seen in this league," Borland said, "and I've been in this league for awhile."

Fast Start, Tight Finish

COLONIE, N.Y. — The first inning was easy
enough. The last eight? Well, not so much.

After taking a 4-0 lead to start the game, the
Senators needed reliever Yorkis Perez to record
the final 10 outs to save a 6-4 victory over
Albany before 3,748 fans at Heritage Park.

YORKIS PEREZ

Perez picked up his third save after replacing
starter Joey Eischen with two outs in the sixth
inning and keeping the Yankees hitless for the
rest of the game. The first of the 10 outs Perez
recorded was the toughest as he entered the game with the bases
loaded and the Senators holding a slim 5-4 lead.

After throwing his first pitch for a ball to Jason Robertson —
who an inning earlier had homered off Eischen — Perez came back
to strike out Robertson swinging at a breaking ball in the dirt.

"He did a fantastic job," manager Jim Tracy said of Perez. "It
was a tough situation, coming in to strike out Robertson."

Perez was perfect in the seventh and eighth, and picked up two
quick outs in the ninth before walking Robertson. Just to spike
everyone's blood pressure, Perez then bounced a wild pitch past
catcher Rob Fitzpatrick before Mike Hankins grounded out to Mike
Hardge at second to end the game.

The Senators led 3-0 before making an out in the first inning
after Cliff Floyd's RBI single and Glenn Murray's two-run double.
The lead grew to 4-0 when Murray — running home on Shane
Andrews' grounder to Hankins at third base — kicked the ball out
of the glove of catcher Jeff Livesey.

The Yankees scored twice off Eischen (8-2) in the second
inning, followed by solo
homers in the fifth and
sixth. In between, Floyd
launched his EL-leading
17th homer, crushing a
pitch from Rafael Quirico
deep over the wall in right
field in the third inning.

EASTERN LEAGUE STANDINGS on June 4			
	Record	Pct.	GB
SENATORS	38- 11	.776	—
Bowie	28 - 19	.596	9
Canton	25 - 24	.510	13
Albany	23 - 24	.489	14
Reading	23 - 25	.479	14 1/2
London	21 - 29	.420	17 1/2
New Britain	19 - 30	.388	19
Binghamton	17 - 32	.347	21

SATURDAY, JUNE 5
DeHart Still Waiting

COLONIE, N.Y. — Rick DeHart waited six days for a second chance to impress the Senators. The first chance resulted in an abysmal start nearly a week ago in an 8-2 loss to Albany on City Island. DeHart was to start this game, only to have that get rained out and rescheduled as part of a Sunday doubleheader. Sigh.

SUNDAY, JUNE 6
Swept Away In Albany

COLONIE, N.Y. — Turned out that Rick DeHart could have waited awhile longer for his second start with the Senators.

Gabe White could have waited, too, as neither pitcher was effective as the Senators were — yikes — swept by the barely .500 Albany Yankees in an afternoon doubleheader before a crowd of 2,204 at Heritage Park.

The first game, started by White, ended 7-3. The second, DeHart's start, was slightly closer at 4-3, but that was after the Yankees took a 3-0 lead to chase DeHart after just two innings.

Highlights were few for the Senators, who in the two games totaled just nine hits. Cliff Floyd drove in two runs in each game with a two-run single in the sixth inning of the opener and a two-run double in the sixth inning of the second game.

The losses came against Mark Carper and Domingo Jean, Albany's starters who entered the game with a combined record of 4-5 that marked only half of Joey Eischen's season win total.

"Different guys in this league are going to step up and want to play their best ball and pitch their best ball against us," manager Jim Tracy said. "When you play the top dog, let's face it, you want to beat them."

For a day, Albany did.

EASTERN LEAGUE STANDINGS on June 6			
	Record	Pct.	GB
SENATORS	38- 13	.745	—
Bowie	30 - 19	.612	7
Albany	25 - 24	.510	12
Canton	26 - 25	.510	12
Reading	23 - 27	.460	14 1/2
London	22 - 30	.423	16 1/2
New Britain	20 - 31	.392	18
Binghamton	18 - 33	.353	20

121

MONDAY, JUNE 7

Losing Here? Really?

NEW BRITAIN, Conn. — The season almost was two months old and the Senators had not yet lost three straight games.

Two? Yes. Just did, actually, in a Sunday doubleheader at Albany.

Thankfully, the New Britain Red Sox — losers in eight of nine games so far to the Senators were next on the schedule.

Uh, oh, make that eight of 10 now as the Red Sox found the league's best offense still napping from Albany and beat the Senators 5-2 before a sparse gathering of 897 at Beehive Field.

The loss was the third straight for the Senators, who had not lost three straight since August 1992. This skid reached three as again the Senators' offense was challenged, totaling only five singles, Rondell White's solo homer in the seventh inning and Cliff Floyd's two-out double in the ninth.

The Senators, though, gave themselves a chance in the ninth after Floyd's double was followed by Glenn Murray's infield single, Shane Andrews' RBI single to left and Tyrone Woods' walk to load the bases. Red Sox closer Joe Ciccarella, though, struck out Rob Fitzpatrick to end the game for his team-high fourth save. Ciccarella had all of New Britain's saves, a testament to just how bad the Red Sox's season had gone.

White's homer to left off Tim Smith actually gave the Senators a 1-0 lead in the top of the seventh. The lead vanished in the bottom of the inning as the Red Sox scored three runs off starter Reid Cornelius and then twice more in the eighth off Yorkis Perez.

The four earned runs off Cornelius (4-2) and Perez pushed the Senators' team earned-run average to 3.02, marking the first time since May 19 that their league-leading ERA was above 3.

The only positive of the day was Floyd being named the EL's player of the month for May, when the Expos' top prospect had 33 hits in 29 games with 12 homers and 34 runs batted in.

EASTERN LEAGUE STANDINGS on June 7			
	Record	Pct.	GB
SENATORS	38- 14	.731	—
Bowie	31 - 20	.608	6 1/2
Albany	26 - 24	.520	11
Canton	26 - 26	.500	12
Reading	24 - 27	.471	13 1/2
London	22 - 31	.415	16 1/2
New Britain	21 - 31	.404	17
Binghamton	19 - 34	.358	19 1/2

TUESDAY, JUNE 8

A Struggle, But A Win

NEW BRITAIN, Conn. — The offense kept sputtering, but that was OK for the Senators since the New Britain Red Sox in the end reverted to being, well, the New Britain Red Sox.

And that meant another victory over a team the Senators had beaten in nine of 11 games. This one for the Senators ended with a 3-2 victory in 10 innings before what was left from a crowd of 1,103 at Beehive Field. This victory was gift wrapped, really.

Curtis Pride started the winning rally with a one-out walk off reliever Zack Dzafic and moved to second when Mike Hardge was awarded first on catcher's interference against Scott Hatteberg.

Rondell White, who had three of the Senators' six hits, then bounced a pitch back to Dzafic, who tried to turn an inning-ending double play. Dzafic threw out Hardge at second base, but then watched as White beat Scott Bethea's relay to first.

With the rally still alive, Dzafic hit Cliff Floyd with a pitch to load the bases and Glenn Murray followed with an infield single to score Pride with the go-ahead run.

Murray's game-winning hit, such as it was, came three innings after the Senators tied the score at 2 on a hitless rally that the Red Sox fueled with a two-base error as center fielder Mike Beams dropped Oreste Marrero's fly ball and Tony Rodriguez botched Rob Fitzpatrick's grounder to short. Chris Martin then picked up an RBI, bizarre as that was, when his pop-up was dropped by Bethea, who recovered in time to force out Fitzpatrick at second base but not before Marrero scored on the play.

The Senators' pitching staff and defense were not as generous.

Miguel Batista worked the first seven innings, allowing two runs while striking out six. Yorkis Perez and Heath Haynes (4-0) combined for two shutout innings before Mario Brito picked up his fourth save after working out of a two-on, none-out jam in the ninth.

Pretty? No.
Still a W? Yes.

EASTERN LEAGUE STANDINGS on June 8			
	Record	Pct.	GB
SENATORS	39- 14	.736	—
Bowie	31 - 20	.608	7
Albany	26 - 25	.510	12
Canton	27 - 26	.509	12
Reading	25 - 27	.481	13 1/2
London	22 - 32	.407	17 1/2
New Britain	21 - 32	.396	18
Binghamton	19 - 34	.358	20

123

Eischen Wins Again

NEW BRITAIN, Conn. — Winning two out of three from the New Britain Red Sox normally was not a cause to celebrate.

The Senators did anyway.

Considering their struggles to pick up hits on this road trip — first at Albany, now here at Beehive Field — the Senators were just fine with getting 10 hits in this game to beat the Red Sox 2-1 before 1,143 fans.

MITCH SIMONS

The encouraging news for the offense came in the form of six doubles that matched the Senators' season high from an 11-5 win here on April 19 and equaled their total from the first five games of this road trip.

Even better news came from starter Joey Eischen, who pitched six scoreless innings before giving up the Red Sox's only run in the seventh on Tony Rodriguez's two-out, bases-loaded, slow-rolling infield single down the third-base line.

Eischen (9-2) allowed only one other hit — a fifth-inning double by Paul Rappoli — over the first six innings. Relievers Heath Haynes, Yorkis Perez and Mario Brito combined for the final two innings with Brito picking up his team-high fifth save.

In a housekeeping matter, manager Jim Tracy finally dusted off Mitch Simons to start at second base for Mike Hardge, who had not missed a game since arriving in Harrisburg on May 19.

In those 20 straight games with Hardge in the lineup, the Senators were 15-5.

Now, they were 1-0 with Simons in the lineup, although Simons, who arrived from Class A West Palm Beach when Tim Barker went on the DL, did not contribute much in this game. He went 0-for-4 with a pair of groundouts and flyouts.

EASTERN LEAGUE STANDINGS on June 9			
	Record	Pct.	GB
SENATORS	40- 14	.741	—
Bowie	32 - 21	.604	7 1/2
Canton	28 - 26	.519	12
Albany	26 - 26	.500	13
Reading	25 - 28	.472	14 1/2
London	23 - 32	.418	17 1/2
New Britain	21 - 33	.389	19
Binghamton	20 - 35	.364	20 1/2

THURSDAY, JUNE 10
Out Of Left Field

HARRISBURG — The idea in spring training was for Cliff Floyd to play some in the outfield while also learning how to play first base.

For the season's first 48 games, Floyd spent all of two innings in the outfield, and that reluctantly was spent in right field after the May 23 melee with London led to right fielder Glenn Murray being ejected from that game and backup outfielder Tyrone Woods being forced to play third base.

Other than that, Floyd had been the Senators' first baseman. Until the start of the latest, six-game road trip, when Floyd played every game in left field. He had 10 chances there, catching nine flies and flubbing a single by Albany's Lyle Mouton for an error.

For this game against Bowie, Floyd was back at first base.

Not because of his play in left field, but because left field at RiverSide Stadium was all but unplayable, thanks to a combination of rains earlier in the week, new sod and a faulty sprinkler system.

"When I walked out there at 4:30, it was unplayable," manager Jim Tracy said.

A few minutes later, Tracy called the Expos to tell them he could not, in good conscience, send their top prospect to play in the muck and mire that now was left field. The Expos did not hesitate in their response: Get Floyd back at first base, give Curtis Pride a snorkel and send *him* out to left field.

With that, Floyd was back at first base and Pride, opportunistic as he had been so far this season, ended up lifting the Senators over Bowie 8-7 before a crowd of 4,473 on the island.

Pride, who already had a single and triple in the game, snapped the 7-7 tie in the eighth as his bases-loaded sacrifice fly to right fielder Stanton Cameron scored Shane Andrews.

"We'd score. They'd score. They'd score again. We'd score again," said catcher Rob Fitzpatrick.

"It felt like a playoff game."

EASTERN LEAGUE STANDINGS on June 10			
	Record	Pct.	GB
SENATORS	41- 14	.745	—
Bowie	32 - 22	.593	8 1/2
Canton	29 - 26	.527	12
Albany	26 - 27	.491	14
Reading	25 - 29	.463	15 1/2
London	24 - 32	.429	17 1/2
New Britain	21 - 34	.382	20
Binghamton	21 - 35	.375	20 1/2

THURSDAY, JUNE 10

If nothing else, it was a weird game.

In a game delayed at the start by 37 minutes to repair the outfield, the teams traded the lead six times before the Senators took the final lead in the eighth inning without an official at-bat.

Andrews walked to start the inning and moved to second when Chris Martin pushed a sacrifice bunt back to pitcher Tom Taylor, whose throw to get Andrews at second was late.

Exit Taylor. Enter Dave Paveloff, who jumped ahead 1-2 in the count to Fitzpatrick, the Senators' No. 8 hitter, before walking him to load the bases. Pride then lined out to Cameron, who had no chance to catch Andrews at the plate.

The recipient of the final lead change was Yorkis Perez (4-2), who could not hold a 7-6 lead in the eighth but escaped when Sam Ferretti was caught trying to steal home to end the inning.

Mario Brito, the fifth Harrisburg pitcher, also survived a leadoff single to T.R. Lewis in the ninth before recording his sixth save.

Well before that, starter Rick DeHart showed he actually could last past the second inning as the left-hander sandwiched four shutout innings around Bowie's three-run rally in the second.

"Relaxation and concentration. That's all it was," DeHart said. "I more or less let things happen in the second inning. I wasn't concentrating enough then."

No worries as DeHart's performance arguably was the most consistent part of a choppy game that took three hours to play, and that was after the initial delay of more than a half-hour.

"There were a lot of strange things out there tonight," Tracy said. "It got sloppy at times. It got lengthy at times. There are going to be ballgames like this, but we did the little things we had to do."

Most of which came in the eighth inning.

"I think we hustled ourselves into a win tonight," Tracy said. "This one makes me earn my money a little bit."

As for Floyd, he was supposed to return to left field as soon as the turf dried.

"Cliff's capable of being a damn good first baseman and he's going to get to that point," Tracy said. "In my opinion, he's a half a season ahead defensively [at first base] as far as where we projected him in spring training."

On The Go

HARRISBURG — All season, manager Jim Tracy gave his blessing for his players to run on their own with pitches in the dirt.

Aggressive baseball, Tracy-style. Run smart. Run often. Run yourself into a victory.

So far, though, the Senators made headlines by hitting homers, not hot-footing around the bases. In this game against Bowie, they ran. A lot.

Using five stolen bases, coupled with three Bowie errors, the Senators beat the Baysox 6-4 before 3,848 fans on City Island.

The victory was the fourth straight for the team with the best record in pro baseball.

"Our running won us a ballgame tonight," Tracy said. "It's not always the home runs or the 10-2, 11-2 games."

The stolen bases came from Shane Andrews, Curtis Pride, Rondell White, Chris Martin and Rob Fitzpatrick.

Andrews' steal came after his leadoff single in the fifth inning triggered a four-run rally off Bowie starter Rick Krivda.

"It's been that way all year," Andrews said of Tracy's never-changing green light. "If we see a pitch in the dirt, we can go."

The game had plenty of sidebars.

Starter Gabe White (4-1) scattered eight hits over eight-plus innings before Heath Haynes recorded the final three outs.

Shortstop Tim Barker, still out with a fractured right thumb, was excused to go home to Salisbury, Maryland, as his wife gave birth to their second child.

Pride was shadowed before the game by the Discovery Channel, which was preparing a documentary on baseball's only deaf player.

And then there was Floyd's return to left field, where in the ninth inning he misjudged Stanton Cameron's routine fly. Floyd said his vision was blocked by the island's indigenous population.

"Mayflies," he said with a smile. "The ball just hit my glove and popped out."

EASTERN LEAGUE STANDINGS on June 11			
	Record	Pct.	GB
SENATORS	42- 14	.750	—
Bowie	32 - 23	.582	9 1/2
Canton	29 - 28	.509	13 1/2
Albany	27 - 28	.491	14 1/2
Reading	27 - 29	.482	15
London	25 - 33	.431	18
Binghamton	22 - 35	.386	20 1/2
New Britain	21 - 35	.375	21

Simons Says: It's A Win

HARRISBURG — The stars in this game were plentiful. Some of their IDs, though, were unlikely.

On the team of highly touted prospects, the Senators were instead led by the unheralded Mitch Simons and the slumping Oreste Marrero as the two combined for four hits and three RBIs in a 6-2 victory over Bowie before a crowd of 5,661.

The crowd was the fourth largest since RiverSide Stadium opened in 1987 and one that pushed the Senators' season total over 100,000 in only 32 home games, marking the franchise's fastest pace to reach that milestone.

Simons, getting a rare start at third base for the injured Shane Andrews, had two singles, while Marrero, owner of just two hits in his previous 22 at-bats, had two RBIs on a double and a single.

"I've been hitting the ball hard, but I couldn't find a hole," Marrero said of his struggles that dropped his batting average from .357 to .296. "There was nothing I could do about it."

Starter Reid Cornelius (5-2) held Bowie to one run on five hits in six innings before Darrin Winston and Archie Corbin combined for the final three innings of one-run, two-hit relief.

Simons drove in the run that would be the difference in the game with a fourth-inning single that gave the Senators a 3-1 lead. Marrero led off that rally with a grounder botched by second baseman Brad Tyler and moved to second on Chris Martin's bunt. Bowie starter Kevin Ryan then moved closer to getting out of the inning when he struck out Rob Fitzpatrick for the second out.

Next up was Simons, the Senators' No. 9 hitter with just one hit in his first 14 at-bats since arriving from Class A West Palm Beach. Simons chewed through nine pitches and ran the count to 3-2 before flaring Ryan's next pitch into right for a single to score Marrero.

"He jammed me. I just wanted to put the ball in play," Simons said. "When you do that, you never know what can happen."

EASTERN LEAGUE STANDINGS on June 12			
	Record	Pct.	GB
SENATORS	43 - 14	.754	—
Bowie	32 - 24	.571	10 1/2
Canton	30 - 28	.517	13 1/2
Albany	28 - 28	.500	14 1/2
Reading	27 - 30	.474	16
London	25 - 34	.424	19
Binghamton	23 - 35	.397	20 1/2
New Britain	21 - 36	.368	22

SUNDAY, JUNE 13
Bottom's Up

HARRISBURG — Rondell White knew the feeling, that dread that came with a slump.

MIKE HARDGE

Mike Hardge knew White knew, so he sought his advice. He also talked with backup outfielder Tyrone Woods, manager Jim Tracy and anybody else he could find in the Senators' clubhouse.

The ever-confident Hardge simply was out of confidence. Hardge, ever the one to look stylish, even ditched his beloved black wristbands for a pair in red.

Not sure which ended up being the cure in this game, but Hardge found some spaces to slap the ball against Bowie, picking up two singles to go along with three walks and three runs scored in a 12-4 rout of the Baysox before a 5,083 fans on City Island.

Hardge combined with Chris Martin and Lance Rice for eight of the Senators' 15 hits, eight of their 12 runs and half of their 12 RBIs. Not bad for the bottom third of any batting order.

"I feel like I took a lot of pressure off myself," Hardge said after the Senators completed a four-game sweep of the Baysox.

Hardge's hits came in the fourth and fifth innings, each going to the opposite field, each falling in front of Bowie right fielder Stanton Cameron and each scoring a run.

Hardge began the afternoon hitless with 11 strikeouts in his previous 24 at-bats. He also had just one RBI in his last 40 at-bats.

"I didn't know what was going to happen from AB to AB," Hardge said.

Just like White a few weeks ago, when he began emerging from an 9-for-78 slump that cut his batting average to .167.

"I had a long talk with Rondell, with Woodsy, with Trace," Hardge said. "I just need to break out of this like Rondell did."

EASTERN LEAGUE STANDINGS on June 13			
	Record	Pct.	GB
SENATORS	44 - 14	.759	—
Bowie	32 - 25	.561	11 1/2
Canton	31 - 28	.525	13 1/2
Albany	29 - 28	.509	14 1/2
Reading	27 - 31	.466	17
London	25 - 35	.417	20
Binghamton	24 - 35	.407	20 1/2
New Britain	21 - 37	.362	23

129

SUNDAY, JUNE 13

"I knew what he was going through," said White, whose two hits in this game raised his batting average to .299. "I've been telling him to look for the pitch on the inside part of the plate."

Bowie's pitchers were more than accommodating there as they seemingly threw most of their pitches over the inside part of the plate to everyone. Especially to Martin, Hardge and Rice — the Senators' No. 7, 8 and 9 hitters. Just over the fourth and fifth innings, the three combined for three hits and three runs as the Senators scored six times off Jose Mercedes.

"That says something for the top of the order to have the bottom third hit like that," said Rice, who was 4-for-4 with four RBIs.

The top third of the Senators' batting order wasn't too bad, either, as Curtis Pride, Mitch Simons and White reached base in seven of their 16 plate appearances with four hits and three walks.

They also accounted for the other six runs not driven home by Martin, Hardge and Rice.

One of Rice's RBIs came in the fifth inning on a safety squeeze that scored Martin for a 7-4 lead.

Mercedes lasted only two more pitches as he was ejected, along with Bowie manager Don Buford, after aiming an 0-1 fastball at Pride's head.

Undeterred, Pride broke open the game two innings later as he drilled a three-run homer off Tom Taylor for an 11-4 lead.

Not lost in the Senators' latest outburst — they had 15 hits in this game and 46 in the four-game sweep — was the best performance of the season by erstwhile closer Archie Corbin.

Corbin (2-1) replaced the struggling Miguel Batista in the top of the fourth inning and needed only 51 pitches to get through the seventh inning. In that time, the Senators turned a 4-1 deficit into an 11-4 lead.

"Our bullpen the last two weeks has been outstanding," Tracy said. "No, not outstanding, phenomenal."

Heath Haynes and Darrin Winston split the final two innings, retiring the final six batters before the Senators packed for an 11-game, 10-day road trip to Canton, Reading and Bowie.

"Everything I threw, I threw for strikes," said Corbin, who spent nearly all of May in a pitching version of Hardge's hitting slump.

"Now," Corbin said, "I have to build on this."

Just like Hardge.

A Thud In The Night

CANTON, Ohio — Wasn't all that long ago in real time when the Canton Indians were the top team — record-wise, anyway — in the Class AA Eastern League. That was less than seven weeks ago, which in baseball time really was an eternity.

CURTIS PRIDE

Since then, the Senators caught Canton for first place and passed the Indians. Really, passed them. Like 13 and a half games passed them, leaving the Indians hovering near .500 while the Senators were piling up baseball's best record.

So something like this game was inevitable as the Senators started a marathon 11-game, 10-day road trip with a 15-6 loss to Canton before 2,113 fans at Thurman Munson Memorial Stadium.

The Senators' effort was much like Munson Stadium itself. Dreary.

In absorbing their worst loss of the season — there had been so few from which to choose with only 15 losses in 59 games — the Senators' vaunted pitching staff gave up 21 hits, and trailed 7-0 after only two innings.

Most of the damage was done against Joey Eischen (9-3), who faced 12 batters with nine of them reaching base and seven of them scoring before he left with none out in the second inning.

The Senators briefly rallied for three runs in the third inning before the Indians scored eight more runs off Darrin Winston and Yorkis Perez to build a 15-4 lead before the end of the seventh.

The Senators' highlights were few.

Curtis Pride had three of their eight hits with a two-run homer to right in the third inning off Albie Lopez and an RBI single off Paul Romagnoli in the ninth.

Cliff Floyd also launched his 18th homer of the season off Romagnoli in the eighth inning. The homer pushed his hitting streak to 11 games.

EASTERN LEAGUE STANDINGS on June 14			
	Record	Pct.	GB
SENATORS	44 - 15	.746	—
Bowie	33 - 25	.569	10 1/2
Canton	32 - 28	.533	12 1/2
Albany	29 - 30	.492	15
Reading	27 - 32	.458	17
Binghamton	26 - 35	.426	19
London	25 - 36	.410	20
New Britain	22 - 37	.373	22

LOOKING BACK
Tobacco Stains

CANTON, Ohio — No more runs.

At least not the ones created by tobacco juice rolling down the front of the jersey.

No more dips. Nor chew. Nor butts, for that matter.

And, for sure, no more errors, because now getting caught with nicotine-laden products was going to be costly to players in the minors.

JOEY EISCHEN

The lords of baseball finally got their wish as, effective June 15, 1993, they instituted a ban on all tobacco products for more than 6,000 minor league players, managers, coaches and umpires.

Spared from the new rule are non-uniformed personnel; major league players, who already were protected by their own collective bargaining agreement; and players sent down from the majors to the minors for injury rehab assignments.

Since the new rule and its ramifications did not apply to their better-paid brethren in the major leaguess, those in the minors predictably reacted with distain.

OK, actually, they were pissed.

"It's ridiculous," said Senators pitcher Joey Eischen, a dipper off the field who never was shy in sharing his opinions on all things baseball.

"We're grown men," Eischen said. "Doesn't this have something to do with our rights? We really need to get a union like they have in the big leagues."

Until that unlikely moment happened, the non-union minor leaguers were told to expect the following:

LOOKING BACK

— No tobacco products, whether they be cigarettes, cigars, chew, dip or — for the more cerebral players — pipes on the field, in the dugouts, bullpens, batting cages, clubhouses or any mode of team travel (that was the plane, trains, automobiles and, now, buses clause).

— A fine of $300 for each violation on the AAA and AA levels, plus an automatic game ejection for player and manager.

— Random inspections by baseball's tobacco police, who theoretically could find a tin of dip in a player's locker at 3 p.m. and eject both player and manager hours before the first pitch

Big money, given first-year players in Class AA were paid only $350 per week.

"I believe in the rule," said third baseman and frequent dipper Shane Andrews, "but I think they're getting a little steep with a $300 fine. I don't do it on the field, but if they see it before the game, you're done and so is the manager."

As a rule, the Montreal Expos did not let their minor leaguers indulge in tobacco products on the field. Nothing, though, about chewing, dipping and smoking away from the field.

"I feel sorry for the guys who are going to have to stop doing it," said Cliff Floyd, who neither smoked nor dipped. "You never know what a chew or dip can do for somebody else when they're playing. It might help them out, but now it's going to be gone. It's a rule and you have to live by it now."

Enforcing the rule would not be as easy as implementing it.

"The umpires can't be looking for it," said manager Jim Tracy, a reformed dipper from his playing days in the majors in the early 1980s. "To have the umpires do that, and take away from the job they already have to do in calling balls and strikes, that's a tough thing to ask those gentlemen. What are they supposed to do? Call timeout to go into the outfield and check out a player?"

Players being players were going to find ways around the rule.

"Guys are going to keep doing it," said pitcher Gabe White, an off-field smoker. "They're just going to hide it better."

What was happening for some was a gradual switch from tobacco products to candy, sunflower seeds and gum.

"Let's just say," Tracy added, "I'm acquiring a very good taste for Dentine this year."

TUESDAY, JUNE 15

Waiting Out Nagy

CANTON, Ohio — For five innings, Charles Nagy dominated the Senators. As he should, given he was a major leaguer, an All-Star pitcher for the Cleveland Indians. For this night, he was a pitcher on an injury rehab assignment with their Class AA team.

Nagy was limited to five innings and 75 pitches, leaving with a 3-0 lead in the first game of a doubleheader against the Senators.

Doubleheaders in the minors, though, were seven innings, so the Senators simply waited out Nagy before roasting Canton's bullpen, scoring four runs in the sixth and two more in the seventh for a 6-3 victory in the first game at Thurman Munson Memorial Stadium.

With no major leaguer All-Stars to bother them in the second game, the Senators rolled to a 10-3 victory before what remained of the 3,156 fans who mostly showed up to see Nagy pitch.

Less than 24 hours after suffering their worst defeat of the year during a 15-6 loss to Canton in which they had just eight hits, the Senators totaled 16 runs on 19 hits in only 14 innings of the doubleheader.

Chris Martin, continuing to play shortstop for the injured Tim Barker, had four of those 19 hits in the doubleheader and scored six runs while driving in four. Cliff Floyd had a single in each game to push his hitting streak to 13 games.

The only concerns — big concerns, actually — were injuries in the opener to outfielders Rondell White and Curtis Pride. White strained a hamstring chasing a fly ball, while Pride tweaked his back diving into second base.

In the opener, Rick DeHart (1-2) finally picked up his first win, outlasting Nagy by two-thirds of an inning and being the pitcher of record in the sixth as the Senators scored four runs off Calvin Jones and Greg McCarthy.

Relievers Rafael Diaz and Heath Haynes split the second game with Diaz going the first four innings and Haynes (5-0) working the final three innings for the win.

EASTERN LEAGUE STANDINGS on June 15			
	Record	Pct.	GB
SENATORS	46 - 15	.754	—
Bowie	33 - 26	.559	12
Canton	32 - 30	.516	14 1/2
Albany	30 - 30	.500	15 1/2
Reading	28 - 32	.467	17 1/2
Binghamton	26 - 36	.419	20 1/2
London	25 - 37	.403	21 1/2
New Britain	23 - 37	.383	22 1/2

White On, White Off

CANTON, Ohio — The Eastern League's most dominant offense was missing two of its hottest hitters as outfielders Rondell White and Curtis Pride sat out with assorted bumps, bruises and muscle pulls

No matter. The Senators had a whole roster full of prospects to torment the Canton Indians.

First, there was Gabe White, the left-hander who started the season as the Montreal Expos' top pitching prospect and so far had done nothing to change that status.

There also was Cliff Floyd, the first baseman-and-sometimes left fielder who simply was the Expos' best prospect.

They combined in this game to do in the Canton Indians 2-0 before a crowd of 3,101 at Thurman Munson Memorial Stadium.

All White did — Gabe, not Rondell — was hold Canton to five singles in posting the Senators' second complete-game shutout.

Floyd gave White (5-1) all of the runs he needed with a two-run homer in the eighth inning of a game that marked the Senators' ninth victory in 10 games since snapping their season-long, three-game losing streak.

Floyd's homer — a line drive to right and his league-leading 19th — came after Mitch Simons, starting at DH for the injured Pride, led off the eighth with a single to left off Apolinar Garcia.

The homer left Floyd only two homers shy of the modern-franchise record of 21 hit by Wes Chamberlain in 1989. The two RBIs gave him 64 in only 61 games — just 29 away from matching Lance Belen's modern-franchise total set in 122 games in 1987.

Did we mention Floyd's 14-game hitting streak?

The homer also was Harrisburg's 84th of the season, leaving them 10 shy of tying the modern-franchise record set in 1991.

That record was destined to fall, given 78 games remained on the regular-season schedule.

EASTERN LEAGUE STANDINGS on June 16			
	Record	Pct.	GB
SENATORS	47 - 15	.758	—
Bowie	34 - 26	.567	12
Canton	32 - 31	.508	15 1/2
Albany	30 - 31	.492	16 1/2
Reading	28 - 33	.459	18 1/2
Binghamton	27 - 36	.429	20 1/2
London	26 - 37	.413	21 1/2
New Britain	23 - 38	.377	23 1/2

135

THURSDAY, JUNE 17

Oh, That Pesky Odor

CANTON, Ohio — The Senators had plenty of chances to win. They had plenty of hits with 11 and seemingly plenty of runs with seven.

They just did not have quite enough in this game as Canton rallied for three runs over the eighth and ninth innings to give the Senators only their second loss in 11 games.

The main culprit was Rouglas Odor, Canton's No. 9 hitter, whose three hits included the game winner in the bottom of the ninth of an 8-7 decision before a crowd of 3,482 at Thurman Munson Memorial Stadium.

The Indians scored twice in the eighth on Miguel Flores' two-out, two-run single to left field off reliever Heath Haynes.

They won the game in the ninth as Odor's two-out single to right off Mario Brito (3-2) easily scored Brian Giles from third.

The hit lifted Odor's batting average against the Senators to .391. He was hitting under .200 against the rest of the EL.

Cliff Floyd — who else? — combined with Mike Hardge and Mitch Simons for seven of the Senators' 11 hits.

They surely would have had more hits and, presumably, more runs had injured top-of-the-order batters Rondell White and Curtis Pride not missed their third straight game with various injuries.

Floyd also sparked a four-run rally in the first inning with a three-run homer to right field off Canton starter Shawn Bryant.

The homer was Floyd's 20th of the season, one shy of matching Wes Chamberlain's modern-franchise record set in 1989.

Chamberlain played in 129 games that season for Harrisburg. This game was Floyd's 62nd.

Floyd drove in 10 runs during the five-game series and extended his hitting streak to 15 games, matching the Senators' season high first reached by still-injured shortstop Tim Barker.

EASTERN LEAGUE STANDINGS on June 17			
	Record	Pct.	GB
SENATORS	47 - 16	.746	—
Bowie	34 - 27	.557	12
Canton	33 - 31	.516	14 1/2
Albany	31 - 31	.500	15 1/2
Reading	29 - 33	.468	17 1/2
Binghamton	27 - 37	.422	20 1/2
London	27 - 37	.422	20 1/2
New Britain	23 - 39	.371	23 1/2

136

FRIDAY, JUNE 18
Managing Just Fine

READING, Pa. — An hour before the first pitch, manager Jim Tracy took inventory of his roster, crossed off three outfielders who were hurt, talked about his injured shortstop and then offered a couple of words.

"We'll manage," Tracy said.

After reworking his lineup, Tracy sent out his team to do what the rest of the EL came to expect: Administer another ass kicking.

On the receiving end in this game were the Reading Phillies, who absorbed a 9-4 loss to the Senators before a mostly muted crowd of 4,497 at old Municipal Stadium.

With outfielders Rondell White (hamstring), Glenn Murray (shoulder) and Curtis Pride (ribs), as well as shortstop Tim Barker (finger), all on the bench with injuries, the Senators used four home runs to wipe out the Phillies. The homers by Tyrone Woods, Oreste Marrero, Shane Andrews and Rob Fitzpatrick gave the Senators their 10th win in the last 12 games.

The homers by Woods, Marrero and Andrews highlighted a pair of four-run rallies in the fourth and fifth innings for an 8-0 lead.

Fitzpatrick's homer, a solo homer in the eighth and his first since April 20, clinched Miguel Batista's first win since May 22.

Batista (6-2), who had three no-decisions and a loss in his previous four starts, allowed seven hits in seven innings before Archie Corbin and Rafael Diaz finished. Batista's only rough spot came in the fifth, when Reading scored all its runs on David Tokheim's bases-loaded triple and Keith Kimberlin's sacrifice fly.

"I was trying to go in a hurry and got out of my rhythm," Batista said.

Batista first put himself out of sync during the Senators' four-run rally in the fourth inning — a rally the light-hitting pitcher highlighted with his first hit of the season, an RBI double to right-center off Reading starter Ron Allen.

EASTERN LEAGUE STANDINGS on June 18			
	Record	Pct.	GB
SENATORS	48 - 16	.750	—
Bowie	34 - 28	.548	13
Canton	34 - 31	.523	14 1/2
Albany	32 - 31	.508	15 1/2
Reading	29 - 34	.460	18 1/2
Binghamton	28 - 37	.431	20 1/2
London	27 - 38	.415	21 1/2
New Britain	23 - 40	.365	24 1/2

137

FRIDAY, JUNE 18

Cliff Floyd, now the owner of a 16-game hitting streak, started that rally with an infield single. Woods then gave the Senators a 2-0 lead when he launched Allen's 1-1 pitch over the wall in left-center for his third homer of the season against Reading.

"We're just trying to pick each other up," Woods said. "If our big dogs aren't doing it one night, then maybe the little puppies can help out."

TYRONE WOODS

Marrero, who like Woods had been among the pups, followed with a walk and moved to second on Andrews' single to right. Both advanced on a passed ball by catcher Steve Bieser before Marrero scored on Fitzpatrick's groundout to second baseman Mica Lewis. Andrews scored when Batista drove Allen's 2-1 pitch past center fielder Jeff Jackson. Batista might have had a triple had he not performed a near-perfect tuck-and-roll after tripping over first base.

"I'm not used to doing that," said Batista, who had been 0-for-7.

Floyd also led off Harrisburg's four-run fifth inning with another infield hit. He then stole second before Woods walked to chase Allen, who was replaced by Blake Doolan.

ORESTE MARRERO

Marrero promptly sliced Doolan's first pitch over the left-field wall for a 7-0 lead. Two pitches later, Andrews homered to straightaway center.

"This is just another example of the character of this team," Tracy said. "We're almost halfway through the season, we're banged up, a day away from getting some people back and we get big hits from guys like Marrero and Woods to pick us up.

"This is what's been going on for 64 games."

ROB FITZPATRICK

Chasing History

READING, Pa. — The Reading Phillies looked sharp, all decked out in replica uniforms from 1953, the year their predecessors rolled to an Eastern League-record 101 victories.

Alas for today's Reading Phillies, the other players in this game were wearing the uniforms of the 1993 Senators, the team hoping to break that 40-year-old record.

The Senators moved a game closer to that record with a 19-4 rout of the Phillies before a crowd of 5,765 on Turn Back the Clock Night at Municipal Stadium.

Their 19 runs and 24 hits both were season-highs for the Senators, who won for the 11th time in 13 games to maintain the best record in pro baseball.

Seven Senators had at least two hits with Curtis Pride picking up five on two homers, two singles and a triple. Pride also drove home a season-high six runs and scored five times himself.

The beneficiary of this largesse was Joey Eischen (10-3), who in coming off his worst outing of the season held Reading to six hits over eight innings. Eischen also had two hits, both doubles, in five at-bats after going hitless in his first four at-bats this season.

Pride, who missed the last four games with a muscle pull in his rib cage, started the game batting .341 — just two percentage points behind Canton's Manny Ramirez for the league lead.

Five hits later, Pride was batting .368.

Cliff Floyd had three more hits to extend his team-high hitting streak to 17 games.

Among Floyd's hits was his 21st homer to tie the modern-franchise record set in 1989 by Wes Chamberlain. Like most of his homers, this one was crushed as he launched Eric Hill's 2-2 pitch deep to right field, clearing the ancient stadium's outer brick wall and leaving motorists on Route 61 with more of a chance to retrieve the ball than right fielder Mickey Hyde.

EASTERN LEAGUE STANDINGS on June 19			
	Record	Pct.	GB
SENATORS	49 - 16	.754	—
Bowie	34 - 29	.540	14
Canton	35 - 31	.530	14 1/2
Albany	33 - 31	.516	15 1/2
Reading	29 - 35	.453	19 1/2
Binghamton	29 - 37	.439	20 1/2
London	27 - 39	.409	22 1/2
New Britain	23 - 41	.359	25 1/2

SUNDAY, JUNE 20
Losing Pride

JIM TRACY WITH CURTIS PRIDE, ONE OF HIS PRIZED PUPILS

READING, Pa. — The Montreal Expos decided they had seen enough of outfielder Curtis Pride in the Eastern League.

Until now, in a career of some highs and many lows, Pride had been a tweener candidate to move up or simply move out.

That was before. Now, Pride most definitely was moving up.

Less than 24 hours after torching the Reading Phillies for two homers, a triple, two singles and six RBIs in a 19-4 rout here at Municipal Stadium, Pride was told he was going to Ottawa.

Bound for Class AAA for the first time in his career.

The news came from manager Jim Tracy after the Senators' latest victory over Reading.

The news overshadowed a 3-1 win, where Rick DeHart allowed just one hit and one run pitching into the eighth while Cliff Floyd went hitless for the first time in 18 games.

SUNDAY, JUNE 20

Predictably, Tracy's words brought tears to the 24-year-old Pride, who in his first seven-plus years of pro ball had yet to play above Class AA.

CURTIS PRIDE

The reasons for the tears were not so predictable.

"I told Jim Tracy that I didn't want to go to Ottawa," Pride remembered 25 years later.

The time, though, had come for the parent to kick the kid, for his own good, out of the house.

"I cried because I wanted to stay," Pride recalled. "This was a great team and I was having my best year. I asked Jim if I could stay. He played such a key role in my hitting, turning it around. He taught me. He really developed my hitting. … I didn't want to go."

After foundering in the lower tiers of the New York Mets' system for seven seasons, Pride signed with the Expos as a minor league free agent in the fall of 1992.

The Expos gave him a contract but no promises, other than getting a chance to compete for a roster spot with the Senators.

Regular playing time? Don't count on it.

Not with a Harrisburg outfield the Expos already planned to stock with wunderkind prospects Cliff Floyd and Rondell White, another Top 10 prospect in Glenn Murray and the hard-hitting, but oft-overlooked Tyrone Woods.

From his mostly forgettable seasons in the Mets' system, Pride arrived in Harrisburg with an underwhelming .247 career batting average.

He had been viewed by some more as a curiosity and less as a player. He had been seen as a person who was born 95-percent deaf, not one with dreams of becoming the majors' first deaf player since Dick Sipek played 82 games for Cincinnati in 1945.

Back in those days, in the closing days of World War II, major league teams were short of talent and players like Sipek and the one-armed Pete Gray received opportunities that did not exist in the game during non-wartime years.

SUNDAY, JUNE 20

The only battle Pride was fighting in 1993 was against the narrow-minded belief that his inability to hear was greater than his ability to play. What the pundits did not see in Pride was his passion, his desire to learn and to succeed.

Pride found no better teacher than Jim Tracy, a former batting champion in the minors whose brief, flickering career in the majors had been swept away in the ashy residue that followed baseball's bitter strike of 1981.

Tracy seemingly needed only 20 minutes in spring training to correct the flaws in Pride's swing. That tutorial came during the heat-filled, humidity-draining training camp the Senators held in a dustbowl known as Lantana, Florida.

"I remember the first day we talked at the batting cage," Pride said 25 years later. "We talked about hand-foot separation, how to pick up my (front) leg, how to keep my head back and how to use my hands, because he knew I had quick hands."

Pride used those hands at the plate, his quickness in the field and his freakish, bull-like strength to turn around his career. For him, one hit begot two hits, two turned into three.

Opportunities came more often.

"Trace saw the ability I had," Pride recalled. "He knew I could run. He knew I could play defense. I just needed consistency. He saw the more I played, the more consistent I played and my average went up."

Pride left for Ottawa batting a team-high .356 with 15 homers, 38 RBIs and 21 stolen bases. All in just 50 games.

When he left for Ottawa, Pride was hitting 45 points higher than the great White and 52 better than the even-greater Floyd.

"I started out at spring training on the Triple-A team, and I thought I was going to open the season with them," Pride said.

"Then as camp went on I went down to Harrisburg. I was kind of disappointed in that, but at the same time I thought I might get more opportunities to play. And then I get to play with Rondell White and Cliff Floyd and Glenn Murray, and that really was nice."

EASTERN LEAGUE STANDINGS on June 20			
	Record	Pct.	GB
SENATORS	50 - 16	.758	—
Bowie	35 - 29	.547	14
Canton	35 - 32	.522	15 1/2
Albany	33 - 32	.508	16 1/2
Reading	29 - 36	.446	20 1/2
Binghamton	29 - 38	.433	21 1/2
London	28 - 39	.418	22 1/2
New Britain	24 - 41	.369	25 1/2

142

MONDAY, JUNE 21

Rain, Shine, Clouds

BALTIMORE — A group of near-sighted groundskeepers, coupled with two downpours, did what few had done: They slowed down the Eastern League-leading Senators.

A second downpour in the third inning put a halt to this game against Bowie, the first of a scheduled doubleheader at Memorial Stadium. When the grounds crew, comprised of volunteers from the stands, failed to properly cover the field, the rains made mud of the right side of the infield and left it unplayable. The game was suspended at 8:43 p.m. — 42 minutes after the volunteers tried to cover the field. At the time, the Senators trailed 2-1, leaving them to try and rally in another doubleheader scheduled for Tuesday.

TUESDAY, JUNE 22

BALTIMORE — One step was made toward history. Another went backward, toward playing like New Britain as the Senators split two games with Bowie, winning 7-2 in the completion of Monday's suspended game before losing 5-0 in the regularly scheduled, seven-inning game. The split kept the Senators on pace to win a league-record 105 games.

The good news: Rondell White's three hits in the two games extended his hitting streak to 13 games, a span over which he was batting .436, while Archie Corbin's four hitless innings of relief were plenty to pick up the victory in the suspended game.

The bad news: Jim Dedrick's five-hitter in the second game made him the first pitcher this season to shut out the Senators.

"We're 50 (wins) away from tying a record set by a (1953 Reading) team that played 154 games," manager Jim Tracy said. "If that's not enough incentive to go after it, then you have to take a long look at yourself.

"But, we can't afford too many games like the second game. We can't have a lackadaisical effort like we had in the second game."

EASTERN LEAGUE STANDINGS on June 22			
	Record	Pct.	GB
SENATORS	51 - 17	.750	—
Bowie	36 - 30	.545	14
Canton	37 - 32	.536	14 1/2
Albany	33 - 33	.500	17
Binghamton	30 - 38	.441	21
Reading	29 - 38	.433	21 1/2
London	29 - 39	.426	22
New Britain	24 - 42	.364	26

143

Taking Off Early

BALTIMORE — A regularly scheduled off day was coming up in less than 24 hours. Alas, the Senators decided to take off early.

First, the offense was a no-show, totaling just six hits in an 11-2 loss to Bowie before a crowd of 1,747 at Baltimore Memorial Stadium.

Second, the pitching was just as AWOL as the Baysox piled up 16 hits, including 11 in only five innings against starter Miguel Batista (6-3).

The outcome marked only the third time the Senators lost consecutive games. And they did

RANDY WILSTEAD

so in such unspectacular style as manager Jim Tracy used the upcoming off day to give an extra day of rest to top prospect Cliff Floyd, third baseman Shane Andrews and catcher Rob Fitzpatrick.

"All resting," Tracy said. "They were sitting there charging their batteries. Floyd had played in 67 of 68 games, and every time we tried to give Andrews a day off someone got hurt or started a fight."

Fitzpatrick, the gritty catcher, simply was wearing down.

"I want them strong in mid-July and early August," Tracy said. "I don't want to run them down here."

While Floyd, Andrews and Fitzpatrick rested, injured shortstop Tim Barker was spotted before the game taking grounders for the first time since fracturing his right thumb on May 23.

The Senators' highlights in this game were few, but included Rondell White and Oreste Marrero pushing their hitting streaks to 14 and 11 games, respectively; newly arrived Randy Wilstead picking up his first RBI after making his Class AA debut 24 hours earlier; and Glenn Murray posting his 14th homer in the sixth inning.

By then, the Baysox were leading 6-1 and the Senators already were into their day-off mode.

EASTERN LEAGUE STANDINGS on June 23			
	Record	Pct.	GB
SENATORS	51 - 18	.739	—
Bowie	37 - 30	.552	13
Canton	37 - 33	.529	14 1/2
Albany	33 - 34	.493	17
Binghamton	32 - 38	.457	19 1/2
Reading	30 - 38	.441	20 1/2
London	30 - 39	.435	21
New Britain	24 - 44	.353	26 1/2

THURSDAY, JUNE 24

Right On The Money

HARRISBURG — The familiar buzz started on the backfields of West Palm Beach's Municipal Stadium, where Cliff Floyd was coming to bat in an otherwise forgettable spring training game.

CLIFF FLOYD AT WORK

Side conversations tended to break out whenever Floyd had a bat in his hands.

Didn't matter when. During batting practice. During spring training games. During the bottom of the ninth with two outs and two on in a game that counted.

Floyd's presence always brought a stir.

"There," Mark LaRosa, a Class A pitcher for Montreal, said in a whisper as Floyd prepared to hit in a March game against Greenville, "there goes a future millionaire."

Three months later, Floyd still squirmed at the notion as he paced around the jail cell-sized cubicle that manager Jim Tracy called his office at RiverSide Stadium.

Floyd, who like the rest of the Senators had today off, mindlessly twirled a bat with his wrists as he wondered aloud if his latest nickname of "Money" was a derisive one.

"I really don't like it," Floyd said to Tracy. "What do they mean?"

The nickname, Floyd was told, denoted respect for his ability.

His performance, Floyd was told, backed it up.

Yet, Floyd did not seem convinced.

Despite his imposing size — 6-foot-4, 220 pounds — and his remarkable composure on the field, the 20-year-old Floyd often could be as sensitive as a child half his age and size.

"I kind of just play it off, because they're joking," Floyd said, "but sometimes jokes get to you, because they don't know how you're feeling.

"In this clubhouse, being a first-rounder doesn't mean anything," he said. "I still have to work like everybody else."

145

THURSDAY, JUNE 24

Cliff Floyd was just two years removed from being the Montreal Expos' top choice and 14th overall pick in baseball's annual amateur player draft.

He was less than a year removed from ravaging the Class A South Atlantic League, where he learned a new position — center field — while leading the SAL with 97 runs batted in, 56 extra-base hits, 261 total bases, a league-record 16 triples and making opposing pitchers cry.

Floyd now was halfway through his first season in the Class AA Eastern League.

He was crushing this league, too.

Floyd, splitting his time with the Senators between first base and left field, easily was ranked the top prospect in an Expos' organization already loaded with prospects.

As the 51-18 Senators neared the season's halfway point, Floyd was hitting .299 in 67 games with a league-leading 21 home runs and 71 runs batted in.

He was, by numbers alone, the leader of the team with the best record in all of baseball.

The concepts of leadership, like some of the nicknames he picked up along the way, hardly were embraced by Floyd.

"He's very capable of being one," Tracy said, "but, early on, he had to be pushed."

"I've been working on it," Floyd said. "I haven't been a leader in the past. I've always been low key. Being a leader is kind of tough sometimes."

To understand Floyd's reluctance was to understand his background, a past that — with a stray bullet here or there — easily could have prevented his present.

In Floyd's former world, at the corner of 79th Street and the Dan Ryan Expressway in Chicago's turbulent South Side, so-called "leaders" often died by gunshot.

Floyd's world now was the northeast corner of the Senators' tiny clubhouse on City Island. The corner was occupied by the self-proclaimed Harrisburg Hood, by players who went by "Rock" and "G-Wiz" and "Woodsy."

Floyd was called "Sleepy."

This Hood was the only gang to successfully recruit Floyd. Others had tried.

146

THURSDAY, JUNE 24

"It was not so much the gangs, but the drug dealers," said Floyd's mother, Olivia. "In our neighborhoods, the kids worried about those shirts and shoes. Guys were always offering, 'If you do this, we'll do this for you.' He had to avoid the peer pressure."

Somehow, Floyd managed.

"You try to block it out," Floyd said of the temptations of his youth. "You know what situation you're in and how to handle it.

"You have a lot of gangs, a lot of violence, a lot of people who were jealous. … Trying to stay off the streets was tough, because you want to have fun. You're still young. You don't want to stop having fun just because guys are shooting guns."

Reminders were plentiful.

"You would hear gunshots at nighttime," Floyd said, "and you tell yourself, 'One day, I have to get out of here.' "

His parents, Cornelius and Olivia Floyd, already started.

Cornelius Floyd, a former Marine, worked double shifts at the local steel plant so the family could live in Markham, a suburb 23 miles south of Chicago.

Cliff Floyd attended nearby Thornwood High, leading the school to an Illinois state title in 1991 before being drafted and signed by the Expos for $290,000.

"He's lucky … he avoided it," said Murray, who once ran with the gangs in Manning, South Carolina. "I probably never would have known Cliff Floyd if he got tied up in that stuff."

Olivia Floyd saw to that. She also had some unexpected help.

"I would tell Clifford, 'I know some of your friends are doing illegal things. I don't want you to do the same,' " she said. "But they would tell him, 'Cliff, we're doing these things, but you don't want to be doing these things.' It's like they wanted him to make something of himself."

Floyd occasionally let his thoughts wander, trying to get a glimpse into just what that something could be one day.

Celebrity was that intoxicating to him in 1993.

"Sometimes I kind of let it get to me a little bit, thinking, 'One day, I'm going to do this and have all of this, see myself on television,' " Floyd said.

"But I have a feeling that when I do see that, I'll still be the same person."

THURSDAY, JUNE 24

Floyd's growth, not just as a player but as a person, was measured by those around him.

"When he first signed, you could see that 'street' in Cliff," said Derrick White, the Senators' first baseman in 1992 who was drafted five rounds behind Floyd in 1991.

DERRICK WHITE

"That first year in the Instructional League, he used to go to the mall with $5,000 in his pocket."

White, who was Floyd's roommate that fall as well as the last two spring trainings, saw through the pretenses.

"He'd do things young people do when they first get a lot of money," White said. "He carried it around, because people expected him to."

The expectation now was for Floyd to reach the majors with Montreal sooner rather than later.

The Expos, of course, remained non-committal as June neared July, saying Floyd needed to find a spot in the field — either first base or left field — before they could move that potent bat of his to the majors.

Some national pundits, of course, speculated that Floyd may reach the majors sometime around the All-Star break.

The timetables meant little to Floyd.

"I know I'm ready now, but that's my opinion," Floyd said. "The defense will come. I'm working hard at it. I feel I can play first base in the big leagues.

"I know I can hit. ... I'll just wait on the call."

Until then, Tracy and the Senators remained the beneficiaries of Floyd's vast talents, both tangible and intangible.

"Beside all the ability," Tracy said, "he has the quality that the more pressure is on, the better he likes it, the better he performs. You can't teach that.

"When a guy lives for something like that," Tracy said, "or a guy shows you he has the innate ability to perform under those type of circumstances ... I think what we're talking about here is a superstar, aren't we?"

FRIDAY, JUNE 25
Back To Work

HARRISBURG — Cliff Floyd, the player, did not want to sit out the Senators' last game at Bowie, but he had no choice.

Jim Tracy, the manager and the man with the final say so, wanted Floyd to rest.

There was no conversation. No argument. No battle.

The player sat. For one game.

Floyd, well rested from sitting out Wednesday's 11-2 loss to the Baysox and the scheduled day off that followed, came back in this game and collected a pair of hits, including one that broke a 2-2 tie, as the Senators beat Reading 7-2 before a crowd of 5,570 at RiverSide Stadium.

Floyd also had two stolen bases and his first assist from left field as he threw out Steve Bieser trying to score from second base with one out in the second inning.

The victory also snapped a modest two-game losing streak for a team that finished the first half of the Eastern League's 140-game season with the best record in pro baseball, majors or minors.

"I needed a rest, but I want to play every day," said Floyd, who had played in 67 of the Senators' first 68 games. "Getting a couple of days off was a tremendous help."

As if he had a choice.

"I didn't even give him a chance to talk about it," Tracy said. "His bat was sluggish."

After striking out in the first inning and flying out to center fielder Jeff Jackson in the third, Floyd singled to left in the fifth inning, scoring Rondell White from second for a 3-2 lead, and then singled to right during his final at-bat in the seventh.

The RBI was Floyd's EL-high 72nd in only 68 games.

The two steals gave him 17, tying him with White for second on the team behind the 21 Curtis Pride totaled before his recent promotion to Class AAA Ottawa.

EASTERN LEAGUE STANDINGS on June 25			
	Record	Pct.	GB
SENATORS	52 - 18	.743	—
Bowie	37 - 31	.544	14
Canton	38 - 33	.535	14 1/2
Albany	34 - 35	.493	17 1/2
Binghamton	32 - 40	.444	21
London	31 - 40	.437	21 1/2
Reading	30 - 39	.435	21 1/2
New Britain	26 - 44	.371	26

FRIDAY, JUNE 25

What ultimately finished the Phillies in this game were home runs. They allowed two more — the 26th and 27th over their last 26 games — to help the Senators set their first milestone of the season.

Mike Hardge's seventh-inning homer off Blake Doolan was the Senators' 95th of the season, one more than the previous modern-franchise record set in 1991 over 140 games.

Hardge's homer to center field on Doolan's first-pitch slider also gave the Senators a 5-2 lead. Floyd followed with a single to right before Glenn Murray drilled Doolan's 1-1 changeup over the left-field wall and toward neighboring Lemoyne.

The homers by Hardge and Murray clinched another victory for Joey Eischen (11-3), who scattered six hits and four runs over seven innings before Archie Corbin closed out the game.

"I held them when I had to hold them," Eischen said. "Then, we finally exploded."

Eischen's defense repeatedly saved him, starting in the second inning when Hardge made a diving stop to his left at second base to throw out Mica Lewis and Floyd followed with a perfect throw to catch Bieser.

Hardge later ended Reading's seventh by going hard to his right to grab Keith Kimberlin's one-out grounder, running over the bag to force out David Tokheim and then throwing out Kimberlin.

"Everybody's saying when you make a great play, you should lead off the next inning," Hardge said of his record-setting homer in the bottom of the seventh, "but I didn't expect that."

JIM TRACY

Tracy To Manage All-Stars

The Senators' winning ways paid off even before the start of the game as Jim Tracy was named to manage the National League players in the third annual Class AA All-Star Game coming up in a couple of weeks in Memphis.

Tracy, being Tracy, refused to take credit, giving that instead to his players and his staff.

"There are 25 reasons why I am the manager of the National League club," Tracy said.

Fine Night for Fitty

HARRISBURG — Another Saturday night for the Senators, another massacre for the Reading Phillies.

For the third time this season, the two teams met on a Saturday night — and, for the third time, the Senators crushed the Phillies.

This time, the beating was administered by the struggling Rob Fitzpatrick, who launched a pair of three-run homers as the Senators rolled to a 15-0 win before 5,226 fans on City Island.

ROB FITZPATRICK

Rondell White and Oreste Marrero added solo homers to extend their hitting streaks to 16 and 13 games, respectively.

Fitzpatrick and White each finished with four hits and combined for nine RBIs. Mike Hardge also had three of the Senators' 17 hits.

Tim Barker, playing for the first time in 33 games after fracturing his right thumb, reached base five times with a pair of singles and three walks.

Fitzpatrick, who began the game with only 17 hits in his last 98 at-bats, used his first three-run homer to cap the Senators' six-run first inning off Greg Brown. His second three-run homer came in the fifth off reliever Eric Hill to push the lead to 11-0.

Gabe White (6-1) struck out 10 batters in seven innings to win his third straight decision. Yorkis Perez and Mario Brito split the last two innings to preserve the Senators' sixth shutout and send the Phillies to their 19th loss in 26 games.

Each of Harrisburg's three Saturday night victories over the Phillies had been lopsided — 7-2 at Reading on May 1, then 19-4 again at Reading last Saturday and now this rout.

For those counting, the Senators outscored Reading 86-41 in the teams' first 12 meetings with Harrisburg winning nine of those 12.

EASTERN LEAGUE STANDINGS on June 26			
	Record	Pct.	GB
SENATORS	53 - 18	.746	—
Canton	39 - 33	.542	14 1/2
Bowie	37 - 32	.536	15
Albany	35 - 35	.500	17 1/2
London	32 - 40	.444	21 1/2
Binghamton	32 - 41	.439	22
Reading	30 - 40	.429	22 1/2
New Britain	26 - 45	.366	27

LOOKING BACK

Barker In, Martin Out

HARRISBURG — The much anticipated return came on June 26 as Tim Barker, the Eastern League's best shortstop before breaking a bone in his right thumb on May 23, finally was back in the Senators' lineup in a 15-0 rout of Reading on City Island.

All was well. Sort of.

While Barker's return enhanced an already gifted lineup, his return significantly cut into Chris Martin's playing time.

Martin deserved better. He was nothing less than outstanding filling in for Barker for 32 games. The Senators won 23 of those 32 games as Martin played the most inspired baseball of his four-year pro career.

CHRIS MARTIN

The Senators would have been fortunate to win, say, 16 games instead of 23 had Martin simply gone through the motions knowing the starting job at shortstop was not his after Barker's recovery.

Instead, Martin hit .304 in Barker's absence to raise his batting average 37 points to .275. He also scored 34 runs in that span. Martin, though, was not going to stay the starter, not with Barker hitting a team-high .354 before his injury.

"It's a difficult, yet a pleasant problem to have," manager Jim Tracy said, knowing the Montreal Expos wanted him to play Barker over Martin.

"I'm well aware of the situation."

So was Martin, who grudgingly had learned to sit, watch and wait.

"I know I'm one of the older guys here," said Martin, who like Barker was 25 years old, "and it's a big deal to me to show them that you have to go about your work the same way whether you're hitting .320 or .220."

Still.

"It's a tough thing," Martin said, "especially when you believe in your heart that you should be playing."

Fast Start For Reading

HARRISBURG — As they typically did
against Reading, the Senators planned to score in
bunches, win another game and give the Phillies
yet another loss. So long, of course, as they kept
the increasingly frustrated Phillies quiet early.

RAFAEL DIAZ

Nice idea. Never happened in this game.

The Phillies used a five-run first inning to
ignite their offense and then scored a couple of
runs late to beat the Senators 7-5 in an afternoon
game before a crowd of 5,270 on City Island.

Starter Rick DeHart managed to wriggle out of
the game with a no-decision, despite allowing six
of the seven batters he faced in the first inning to reach base. He
never saw an eighth batter as he was quickly replaced by Rafael
Diaz, who allowed only two hits and a walk to get through the
fifth.

By then, the Senators rallied for four runs on Shane Andrews'
two-run homer in the second inning, and back-to-back solo homers
by Tim Barker and Rondell White in the fifth.

Another solo homer by Tyrone Woods in the sixth tied the score
at 5 before Reading broke that tie in the seventh with a run off
Archie Corbin (3-2) and added its final run with another run in the
ninth off Yorkis Perez. While White's homer in the fifth extended
his hitting streak to 17 games, Oreste Marrero needed a single as a
pinch-hitter with two outs in the ninth to push his streak to 15.

"I thought going in that the only way they could beat us was to
do just what they did in the first inning," said manager Jim Tracy,
who could indulge in such thoughts, given the Senators had won
five straight from Reading.

"If we shut them down
early, I knew we were
going to score runs, but
that first inning changed
the whole complexion."

EASTERN LEAGUE STANDINGS on June 27			
	Record	Pct.	GB
SENATORS	53 - 19	.736	—
Canton	40 - 33	.548	13 1/2
Bowie	37 - 33	.529	15
Albany	36 - 35	.507	16 1/2
London	33 - 40	.452	20 1/2
Reading	31 - 40	.437	21 1/2
Binghamton	32 - 42	.432	22
New Britain	26 - 46	.361	27

Waiting Around

HARRISBURG — You could expect a series opener between the league's two best teams would produce a nice, tight game.

If you figured that for this game, well, you figured wrong as the Senators and Canton combined for six errors, nine walks and a mental mistake that cost the Senators a run in a listless 9-6 loss to the Indians before a crowd of 3,177 on City Island.

After trailing early, the Senators took a 6-5 lead with a three-run rally in the fifth. They enjoyed the lead for all of one inning before Canton scored twice in the seventh off Archie Corbin (3-3), who might have avoided the loss had normally heads-up shortstop Tim Barker not committed a thumbs-down mental error in the seventh.

Corbin walked Omar Ramirez to lead off the inning before striking out Miguel Flores, giving up a single to Manny Ramirez and then striking out Herbert Perry for the second out. Corbin appeared to get out of the inning when second baseman Mike Hardge made a diving stop to his right on Brian Giles' sharp grounder up the middle and flipped the ball to Barker covering second for the would-be, inning-ending forceout.

Only umpire Scott Simonides instead ruled Manny Ramirez safe, leaving Barker to drop his head in disbelief as Omar Ramirez, who had pulled up at third base, bolted home with the tying run. Corbin then gave up an infield single to Mike Sarbaugh to load the bases and walked David Bell to force home the go-ahead run.

"We made some mental mistakes, and we didn't pitch very well," manager Jim Tracy said. "And we can't stand around and wait for an ump to make a call knowing they might be bringing the guy around. That's just not heads up."

Hardge's two errors on one play in the ninth led to Canton's final two runs.

"We ended up sitting around waiting for good things to happen," Tracy said. "That's not how this team got 53 wins in 73 games played."

EASTERN LEAGUE STANDINGS on June 28			
	Record	Pct.	GB
SENATORS	53 - 20	.726	—
Canton	41 - 33	.554	12 1/2
Bowie	38 - 34	.528	14 1/2
Albany	37 - 35	.514	15 1/2
London	33 - 41	.446	20 1/2
Binghamton	33 - 42	.440	21
Reading	32 - 41	.438	21
New Britain	26 - 47	.356	27

Locked And Loaded

HARRISBURG — Glenn Murray had just missed fully connecting on the pitch, driving Paul Shuey's 1-2 fastball to the warning track in left field for an out to start the eighth inning.

On his way back to the dugout, Murray said nothing to on-deck hitter Shane Andrews about what was coming next. No need.

Andrews already knew. Fastball.

Andrews did not miss it, either, as he drilled Shuey's first-pitch fastball deep over the wall in left-center to snap a 2-2 tie and lift the Senators over Canton 3-2 before a crowd of 5,132 on City Island.

"There was nothing to say. He knew what was coming," Murray said of Andrews. "Shuey was coming fastball to get ahead."

All-Star Picks

To the surprise of no one, first baseman-left fielder Cliff Floyd, center fielder Rondell White and pitcher Joey Eischen were selected to join manager Jim Tracy on the National League team at next month's third annual Class AA All-Star Game in Memphis.

Instead, Shuey and the Indians fell behind as Andrews hit his 12th homer, six of which came in June.

"He is a fastball pitcher, and he left it up a little," Andrews said. "I felt it off the bat."

Mario Brito (4-2) picked up the win as he navigated the final two innings after Miguel Batista allowed only five hits and three walks in seven innings of one-run, coming-right-at-you pitching.

"A tremendous performance," manager Jim Tracy said of Batista. "He was aggressive and went after hitters. It's something he hasn't done in his last couple starts, but he shouldn't be afraid."

Twice Batista worked out of big-time jams in the second and seventh innings.

"I was nervous because I wanted to do the job," Batista said. "We knew the hitters were getting it done and the pitchers wanted to do their jobs, too."

EASTERN LEAGUE STANDINGS on June 29			
	Record	Pct.	GB
SENATORS	54 - 20	.730	—
Canton	41 - 34	.547	13 1/2
Bowie	39 - 34	.534	14 1/2
Albany	38 - 35	.521	15 1/2
Binghamton	34 - 42	.447	21
London	33 - 42	.440	21 1/2
Reading	32 - 42	.432	22
New Britain	26 - 48	.351	28

WEDNESDAY, JUNE 30

Eischen Rebounds

HARRISBURG — Earlier this season, the one inning might have been enough to finish off starter Joey Eischen.

Eischen, whose ERA in the early innings once pointed toward infinity, found himself in this game with a bases-loaded, none-out bind against Canton, the Eastern League's second-best hitting team.

A similar bind two weeks ago saw the Indians rip Eischen for seven runs in an inning-plus of torture.

No such problems here, though, as Eischen recovered to escape the top of the first inning without allowing a run. The Senators then scored three times in the bottom of the inning to jump-start their 8-4 victory before a crowd of 4,054 at RiverSide Stadium.

"The last start against them doesn't mean anything," said Eischen, the EL's runaway leader in victories with 12 but one who entered the game with an 8.36 ERA in three starts against Canton.

"After the first couple of innings, it's easier for me," he said.

The Senators' offense saw to that, scoring three times in the bottom of the first on RBI singles by Cliff Floyd and Glenn Murray before a sacrifice fly by Oreste Marrero, who was 24 hours removed from having his hitting streak snapped at 15 games.

Rondell White, owner of a 20-game hitting streak, started a rally in the fifth inning with a leadoff single off Mike Dyer. The rally culminated when Murray lined Dyer's first-pitch fastball to him off the scoreboard in right-center for a three-run homer and 6-1 lead.

Eischen lasted one more inning following Murray's homer, leaving with a 6-2 lead after allowing six hits and four walks while striking out eight.

"I don't want to make light of the other five innings he pitched," manager Jim Tracy said of Eischen, who had won 12 of his last 14 decisions.

"But Joey Eischen won that game in the first inning. Just one inning, six outs (for both teams).

"That changed the whole complexion of the game."

EASTERN LEAGUE STANDINGS on June 30			
	Record	Pct.	GB
SENATORS	55 - 20	.733	—
Bowie	40 - 34	.541	14 1/2
Canton	41 - 35	.539	14 1/2
Albany	39 - 35	.527	15 1/2
Binghamton	35 - 42	.455	21
London	33 - 43	.434	22 1/2
Reading	32 - 43	.427	23
New Britain	26 - 49	.347	29

156

Gabe's Twisted Tale

LONDON, Ont. — Gabe White lost, won and lost again. All in just a few hours.

First, the Senators' left-hander was tagged with the loss in a 3-1 decision against the London Tigers before a crowd of 5,018 at Labatt Memorial Park. Then, he was promoted after the game by the Montreal Expos to Class AAA Ottawa.

Before the end of the night, though, White was headed to the Senators' disabled list with a severely sprained right ankle, an injury he suffered tripping on a flight of stairs shortly after learning of his promotion.

"I was trying to go over things in my mind of what I was going to do once I was up there," White said. "I was walking down some stairs and turned my ankle pretty bad."

In what was supposed to be his final game for the Senators, White worked eight innings, allowing three runs on five hits and striking out six. The only run of support for White (6-2) came on Tyrone Woods' leadoff homer in the third off Ben Blomdahl.

Woods' homer was one of just four hits the Senators had against Blomdahl, and relievers Henrique Gomez and Tom Schwarber. One of those four hits came on Rondell White's first-inning single to center that extended his hitting streak to 21 games.

The loss was the first for the Senators in eight games against the Tigers, who they routinely smacked around on the scoreboard and, on May 23, in a bench-clearing brawl on City Island.

The injury was the second this season for White, who strained his left shoulder May 10 while pitching in the Expos' exhibition game at Ottawa.

White did not return from that injury until May 20. This one figured to last longer.

"It's been tough," White said of his star-crossed season.

"I'm just trying to stay focused on what I'm supposed to do."

EASTERN LEAGUE STANDINGS on July 1			
	Record	Pct.	GB
SENATORS	55 - 21	.724	—
Bowie	41 - 35	.539	14
Albany	40 - 35	.533	14 1/2
Canton	41 - 36	.532	14 1/2
Binghamton	36 - 42	.462	20
London	34 - 43	.442	21 1/2
Reading	32 - 44	.421	23
New Britain	27 - 50	.351	28 1/2

FRIDAY, JULY 2
"Rudy, Rudy, Rudy"

LONDON, Ont. — Rudy Pemberton was one of the few highlights in what otherwise was London's disappointing season.

In this game, he simply was a pain in the, well, backside for the Senators as he single-handedly tied the score in the ninth inning before hitting a grand slam in the 13th as the Tigers won 13-9 in a wild, weird and wet game played here before 958 fans.

Not that many fans at Labatt Memorial Park lasted to the end of a game that took 4 hours and 49 minutes to complete — including two rain delays — and did not finish until early Saturday morning.

Did we mention the Senators put together nine runs on 14 hits in the first nine innings and still lost? And, yes, Rondell White had two of them to push his hitting streak to 22 games.

Blame Pemberton and some shoddy defense in the ninth inning. With the Senators leading 9-8 and Yorkis Perez pitching, Pemberton walked with two outs in the ninth, stole second, moved to third when catcher Rob Fitzpatrick's throw sailed into center field and scored on the play as Glenn Murray's return throw from center eluded Shane Andrews at third.

Four innings later, Pemberton ended the game with a one-out grand slam off Mario Brito (4-3), whose problems in the 13th started with a leadoff walk to Shannon Penn and a double by Dean DeCillis. Brito then struck out Rick Sellers before intentionally walking Mike Rendina and setting up a potential inning-ending double play with Pemberton at the plate. Instead of hitting a grounder to an infielder, though, Pemberton lined his 10th homer of the season over the wall in left-center.

Not that anybody on London's staff was around at the end to file a report back to the Detroit Tigers as manager Tom Runnells, and his coaches, Dan Riley and Sid Monge, all were ejected during the game for arguing with umpires Brian Gilbert, Mike Whitty and Jeff Nelson.

EASTERN LEAGUE STANDINGS on July 2			
	Record	Pct.	GB
SENATORS	55 - 22	.714	—
Bowie	41 - 35	.539	13 1/2
Albany	40 - 35	.533	14
Canton	41 - 37	.526	14 1/2
Binghamton	37 - 42	.468	19
London	35 - 43	.449	20 1/2
Reading	32 - 44	.421	22 1/2
New Britain	27 - 50	.351	28

Late Rally Slows Skid

LONDON, Ont. — This had been the toughest stretch of the season for the Senators, losers in six of their previous 10 games.

Seven of 11 seemed like a possibility, too, after the Senators frittered away leads of 4-0 and 5-1 before rallying for five runs over the final two innings to beat London 10-8 before a crowd of 1,843 at Labatt Memorial Park.

Having tied the score at 8 in the eighth on Chris Martin's two-run double and Tim Barker's game-tying steal of home, the Senators scored twice in the ninth on Shane Andrews' RBI double to right and Lance Rice's RBI single to left.

Heath Haynes (6-0) picked up the victory after recording the final out of the eighth inning in relief of Rick DeHart.

Mario Brito, less than 24 hours removed from giving up a game-ending grand slam to Rudy Pemberton, dodged a two-out double by Pemberton in the ninth inning. Bobby Higginson then flied out to left fielder Cliff Floyd, ending the game and giving Brito his team-high 10th save.

Floyd's three-run homer in the first inning punctuated a four-run rally off Felipe Lira that gave the Senators a 4-0 lead after just four batters. Rondell White preceded Floyd's 22nd homer — a modern-franchise, single-season record — with a double off the bag at second to extend his hitting streak to 23 games. The three RBIs gave Floyd a league-high 79 in just the 76 games.

The lead grew to 5-1 in the fourth inning on White's two-out RBI single to left, but London eventually scored five runs off starter Reid Cornelius over the fourth, fifth and sixth innings before scoring twice off DeHart in the seventh for an 8-5 lead.

By the time the Senators finished their late-inning rallies, they had totaled 18 hits off six pitchers with the top five hitters in their batting order — Barker, Martin, White, Floyd and Glenn Murray — combining for 12 of them.

EASTERN LEAGUE STANDINGS on July 3			
	Record	Pct.	GB
SENATORS	56 - 22	.718	—
Bowie	42 - 36	.538	14
Albany	40 - 36	.526	15
Canton	41 - 38	.519	15 1/2
Binghamton	38 - 42	.475	19
London	35 - 44	.443	21 1/2
Reading	32 - 45	.416	23 1/2
New Britain	29 - 50	.367	27 1/2

LOOKING BACK
Move Over Wes

LONDON, Ont. — The image of this particular at-bat by Cliff Floyd was a lasting one, the one of Floyd's top hand coming off the bat as the baseball cut through the Berks County night before landing outside Reading's old Municipal Stadium.

CLIFF FLOYD

Typical home run for Floyd, an arcing drive to parts rarely traveled. Passing motorists along that busy stretch of Reading's Route 61 be damned.

With his prodigious shot off Reading's Eric Hill that night, Floyd ended Wes Chamberlain's exclusive hold on the Senators' modern-era, single-season record of 21 homers set in 1989.

Two weeks passed before No. 22 came on July 3 off London's Felipe Lira, a three-run drive to right that gave the Senators a 4-0 lead in the first inning of a game they won 10-8.

"I haven't been patient," Floyd said, "and, if you're not patient, bad things will happen."

Bad things did as Floyd went homerless in 45 at-bats before his record-setting homer off Lira.

Floyd admitted, well sort of, that he was pressing during his chase of Chamberlain.

"Yeah," said Floyd, who had been averaging one homer every 11.5 at-bats when he hit his record-tying 21st on June 19.

"But, no," Floyd quickly added. "I haven't been trying for anything. I'm just trying to meet the ball and hit it hard."

Floyd, only 20 years old but dominating his second league in just two full pro seasons, again was hitting the ball hard.

LOOKING BACK

That was, of course, when Eastern League pitchers decided to actually give Floyd anything worth hitting.

After a 4-for-33 post-homer slide, Floyd lined three hits Wednesday in an 8-4 victory over Canton and then had five more hits in the first three games of a four-game series at London to raise his average to .296.

Until this game, though, there were no home runs, but then no worries, either. At least not for manager Jim Tracy.

"Cliff Floyd's back to the position where he got all those home runs," Tracy said.

"He's back to driving the ball," Tracy said. "I don't know where it's been the last five or six games (before the London series). You know, he sees guys in scoring position and he wants them. He started swinging at balls out of his zone."

Tracy also offered Floyd some of his very best homespun, fly-fishing philosophy.

"I told him, 'Don't be some fish out there and let (the opposing pitchers) be the fishermen using some little minnow as bait,' " Tracy said.

"I told him not to go after the minnows."

Floyd's record-setting homer came in his 76th game of the season. Chamberlain's 21st in 1989 came in his 128th game.

Floyd still needed another 11 homers over the Senators' final 62 regular-season games to match Joe Munson's all-time Harrisburg record of 33 set in 1925.

Floyd, though, was not expected to stay that long in Class AA.

His recent struggles hardly altered Montreal's opinion of their top prospect.

Expos general manager Dan Duquette recently shut down club president Claude Brochu when Brochu asked him of the possibilities of acquiring All-Star first baseman Fred McGriff from San Diego.

Duquette, never one to shy away from being blunt, promptly told Brochu that he believed "we've got a McGriff coming up in Double-A."

SUNDAY, JULY 4

Big Bats > Small Park

LONDON, Ont. — Hmm. Let's see. London's smallish Labatt Memorial Park against the Senators' tremendous power.

This was, once again, a bad combination for the Tigers' pitching staff as Glenn Murray, Cliff Floyd and Shane Andrews each homered as the Senators won 10-3 before a crowd of 1,014.

In the final three games of the four-game series, the Senators totaled 29 runs on 45 hits, 10 of which found gaps in the outfield for doubles with another five simply going over the fence.

MIGUEL BATISTA

Andrews had three of the Senators' 12 hits in the series finale. Rondell White had two singles to extend his hitting streak to 24 games, eight shy of the modern-franchise record set in 1987 by Jim Reboulet.

Murray's two-run homer in the third off Justin Thompson, and solo homers in the fifth by Floyd and Andrews off Thompson, gave the Senators at least one homer in 11 straight games. Twenty of the Senators' league-high 113 homers came in that span.

Andrews' homer gave the Senators a 6-1 lead, more than enough for starter Miguel Batista (7-3). In winning for just the

second time since May 22, Batista allowed only two runs in seven innings as he dodged nine hits and a walk along the way. Batista also struck out seven before Darrin Winston worked the last two innings.

The Senators had just as much fun running the bases. Mike Hardge, who reached base four times with three walks and a single, had three steals, while White had

MIKE HARDGE another stolen base to give the Senators 120 steals — another Eastern League high — in only 79 games.

EASTERN LEAGUE STANDINGS on July 4			
	Record	Pct.	GB
SENATORS	57 - 22	.722	—
Bowie	42 - 37	.532	15
Canton	42 - 38	.525	15 1/2
Albany	40 - 37	.519	16
Binghamton	38 - 43	.469	20
London	35 - 45	.438	22 1/2
Reading	33 - 45	.423	23 1/2
New Britain	30 - 51	.375	28

162

Surviving The Heat

HARRISBURG — A blistering late afternoon on City Island was followed by fireworks above it.

In between, the Senators beat the Binghamton Mets 5-3 before 4,525 fans who sat through a game that ran 14 minutes shy of three hours in temperatures that peaked at 92.

Cliff Floyd had three more hits — a single, triple and homer — that gave him nine hits in his last 14 at-bats, as well as homers in three straight games.

Hard to tell which of his hits was the most impressive. Not the homer since everyone had become used to those. First, there was his bunt single to lead off the second inning and jump-start a two-run rally. Then, there was his RBI triple into the right-field corner in the fifth inning that scored Mike Hardge for a 4-1 lead.

"I like to use my speed," Floyd said. "I'll steal a few bags, run around, just to make (other teams) think a little. My mom ran real fast when she was younger and I guess I take after her."

Alas, for the first time in 25 games, Rondell White went hitless.

And, for the umpteenth time, Joey Eischen started out slow, allowing the first three Mets to reach base before escaping the first inning down only 1-0.

The Senators quickly regained the lead at 2-1 in the second inning on Oreste Marrero's RBI single and Shane Andrews' RBI groundout. Hardge hit a solo homer in the third for a 3-1 lead. Floyd chased home Hardge with his triple in the fifth before hitting a solo homer in the eighth for a 5-3 lead.

From there, Heath Haynes — with closer Mario Brito promoted earlier in the day to Class AAA Ottawa — retired all seven batters he faced after replacing Eischen (13-3) in the seventh inning.

"I think Eischen is beginning to establish that if you're going to get him, you better get him quick," said manager Jim Tracy.

"Or you're not going to get him."

EASTERN LEAGUE STANDINGS on July 5			
	Record	Pct.	GB
SENATORS	58 - 22	.725	—
Bowie	43 - 37	.538	15
Canton	43 - 38	.531	15 1/2
Albany	40 - 38	.513	17
Binghamton	38 - 44	.463	21
London	35 - 46	.432	23 1/2
Reading	34 - 45	.430	23 1/2
New Britain	30 - 51	.370	28 1/2

TUESDAY, JULY 6

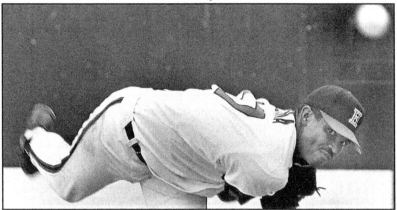

UGUETH URBINA ALLOWED JUST ONE RUN IN 7 INNINGS OF HIS AA DEBUT

Bringing The Heat

HARRISBURG — Top pitching prospect Gabe White still was hobbled by a sprained right ankle, and Rick DeHart already was demoted to the bullpen. So, naturally, the Expos gave the Senators yet another top prospect to continue their conquest of the EL.

Enter Ugueth Urbina, a right-hander who at 19 became the Senators' youngest player since their return to City Island in 1987.

Urbina made his Class AA debut in this game, but was not part of the decision as the bullpen faltered over the final two innings of a 4-1 loss to Binghamton before a crowd of 2,057 on City Island.

The outcome did not matter as much as the impression made by Urbina, who was 10-1 with a 1.99 ERA at Class A Burlington before joining Harrisburg's rotation. After averaging a strikeout an inning at Burlington, Urbina had just one in this game but allowed only one run in seven innings on four hits and five walks.

"For a 19-year-old kid in his first Double-A game, I thought he did well," manager Jim Tracy said. "I expect to get some good performances out of him."

EASTERN LEAGUE STANDINGS on July 6			
	Record	Pct.	GB
SENATORS	58 - 23	.716	—
Bowie	44 - 37	.543	14
Canton	44 - 38	.537	14 1/2
Albany	40 - 39	.506	17
Binghamton	39 - 44	.470	20
London	35 - 47	.427	23 1/2
Reading	34 - 46	.425	23 1/2
New Britain	31 - 51	.378	27 1/2

A Win From Afar

HARRISBURG — There were few cheers for this game, a sloppy, rain-shortened, tarp-flapping-in-the-wind 4-0 loss to Binghamton on City Island.

The only real cheer from the crowd of 2,210, or what was left of it after a 69-minute rain delay, came after learning Kirk Rueter won his major league debut in Montreal as the Expos shut out San Francisco 3-0. Rueter, who opened the season as the Senators' No. 4 starter, was the first player from the Class of '93 to reach Class AAA Ottawa and, now, the majors.

That was the only good news for the Senators on an otherwise wasted night on the island as they were shut out for only the second time in 82 games. The Mets scored all of their runs in the fifth inning off reliever-turned-starter Rafael Diaz (2-2).

Only two of those runs were earned, thanks to an error by outfielder-turned-first baseman Tyrone Woods, whose error was one of three committed by the Senators.

Actually, there were four.

The last one went to the grounds crew that lost its tarp race against a fast-moving, 13-minute thunderstorm. The result left half of the infield flooded and unplayable, forcing the umpires to call the game at 10:39 p.m. — 69 minutes after pinch-hitter Tim Barker flied out to right fielder Alan Zinter to start the seventh inning.

Mike Thomas, who joined the Senators earlier in the day from Class A West Palm Beach when reliever Yorkis Perez was sent to Ottawa, was set to pitch in an eighth inning that never came.

"I would have loved to go back out there," shortstop Chris Martin said. "We still had two more chances. Four runs isn't a lot for our team."

They would have needed snorkels to continue.

"It wouldn't have mattered to me," said third baseman Shane Andrews, "because you never know what can happen with this team."

EASTERN LEAGUE STANDINGS on July 7			
	Record	Pct.	GB
SENATORS	58 - 24	.707	—
Bowie	44 - 39	.530	14 1/2
Canton	44 - 39	.530	14 1/2
Albany	42 - 39	.519	15 1/2
Binghamton	40 - 44	.476	19
London	36 - 47	.434	22 1/2
Reading	34 - 46	.425	23
New Britain	31 - 51	.378	27

THURSDAY, JULY 8

Slumbering Bats

HARRISBURG — Every championship team had moments like this, when winning turned into losing. Even if just for a short time. This was where the Senators found themselves after a 3-1 loss to the London Tigers before a crowd of 2,362 on City Island. The loss was the third straight for the Senators, matching a season-low and sending the league's best team to their ninth loss in 16 games.

For the first time since May 11, their winning percentage dropped below .700 — a ridiculously high number at any point of a summer, let alone 83 games into a season.

The Senators totaled only six hits against London starter Felipe Lira and three relievers, giving them just 13 hits and — gasp — only two runs during their three-game skid.

"We're not slumping," manager Jim Tracy said, using the dreaded "S" word. "We've been through five or six player moves in the last five, six days. That creates a little uncertainty. Some people may not be concentrating as much as they're supposed to."

Lira merely added to the confusion, striking out every Senator except Tyrone Woods at least once as he finished with 10 strikeouts in seven innings. He threw 108 pitches, 40 percent of which were breaking balls.

"He threw a lot of sliders," said Tim Barker, who had two of the Senators' six hits, both doubles. "He was keeping those sliders away. You can't hit those out of the park."

"Everybody on that team can hit," Lira said. "They can hit fastballs, breaking balls. They're a great team."

His was a great effort. The only run Lira allowed came in the fourth, a run that cut the Tigers' lead to 2-1 before they added their third and final run off Reid Cornelius in the seventh inning.

"He pitched well enough to win," Tracy said of Cornelius (5-4), a winner in only one of his last eight starts. "We didn't help him out much offensively."

EASTERN LEAGUE STANDINGS on July 8			
	Record	Pct.	GB
SENATORS	58 - 25	.699	—
Canton	45 - 39	.536	13 1/2
Bowie	44 - 39	.530	14
Albany	42 - 40	.512	15 1/2
Binghamton	40 - 45	.471	19
London	37 - 47	.440	21 1/2
Reading	35 - 46	.432	22
New Britain	31 - 51	.378	26 1/2

Cliff's Countdown

HARRISBURG — Just how much longer Cliff Floyd would remain with the Senators was open to speculation.

For now, the Montreal Expos were keeping their top prospect on City Island, where he continued to shred the Eastern League with two more hits and three more RBIs in a 5-4 victory over the London Tigers before 3,401 fans at RiverSide Stadium.

Floyd's second hit — a triple into the left-field corner — snapped a 4-4 tie in the eighth and lifted the Senators to their first win in four games.

CLIFF FLOYD

Floyd's triple easily scored Rondell White, who led off the eighth with a single to center. His sacrifice fly in the first inning gave the Senators a 2-0 lead and his two-out single to center in the third pushed that lead to 3-0.

White and Tyrone Woods accounted for the Senators' other runs with a first-inning sacrifice fly by White and an opposite-field, solo homer by Woods to right-center in the seventh.

Reliever Archie Corbin (4-3) picked up the victory, despite allowing a pair of runs in the top of the eighth to tie the score at 4. Heath Haynes, the closer after this week's promotions of Mario Brito and Yorkis Perez to Class AAA Ottawa, pitched a perfect ninth inning for his fourth save.

With each of Floyd's hits and RBIs came more questions of when he would join either Class AAA Ottawa or Montreal. And, yes, Floyd was getting frustrated by the attention. Unfortunately, for EL teams, he took out that frustration against their pitchers.

"I hear I'm going up after the All-Star break," Floyd said. "Then, I hear I'm going up next week.

"I hear it every day, but I'll be here every day until they tell me I'm going up."

EASTERN LEAGUE STANDINGS on July 9			
	Record	Pct.	GB
SENATORS	59 - 25	.702	—
Bowie	46 - 39	.541	13 1/2
Canton	46 - 39	.541	13 1/2
Albany	42 - 41	.506	16 1/2
Binghamton	40 - 46	.465	20
Reading	36 - 46	.439	22
London	37 - 48	.435	22 1/2
New Britain	31 - 53	.369	28

SATURDAY, JULY 10
Saving Eischen

HARRISBURG — There were the 131 pitches Joey Eischen threw in his last start and the blisters that kept popping up on his left hand. Then there was the Class AA All-Star Game coming up in two days, and the possibility that Eischen would start the game for the National League.

Actually, there was an excellent chance for that since the NL manager was Jim Tracy, the same Jim Tracy who as the Senators' manager decided for this game to skip Eischen in the rotation.

With the EL's winningest pitcher at 13-3 watching from the dugout, reliever Rick DeHart was given another chance to start.

Worked well enough for a few innings, too, but then the London Tigers did what the rest of the league did in DeHart's few starts and waited him out.

That came in the middle innings as London scored three times over the fifth and sixth innings to chase DeHart from the game en route to an 8-2 victory before a crowd of 3,989 on City Island.

Struggling, too, were relievers Archie Corbin and Darrin Winston, who combined with DeHart (2-4) to give up eight runs on 11 hits and 10 walks. DeHart's inattentiveness also led to London stealing four bases off the left-hander, including three in the sixth inning before Corbin replaced DeHart with the Senators down 5-1.

"I don't care what kind of league you're in," Tracy said. "You can't give up — what? — 11 hits and 10 walks and expect to win. We flat out didn't get the pitching."

Didn't get much hitting, either, as the enormously talented but previously luckless Jose Lima (3-10) held the Senators to five singles before leaving in the eighth. Lima's start mirrored that of Felipe Lira in London's 3-1 victory 48 hours earlier.

"He's a lot like Lira," Tracy said. "They both like to get you out on sliders and changeups, and here we are trying to pull those pitches and hit them in the air."

EASTERN LEAGUE STANDINGS on July 10			
	Record	Pct.	GB
SENATORS	59 - 26	.694	—
Bowie	47 - 39	.547	12 1/2
Canton	47 - 39	.547	12 1/2
Albany	43 - 41	.512	15 1/2
Binghamton	40 - 47	.460	20
London	38 - 48	.442	21 1/2
Reading	36 - 47	.434	22
New Britain	31 - 54	.365	28

The Child Shall Lead

HARRISBURG — In a dizzying week in which the offense struggled, spot starters scuffled and a couple of key relievers moved up to Class AAA Ottawa, the Senators were due for a little normalcy.

Enter Ugueth Urtain Urbina, the 19-year-old Venezuelan whose seemingly perpetual scowl became his persona on the mound.

Urbina, the Eastern League's youngest player and the Senators' youngest player since their return to City Island in 1987, made his second start after last week's promotion from Class A Burlington.

He received a no-decision in his first start five days ago against Binghamton. Urbina had a decision — and then some — in this game against London as he scattered eight hits and walked none in a 10-0 shutout before an afternoon crowd of 3,083 on City Island.

The game was the Senators' last before the All-Star break, which arrived just as they won for only the fifth time in 11 games.

Urbina joined Kirk Rueter, already in the majors with Montreal, and Gabe White, on the disabled list with a sprained ankle, as the only Senators this season to throw complete-game shutouts.

"I didn't expect it to be this good," Urbina said. "This is a tough league."

For this day, it was Urbina's league as he threw 83 of 121 pitches for strikes with his fastball topping out at 94 mph. That was in the first inning. His 121st pitch was a 91-mph slider that produced a game-ending grounder to first baseman Oreste Marrero.

"If he keeps pitching like this, and at his age, he'll be in the majors soon," Marrero said. "He just has to get experience."

Marrero was one of five Senators with two hits. He also had three RBIs, starting with a sacrifice fly for a 1-0 lead in the second.

"We've lost people, but we continue to play a tough brand of baseball," manager Jim Tracy said.

"We're trying to rebuild from there," Tracy said, "and you're starting to see some of that now."

EASTERN LEAGUE STANDINGS on July 11			
	Record	Pct.	GB
SENATORS	60 - 26	.698	—
Bowie	48 - 39	.552	12 1/2
Canton	48 - 39	.552	12 1/2
Albany	44 - 41	.518	15 1/2
Binghamton	40 - 48	.455	21
London	38 - 49	.437	22 1/2
Reading	36 - 48	.429	23
New Britain	31 - 55	.360	29

LOOKING BACK
Keeping A Promise

HARRISBURG — When Rondell White was at the lowest point of his well-chronicled 9-for-78 slump, he made the boldest of statements.

By the All-Star break, he vowed, his batting average would be over .300.

White was not bragging. He was much too humble for that. He was just being, well, matter of fact.

Some might have thought he was just being, well, delusional, especially since he was hitting .167 after the first week of May.

"I've always started slow," White said, "but not this slow."

Slow soon gave way to fast.

Since May 9, when his average bottomed out, the 21-year-old White had been the Eastern League's hottest hitter — even hotter than teammate, natural headline magnet and everyone's top prospect Cliff Floyd.

Through a 10-0 victory over London on July 11 in the Senators' final game before the All-Star break, White batted .391 over his last 58 games with 93 hits in only 238 at-bats to raise his average to .326. Over those 58 games, he had nine of his 11 home runs, 33 of his 46 RBIs and 16 of his 21 stolen bases.

"*Geeezus*," an exasperated Floyd said, looking at White's stats.

Listening as Floyd spoke, White simply shrugged his shoulders. Others did not shrug.

"Instead of trying to hit 30 or 40 home runs and trying to drive in 120 runs, he's getting on base now, he's stealing his bases and getting his doubles," Reading Phillies manager Don McCormack said, comparing the then-and-now White.

"That's all Rondell White is doing now," McCormack said. "He's just being himself."

Rondell just being Rondell already was drawing comparisons to Marquis Grissom, Montreal's all-everything center fielder.

"He's this close now to Grissom," Gomer Hodge, the Expos' roving hitting instructor, said while closing the gap between his thumb and index finger to, maybe, a quarter-inch.

Maybe closer.

LOOKING BACK

Rondell's Reckoning

During spring training, Senators manager Jim Tracy seemingly needed only a few minutes to rebuild Curtis Pride's flawed swing.

A couple of months later, he was telling Pride — a career .247 hitter in the minors before Tracy started working with him — he was being promoted to Class AAA Ottawa on his way, eventually, to the major leagues.

Less than a month into the 1993 season, Tracy found another project, another broken hitter in a 21-year-old, top prospect who had known few, if any, real struggles in the game.

That project was Rondell White, a natural-born hitter going through a most unnatural slump to start the 1993 season.

Everybody had suggestions, even relief pitcher Archie Corbin, who told White he was not getting enough bend in his front leg.

White's problems became a regular talking point for Tracy, coach Greg Fulton and Expos roving hitting guru Gomer Hodge.

A quarter-century later, Tracy remembered the beginning of White's turnaround from his disastrous start to becoming the Eastern League's most feared hitter before the All-Star break.

And you quickly learned that when Tracy talked about hitting to just stay out of the way of the answer, because nobody could top Tracy when analyzing a hitter's problems.

"We all know how bad of a slump this was," Tracy recalled 25 years later. "He was virtually lost, and between Gomer, Fulty, and myself, we had talked about and tried just about everything that you could with him mechanically. It got to a point where I felt like he had gotten to information overload and was thinking himself into deeper and deeper trouble with each and every at-bat.

"Enough was enough. We were playing Bowie in Memorial Stadium in Baltimore (in early May). I called him into my office that afternoon and told him that he and I were going to play hit-and-run with his at-bats the entire game, even if he was up and there was nobody on base. I told him he had to look down at me prior to every pitch like we were in Little League — I got a wry smile and a chuckle out of him when I told him that — and even with nobody on, if I gave him a hit-and-run, he was to react and swing at that particular pitch.

LOOKING BACK

"The purpose of the exercise was to take the mechanical aspect of his hitting out of the equation and force him to just react, find the ball and hit it. Just hit the ball where it was pitched.

"Well, you know how players are. They want results and they certainly don't want to be giving at-bats away with nothing to show for it.

"So, without a word being said about it, we both knew that this was going to be very hard for him and could possibly make him feel even worse mentally at the end of the day.

"A lot of other things had been tried, but to no avail. There was not one person that was associated with the Harrisburg Senators that wasn't rooting their asses off for this kid because of who he was, his personality, his unselfishness, his overall character. He was a man's man, and was revered by every one of his teammates and our entire coaching staff and Montreal organization, as well.

"In one of his at-bats early in the game with nobody on, he worked himself into a fastball count and looked down at me. I put on the hit-and-run and he squared a ball up and hit it pretty well, but it went for an out. You could tell by the body language that he was disenchanted, because it did not result with a hit.

"So, there we are in the eighth inning. I don't know what the score was and I also can't remember if we had just a runner on first or runners on first and second. Anyway, we got into another fastball count and he looks down and I put on another hit-and-run. The expression on his face said, 'I don't really want to do this.'

"Believe me, to tell you that he absolutely crushed this pitch would be an understatement. He hit this ball about three-quarters of the way up in the bleachers in left-center field in (Baltimore's) Memorial Stadium. Regardless of how this home run impacted the game is immaterial. Our entire dugout erupted as if we had just won the Eastern League championship.

"That's how happy they all were for one very special teammate. That's when he started hitting like Rondell White and he never stopped. During his remaining time with us, there was hell to pay as far as the rest of the Eastern League was concerned. He put a hurtin' on our league from that point forward."

No * For White

MEMPHIS — Events at an All-Star Game were fairly standard, regardless of the level. Majors or minors. Didn't matter. You had the players' luncheon during the day, where the sponsors and higher-ups had a chance to break croutons with the All-Stars. Then came the media stuff, where the questions usually were the same with answers just as predictable.

JOEY EISCHEN

Eventually, there was the game, where batters wanted to see how hard and how far they could hit a baseball and pitchers just hoped to throw an inning and escape unscathed.

A good time was had by all. Well, almost all.

Rondell White did not have a good time, at least not at the luncheon before the third annual Class AA All-Star Game, where the brightest prospects from the National League played against their American League counterparts.

CLIFF FLOYD

White had perused the program made for the luncheon. Nice program. Had a list of the players originally selected to the game, as well as a list of last-minute additions to the roster. The names of the late adds were accompanied by an asterisk.

White's name inadvertently was listed with an asterisk. Just an oversight, since he was going to be in the starting lineup along with two other Senators — left fielder-first baseman Cliff Floyd and pitcher Joey Eischen.

RONDELL WHITE

White already had been told he would start by Senators manager Jim Tracy, who was in the best position to know since he was the National League's manager for this game.

Still, White was not amused.

"He saw an asterisk by his name that said he was added as a reserve," Tracy said. "When things like that happen to Rondell, that's not good for the opposition."

MONDAY, JULY 12

Still ticked off at the lunchtime slight, White had two hits and drove in two runs to help the National League All-Stars to a 12-7 victory before a crowd of 6,335 at Tim McCarver Stadium.

The attending media selected White as the Eastern League's top star, as well as Wichita's Dwayne Hosey as the Texas League's top player and Memphis' Les Norman as the Southern League's best.

Hosey also was named the game's MVP for his 3-for-4 night that included a single, triple, home run, three RBIs, a stolen base and four runs scored. Unlike White, Hosey was a last-minute add.

Floyd started at first base and went 0-for-3.

Eischen pitched the first inning and, in typical Eischen fashion, started slow and allowed four runs. No one cared, so long as those recent — and definitely nasty — blisters on his pitching hand did not bother him.

No team was allowed more than three players in the game.

Tracy, of course, was ready to take more.

"I'd take my whole team down there to play," Tracy said.

While Tracy managed the National League team, Bowie's Don Buford ran the American League.

Both had help in the dugout. Syndicated talk show host and noted vitamin supplement hustler Larry King lent his expertise to Buford, while longtime sportscaster Bob Costas shadowed Tracy.

The Senators' traveling party that included general manager Todd Vander Woude and clubhouse manager extraordinaire Steve Purvis brought along a Harrisburg road gray jersey with the No. 42 and "Costas" on the nameplate.

"If Bob Costas wants to be in our dugout," Purvis said then, "he has to wear our uniform."

Other than being Costas' tailor, Purvis had an easy night.

"I didn't really go to work the game, but to make sure our guys, along with Trace, were taken care of," Purvis remembered a quarter-century later. "The front office was going and they invited me to go along. I couldn't pass it up."

Of course, everyone had a chance to say hello to Costas and to, ahem, measure themselves against the diminutive broadcaster.

"It was a great thrill to meet him and we did have a conversation about baseball," Vander Woude recalled 25 years later, "and, yes, I was surprised on how short he really is."

The Isle of White

HARRISBURG — While three of his teammates were returning home from Memphis after playing in the Class AA All-Star Game, Gabe White found himself alone on City Island continuing to rehab his sprained right ankle.

A dozen days had passed since White tripped on a flight of stairs in London, Ontario, after learning he was being promoted to Class AAA Ottawa.

At the time, White, the Montreal Expos' top pitching prospect, was 6-2 in 14 starts with a 2.22 earned-run average.

He hasn't thrown a ball in anger since pitching a complete game July 1 at London and likely will not work in another game anytime soon.

"It will be every bit of three weeks," manager Jim Tracy said, adding that he did not expect White to pitch again until August.

"And," Tracy said, "it's going to take a long time just to get to that point. You're talking about time to rehab, time to throw off flat ground,

GABE WHITE

time to work off the mound in the bullpen, maybe throw in a simulated game and then, maybe, three or four innings. We're talking about some time here. It's not going to be an overnight thing."

White called his injury "just a little setback."

"Everything bad that happens has good in it," the 21-year-old White said. "I just haven't figured out what the good in this is yet. I'm trying to stay positive."

175

WEDNESDAY, JULY 14
Missing Pieces

HARRISBURG — When the Senators boarded the team bus for a four-game trip to Binghamton, they were short-handed with only 19 available players, four under the Eastern League roster limit.

ARCHIE CORBIN

Among the missing was relief pitcher Archie Corbin, who returned home to Beaumont, Texas, to be with his wife and their newborn son, who arrived earlier this week with what manager Jim Tracy called "terrible complications."

Corbin's return date was unknown.

"That's one we're going to handle very carefully," Tracy said. "We're going to take it one day at a time and see where it leads us. We may put Archie on the inactive list, but we want to talk to him first."

RANDY WILSTEAD

Also unavailable was outfielder Glenn Murray, who returned home to Manning, S.C., to attend his cousin's funeral. He was expected to miss the Mets series before rejoining the team to start a four-game home series against Albany.

Meanwhile, injured first baseman Randy Wilstead and pitcher Gabe White traveled with the team, but were not expected to play.

Wilstead had just one hit in 12 at-bats since injuring his left shoulder during an 11-2 loss to Bowie on June 23 in Baltimore.

White had not pitched since spraining his right ankle tripping on a flight of steps following the Senators' 3-1 loss on July 1 at London.

Still with the team was left fielder-first baseman Cliff Floyd, who continued to lead the Senators and the Eastern League with 24 homers, 89 RBIs and non-stop speculation of being promoted at any moment either to Class AAA Ottawa or directly to Montreal.

"If they call me up, fine," Floyd said. "I know everybody here is going to be up there one day, so I wouldn't be leaving the guys for good. Just for now."

REID CORNELIUS

Quieting the Mets

BINGHAMTON, N.Y. — With so many of the headlines this season having gone to the Senators' vaunted offense, the pitching staff sometimes had been overlooked. Easy to do.

Prior to the All-Star break, though, the Senators' pitchers had held Eastern League hitters to a .240 batting average.

Reid Cornelius added to the EL's miseries here, allowing just four hits in seven innings of a 7-4 victory over the Binghamton Mets before a crowd of 4,012 at Memorial Stadium.

Cornelius (6-4) was stingy early on, holding the Mets without a hit until Butch Huskey's leadoff single in the fifth. He left after seven innings with a 6-2 lead.

The Senators' offense totaled 12 hits with Rondell White, Cliff Floyd, Shane Andrews and Rob Fitzpatrick each collecting two. The quartet also combined for four doubles and a homer, that from Andrews off Jason Jacome in the second. Andrews also drove in the final run with a two-out double in the ninth.

Floyd, being Floyd, also had two walks, two steals to give him a team-high 27 and another RBI for his league-leading 90th.

EASTERN LEAGUE STANDINGS on July 15			
	Record	Pct.	GB
SENATORS	61 - 26	.701	—
Canton	49 - 39	.557	12 1/2
Bowie	49 - 40	.551	13
Albany	45 - 42	.517	16
Binghamton	40 - 49	.449	22
London	38 - 50	.432	23 1/2
Reading	37 - 49	.430	23 1/2
New Britain	32 - 56	.364	29 1/2

FRIDAY, JULY 16
A Long Night

BINGHAMTON, N.Y. — Considering New Britain had beaten the Senators only twice in their first 12 meetings, then what Steve Long did against the Senators was extraordinary.

SHANE ANDREWS

Long, who spent spring training with the Senators before the Expos traded him to the New York Mets in late March, scattered eight hits and four walks over six innings as Binghamton beat the Senators 12-7 here before a crowd of 3,528.

The victory was the Mets' third in their last four games against the Senators, an impressive accomplishment. More impressive was Long, who beat his former teammates for the third time this season. Long was not especially sharp in his six innings as he gave up four runs, including two on Shane Andrews' second homer in as many games.

Then again, Long did not have to be especially sharp as the Mets piled up 16 hits, including six for extra bases. Every position player had at least one hit with light-hitting catcher Javier Gonzalez getting three hits and driving in two runs.

Half of the hits came off starter Miguel Batista (7-4), who was chased after Alan Zinter's two-run homer in the fifth gave the Mets a 6-1 lead. Batista's successors — Rafael Diaz, Darrin Winston and Rick DeHart — were equally infective, allowing six more runs on another eight hits.

Andrews, Cliff Floyd and Oreste Marrero each had two of the Senators' 12 hits, eight of which went for extra bases but none of which truly mattered after the Mets built their early lead.

Floyd also drove in the Senators' final run with a ninth-inning double, adding to his league-high 91 RBIs and moving just two behind the modern-franchise record set by Lance Belen in 1987.

Eight of Floyd's RBIs came in the last five games.

EASTERN LEAGUE STANDINGS on July 16			
	Record	Pct.	GB
SENATORS	61 - 27	.693	—
Bowie	50 - 40	.556	12
Canton	49 - 40	.551	12 1/2
Albany	45 - 43	.511	16
Binghamton	41 - 49	.456	21
London	39 - 50	.438	22 1/2
Reading	38 - 49	.437	22 1/2
New Britain	31 - 57	.352	30

178

Two Flies Too Many

BINGHAMTON, N.Y. — The prevailing thought around the Eastern League was that to get to Joey Eischen was to get to him early.

Not that Eischen lost many games this season. Just that he gave up most of his runs in the first few innings.

JOEY EISCHEN

Eischen reduced the opportunities to one inning in this game, but the Binghamton Mets maximized that chance with a pair of sixth-inning sacrifice flies to top Eischen and the Senators 2-1 before a crowd of 5,905 at Municipal Stadium.

The loss was the sixth in nine games for the Eastern League's best team with four of those losses coming to a so-so Mets team.

Eischen (13-4) rolled through the first five innings, allowing just a single to center by Quivlio Veras in the third inning, before the Mets scored their runs in the sixth on sacrifice flies by Bert Hunter and Chris Butterfield.

Eischen, the EL's winningest pitcher, allowed only three hits before leaving with two outs in the seventh.

He did, though, allow a season-high six walks.

Loss In The Family

The Senators' attention understandably was split as the game became secondary to the grief of teammate Archie Corbin, whose newborn son passed away at home in Beaumont, Texas, just a few days after being born with what manager Jim Tracy called "terrible complications."

No date was given for the relief pitcher's return.

Less than 24 hours after totaling six doubles, a triple and a homer in a 12-7 loss to the Mets, the Senators managed only seven singles off Denny Harriger and Pete Walker. Rondell White had two of those singles, extending his latest hitting streak to nine games and 33 of his last 34 games — a span over which he was batting .393.

EASTERN LEAGUE STANDINGS on July 17			
	Record	Pct.	GB
SENATORS	61 - 28	.685	—
Canton	49 - 41	.544	12 1/2
Bowie	50 - 42	.543	12 1/2
Albany	46 - 43	.517	15
Binghamton	42 - 49	.462	20
London	40 - 50	.444	21 1/2
Reading	39 - 49	.443	21 1/2
New Britain	32 - 57	.360	29

Slump? What Slump?

BINGHAMTON, N.Y. — For the last two
weeks, Mike Hardge had a stock, two-word
answer when anyone asked how he was doing.
"Not me," Hardge would say.
A 2-for-29 slump can have that effect.
Hardge's answer was different after this game
as he picked up three hits, including two homers,
to lead the Senators over Binghamton 14-4
before a crowd of 5,573 at Municipal Stadium.
For the second straight game, a near-capacity
crowd turned out hoping to see New York Mets
pitcher Sid Fernandez make an injury rehab start.

MIKE HARDGE

For the second straight game, Fernandez was a no-show.
Instead, Hardge gave them plenty to watch, starting with his
solo homer to left field in the fifth that gave the Senators a 4-2 lead
and finishing with a three-run homer to center in the sixth that
pushed the lead to 7-3. More than enough runs to make a winner of
Ugueth Urbina (2-0), who allowed four runs in six innings before
Mike Thomas and Heath Haynes split the final three innings.
Just part of an afternoon in which the Senators' offense totaled
14 runs on 18 hits, including five doubles, a triple and four homers.
For those counting:
— Rondell White had three hits, including a first-inning homer,
to extend his hitting streak to 10 straight games and 34 of 35.
— Shane Andrews also had three hits and drove in four runs
with three of those coming on a bases-loaded double in the eighth.
— Chris Martin joined Hardge as the only other Senator this
season with an inside-the-park homer when his drive to left in the
seventh eluded Jay Davis.
The runs were the most
for the Senators since their
15-0 rout of Reading on
June 26 at RiverSide. The
18 hits were their most
since posting 24 in a 19-4
win June 19 at Reading.

EASTERN LEAGUE STANDINGS on July 18			
	Record	Pct.	GB
SENATORS	62 - 28	.689	—
Canton	50 - 41	.549	12 1/2
Bowie	49 - 43	.533	14
Albany	47 - 43	.522	15
Binghamton	42 - 50	.457	21
London	40 - 51	.440	22 1/2
Reading	39 - 50	.438	22 1/2
New Britain	34 - 57	.374	28 1/2

All's Well For Barnwell

HARRISBURG — Through his first 37 games out of the bullpen, Heath Haynes was nothing short of outstanding. No Senator reliever had worked more with as much success as Haynes, who was 6-0 with four saves and a 2.74 earned-run average.

High-leverage situations were Haynes' specialty, so calling on him with two outs in the sixth inning to protect a 3-2 lead with the bases loaded and Albany's Richard Barnwell at the plate was an easy decision for manager Jim Tracy.

Not so easy, though, was watching Haynes fall behind 2-0 in the count and then be forced to throw a strike.

He did, and Barnwell did not miss it, launching Haynes' 2-0 fastball over the wall in left to cap a six-run inning and lift Albany over the Senators 6-4 before a crowd of 2,487 on City Island.

"That might've been the hardest ball I've ever hit," Barnwell said of a pitch he hit so hard that left fielder Cliff Floyd did not even bother to pursue as it whizzed over his head.

"He had been tough on me in the past," Barnwell said of Haynes. "He's got a real good 'out' pitch, either a forkball or a slow curve. But at 2-0, he really couldn't come after me with it."

In fairness to Haynes, he did not load the bases for Barnwell to unload them. That was done by Brian Looney (0-1), fresh up from Class A West Palm Beach who prior to the sixth inning had pitched quite well in his Class AA debut.

Looney took a 3-0 lead into the sixth before allowing Mike Hankins' two-out RBI single and then walking Jason Robertson and Joe DeBerry to load the bases. Another walk to No. 9 hitter Gordon Sanchez brought in Albany's second run and Haynes from the bullpen to face Barnwell.

Tracy, being Tracy, found some positives.

"Looney threw strikes for the most part and showed me a real good changeup," Tracy said. "He's going to help us the rest of the way.

EASTERN LEAGUE STANDINGS on July 19			
	Record	Pct.	GB
SENATORS	62 - 29	.681	—
Canton	51 - 41	.554	11 1/2
Albany	48 - 43	.527	14
Bowie	49 - 44	.527	14
Reading	41 - 50	.451	21
Binghamton	42 - 52	.447	21 1/2
London	41 - 51	.446	21 1/2
New Britain	34 - 58	.374	28 1/2

TUESDAY, JULY 20
"We Stunk ..."

HARRISBURG — Let's see. How to nicely describe this game. That was the challenge. OK, there was no nice way.

Seven errors. Eight unearned runs. An 11-6 loss to Albany before a crowd of 3,884 at RiverSide Stadium.

"I'm not going to sugarcoat this," manager Jim Tracy said. "We played piss poor defensively. You can get all the hits in the world; if you don't make the plays that have to be made, it doesn't matter.

"We stunk defensively."

And, for the first time since June 14, the Senators' lead in the Eastern League race fell below 11 games.

BRIEN TAYLOR

"If we play many more games like this in a row," Tracy said, "we can f--- this up real quickly."

Lost in the glare of the Senators' abominations in the field was a fine start by Reid Cornelius and a scintillating performance from Albany's Brien Taylor.

While Cornelius (6-5) was tagged for seven runs, only one was earned as four of the Senators' seven errors were committed during his six innings of work. The other three came during an extended three-inning, save-the-bullpen effort by reliever Darrin Winston.

As for Taylor, the first overall pick of the 1991 amateur draft struck out 11 batters in seven innings and left with a 9-3 lead.

He threw strikes on 70 of his 108 pitches. Quite the contrast from his last two starts against the Senators, starts in which Taylor lasted just 10 innings with a 5.90 ERA against the EL's best offense.

"This was his best performance by far against us," Tracy said. "Let me tell you something, Brien Taylor impressed me a little bit tonight."

EASTERN LEAGUE STANDINGS on July 20		
	Record	Pct.	GB
SENATORS	62 - 30	.674	—
Canton	52 - 41	.559	10 1/2
Albany	49 - 43	.533	13
Bowie	50 - 44	.532	13
Binghamton	43 - 52	.453	20 1/2
Reading	41 - 51	.446	21
London	41 - 52	.441	21 1/2
New Britain	34 - 59	.366	28 1/2

182

WEDNESDAY, JULY 21

MIGUEL BATISTA LOOKS TO SEE WHERE KEVIN JORDAN'S SLAM LANDS

Slide Continues

HARRISBURG — The game was over for 10 minutes when the best move of the night was made. By a cat.

Appropriately enough, a black cat that made a mad dash in mere seconds from the Senators' dugout by the first-base line to deep left field. Apparently, even the stray cat did not want to hang too close to the Senators, who lost again to the Albany Yankees 8-4 before a crowd of 3,924 at RiverSide Stadium.

"Oh, we need to get some wins," center fielder Rondell White said with a whisper in an already quiet clubhouse.

Lord knows, the Senators had been racking up plenty of losses.

This one was their fifth in the last six games and ninth in the last 13 as the Senators saw their still comfortable lead in the Eastern League fall below 10 games for the first time since June 11.

EASTERN LEAGUE STANDINGS on July 21			
	Record	Pct.	GB
SENATORS	62 - 31	.667	—
Canton	53 - 41	.564	9 1/2
Albany	50 - 43	.538	12
Bowie	50 - 45	.526	13
Binghamton	44 - 52	.458	19 1/2
London	42 - 52	.447	20 1/2
Reading	41 - 52	.441	21
New Britain	34 - 60	.362	28 1/2

WEDNESDAY, JULY 21

This loss — fueled by Kevin Jordan's grand slam during Albany's six-run third inning — marked the first time this season the Senators were swept in a series.

"We have not played good baseball over the last two weeks," manager Jim Tracy said, "but I can still sit here and see we're 31 games over .500. That tells me we were doing something good."

Not exactly a promotion for playoff tickets, but then again not exactly the beginning notations on an autopsy report.

"We'll bounce back," Tracy said.

The Senators started doing that in this game, but the comeback lasted only two innings. As they did in the first two games of the series, the Senators failed to hold an early lead.

The ball that Shane Andrews hit over the wall in left-center for a 2-0 lead in the bottom of the second barely had developed grass stains before the Yankees broke open the game with a six-run rally in the third inning off Miguel Batista (7-5). Actually, Batista never saw the end of the inning, which Jordan punctuated when he drove a 2-1 pitch over the wall in left-center for a 6-2 lead.

"I'm not going to come in here and turn over the spread table because of this," Tracy said. "They put up a touchdown on us and we couldn't come back."

Relief On The Way

A familiar face was back in the 'burg, and the timing was perfect for a beleaguered bullpen.

Joe Ausanio, the Senators' closer in 1990 during their final season as the Pittsburgh Pirates' Class AA affiliate, had arrived from the Expos' rookie-level Gulf Coast League affiliate, where he was rehabbing his once-ailing right elbow.

Ausanio, who at 27 immediately became a seasoned citizen on the Senators' roster, took the

JOE AUSANIO

place of Rick DeHart, who struggled in 12 appearances with a 2-4 record and 7.68 earned-run average.

The bullpen was expected to gain more depth in a few days with the pending return of Archie Corbin, who was placed on the temporary inactive list following the death of his newborn son in Beaumont, Texas.

For Sale: One Team

JERRY MILEUR

HARRISBURG — Jerry Mileur has sold the Senators. Sort of.

Mileur, a political science professor from the University of Massachusetts, agreed to sell his Class AA franchise to a New York entrepreneur named Van Farber.

Only problem was that neither Mileur nor Farber signed the preliminary paperwork sent to the Eastern League office.

"To be quite honest about it," EL president John Levenda said, "I opened the envelope and have not looked at it. I will not look at it until I get a signed copy from both the seller and the buyer."

Mileur originally purchased the Senators for $85,000 in 1981, when the team was located in Holyoke, Massachusetts. He promptly moved the team to Nashua, New Hampshire. He again moved the franchise in the winter of 1986-87 to Harrisburg.

Mileur said he wanted the sale contingent on the new owner promising to keep the Senators in Harrisburg in perpetuity.

Sounded great from a PR perspective, but hardly enforceable.

"I'm 59 years old … it's just time to get out," Mileur said. "I want to simplify my life."

Not that Mileur was directly involved with the team. Other than making a pilgrimage or two each summer to City Island with friends, Mileur entrusted the operation to team president Scott Carter and general manager Todd Vander Woude.

"It's been fun," Mileur said, "but Scott Carter wants to move on to other things. We've been able to do this in a way to make time to get an appropriate buyer."

Seemed all the seller and buyer needed, though, was a pen to sign the paperwork.

THURSDAY, JULY 22
Cure For A Slump

HARRISBURG — After watching the Senators being swept, at home no less, by the Albany Yankees, manager Jim Tracy made a statement that partly was a prediction and partly a challenge to his suddenly mortal team.

"It's time," Tracy said, "to tear into somebody. It doesn't matter who. We don't need to win 13 in a row, but five or six in a row would be fine."

A day later, the New Britain Red Sox arrived on City Island. A near-guaranteed cure for any team in a slump. If Pavlov could make his dog salivate at the sound of a dinner bell, then the Senators could make the Red Sox roll over and play dead.

Cliff Floyd started and ended a much-needed, 4-3 victory over the woebegone Red Sox before 4,019 fans at RiverSide Stadium.

His two-run homer inside the right-field foul pole in the first inning gave the Senators a 2-0 lead, which they eventually gave away as they had done so often of late. The Red Sox scored all of their runs early off Joey Eischen, who recovered to finish with 10 strikeouts before leaving after eight with the score tied at 3. The tie came courtesy of a seventh-inning homer by Oreste Marrero, who drilled Tim Vanegmond's 0-2 changeup over the fence in center.

Floyd then started the ninth inning with a walk against John Shea and moved to second on Chris Martin's sacrifice bunt. Two batters later, Glenn Murray bounced an 0-2 pitch from reliever Steve Mintz under the glove of second baseman Jim Crowley to allow Floyd to score the winning run.

"We've made our errors in the last couple of games," Senators second baseman Mike Hardge said, "so I know how they feel."

Floyd's homer gave him 94 RBIs to top Lance Belen's modern-franchise record of 93 set in 1987.

"I don't like to wish ill will on anybody," Tracy said of the Sox, "but the way things have gone against us the last couple of days ... you need a break like this to get rejuvenated."

EASTERN LEAGUE STANDINGS on July 22		
	Record	Pct.	GB
SENATORS	63 - 31	.670	—
Canton	54 - 41	.568	9 1/2
Albany	50 - 44	.532	13
Bowie	50 - 46	.521	14
Binghamton	45 - 52	.464	19 1/2
Reading	42 - 52	.447	21
London	42 - 53	.442	21 1/2
New Britain	34 - 61	.358	29 1/2

FRIDAY, JULY 23
A Ringer At 19

HARRISBURG — To watch Ugueth Urbina was to believe you were watching a major league All-Star taking some time off to troll the minors for a few easy wins.

Hard to remember that Urbina was just 19 years old.

Unfair, really, to unleash him against New Britain, but that is what happened in this game and the results were predictable as Urbina gave up just three singles in beating Red Sox 3-1 in front of 4,503 fans at RiverSide Stadium.

The victory was the third straight for Urbina (3-0). The complete game was his second in a row since arriving from Class A Burlington. The earned-run average? Well, that dropped to 1.74. He threw only 110 pitches, 71 of which were strikes. At one point, he retired 15 straight batters.

NOT MUCH STRATEGY NEEDED HERE FOR ROB FITZPATRICK AND UGUETH URBINA

"I feel really comfortable here," Urbina said. "I'm trying to prove I can pitch here."

Cliff Floyd, the cleanup hitter and No. 1 among the Senators' wunderkinds, had as many hits as New Britain with three singles. Two of those singles never left the infield, yet they accounted for the second of the Senators' two runs in the third inning and their final run in the seventh. The last one came on a two-out bunt after Rondell White tripled just before him.

"Got some help from my teammate there," Floyd said, pointing toward Mike Hardge.

"Mike saw they were playing deep. I wasn't even thinking about bunting," Floyd said, "but he said to give it a shot. I'll take 'em any way I can."

EASTERN LEAGUE STANDINGS on July 23			
	Record	Pct.	GB
SENATORS	64 - 31	.674	—
Canton	55 - 41	.573	9 1/2
Albany	50 - 45	.526	14
Bowie	50 - 47	.515	15
Binghamton	46 - 52	.469	19 1/2
Reading	43 - 52	.453	21
London	42 - 54	.438	22 1/2
New Britain	34 - 62	.354	30 1/2

FRIDAY, JULY 23
Moving The Rock

HARRISBURG — The last hit for Rondell White came in the seventh inning, a triple to the gap in right-center that skipped past New Britain outfielders Bruce Chick and Jim Morrison.

RONDELL WHITE

The triple was White's 10th of the season, joining Matt Stairs as the only other player in the Senators' modern era to record a triple-double in one season. In White's case, that was 16 doubles, 10 triples and 12 homers.

He did not get a chance to add to the total, though, as moments after the Senators' 3-1 victory over New Britain White was told his next game would be played for the Montreal Expos' Class AAA team in Ottawa.

The player whom teammates fondly called "Rock" received the promotion just 11 weeks after his batting average bottomed out at .167.

Back then, one of the Expos' top prospects was one of their worst hitters. Now, no one in the organization was hotter.

Actually, no one in the Class AA Eastern League was hotter than the 21-year-old White. He left the Senators batting .328 in 90 games, having batted .384 over his final 67 games.

"It was probably scary to watch if you were a part of the opposition," manager Jim Tracy remembered a quarter-century after White's phenomenal turnaround. "That's how hard he hit the ball virtually every time that he walked up to home plate."

Like Curtis Pride before him, White was apprehensive to leave the Senators. The promotion was great, of course. He simply did not want to leave the Senators in the middle of what had been a special season.

"I loved playing here," White said. "I'm going to hate leaving the crew, but it's time to go."

Looney Tunes

HARRISBURG — So much changed, and yet nothing changed.

Players left — either onward to Class AAA Ottawa or out of the Expos' organization — and the Senators still were winning games.

To the rest of the Eastern League, this was just another injustice, a case of the rich getting richer.

Especially to the New Britain Red Sox, again a 3-1 loser for the second straight game on City Island.

The game, this one played out before a crowd of 5,425, marked the 13th time in 15 games this season the Senators beat the Red Sox and the 30th time in their last 35 meetings.

With nine of the 23 players who started the season gone through

BRIAN LOONEY

promotion, demotion or retirement, the Senators used a couple of relatively new faces to beat the Sox.

First, there was Brian Looney, the newest of the Senators who in only his second start struck out 13 batters in seven innings.

Next, there was Lance Rice, normally the backup catcher, who as a pinch-hitter for DH Oreste Marrero in the eighth inning delivered an RBI single to break a 1-1 tie.

Rice's single to left came off John Shea, a left-hander who had just entered the game specifically to face the league's premier power hitter in Cliff Floyd with Tim Barker already on first and one out. Shea promptly walked Floyd to move Barker to second.

Rice then drove Shea's 1-1 pitch into left field to easily score Barker, who was running on the pitch.

EASTERN LEAGUE STANDINGS on July 24			
	Record	Pct.	GB
SENATORS	65 - 31	.677	—
Canton	56 - 41	.577	9 1/2
Albany	50 - 46	.521	15
Bowie	51 - 47	.520	15
Binghamton	46 - 53	.465	20 1/2
Reading	43 - 53	.448	22
London	43 - 54	.443	22 1/2
New Britain	34 - 63	.351	31 1/2

189

SATURDAY, JULY 24

Rice's single chased Shea from the game. Glenn Murray then chased home Floyd from second base when he singled to right field off reliever Steve Mintz.

LANCE RICE

The two-run rally made a winner of Heath Haynes (7-0), who in relief of Looney struck out four in two perfect innings.

"There are a lot of people on this ballclub who know how to handle the bat," manager Jim Tracy said, "and Lance Rice is one of them."

Which is why Tracy started Barker from second and Floyd from first for a hit-and-run on Shea's 1-1 pitch to Rice.

"I just wanted to get on top of the ball," Rice said, "because the infield was going to be in motion on the play."

Floyd scored when Murray shot a single past Jim Crowley, who was trying to hold Floyd close to second base.

"He played in that spot in my first at-bat, when I grounded out," Murray said. "I knew where he was."

Looney, in just his second start since arriving from Class A West Palm Beach, pitched behind in the count to only seven of the 27 batters he faced.

His 13 strikeouts were the most this season by a Senator.

"I don't understand a lot of strikeouts I get," Looney said.

"People say I'm a strikeout pitcher, but I'm not. I was getting ahead of them, and when you do that, you can make bad pitches look good."

The Red Sox waited until Looney reached 100 pitches before they scored their only run off him in the seventh inning, tying the score 1-1 on Jason Friedman's bases-loaded sacrifice fly.

"I was getting a little tired," said Looney, who finished with 117 pitches. "I was getting the ball up in that inning."

The game was the Senators' first since Rondell White's promotion to Ottawa, where the Senators already had sent starting pitcher Kirk Rueter, outfielder Curtis Pride, and relief pitchers Mario Brito and Yorkis Perez.

"We've lost some very, very good people," Tracy said, "but there's still a helluva lot of players in this clubhouse."

Paging Bob Feller

HARRISBURG — The thought was tempting, especially by the sixth inning as the Senators were heading to their worst beating of the season. To the freakin' New Britain Red Sox, no less.

Alas, by the time the sixth came along, Bob Feller had cooled down and no longer was available to pitch. A short time earlier, he broke off a decent curveball for the game's ceremonial first pitch. The Senators could have used him in this game.

So what if Feller was 74. The call, though, never came for him.

Instead, the Hall of Famer stayed behind the grandstand signing autographs, while the Senators were in front of the grandstand absorbing an 11-1 loss to the Eastern League's worst team, a team the Senators had beaten in 13 of their first 15 meetings this season.

The Senators stumbled early as second baseman Chris Martin and first baseman Cliff Floyd combined for three errors in the first two innings as the Red Sox scored five unearned runs for a 5-0 lead.

"I don't want to see this ballclub, after all they've done this season, go out and embarrass themselves like they did," manager Jim Tracy said. "I don't want to sit here for the last 40 games and watch this on a regular basis."

Tracy had no choice but to watch the entire game. Others, like the crowd of 3,435, had options and most of them fled by seventh.

Starter Reid Cornelius was gone, too, leaving in the middle of the Red Sox's six-run rally in the fifth. Cornelius (6-6) allowed 16 runs over his last two starts, but 11 of those runs were unearned thanks to a defense that committed 10 errors behind him in those two starts.

There were a couple of positives:

— Joe Ausanio, who saved 15 games for Harrisburg in 1990, marked his return to the Senators by working a perfect ninth. He had been in Florida to rehab his right elbow.

— Tyrone Horne, just promoted from Class A West Palm Beach after center fielder Rondell White moved up to Class AAA Ottawa, started in left field and went 1-for-3.

EASTERN LEAGUE STANDINGS on July 25			
	Record	Pct.	GB
SENATORS	65 - 32	.670	—
Canton	57 - 41	.582	8 1/2
Bowie	52 - 47	.525	14
Albany	50 - 47	.515	15
Binghamton	46 - 54	.460	20 1/2
London	44 - 54	.449	21 1/2
Reading	43 - 54	.443	22
New Britain	35 - 63	.357	30 1/2

MONDAY, JULY 26
Those Damn Yankees

COLONIE, N.Y. — The Senators had made a habit so far of dominating every team in the Eastern League.

Except one.

Those damn Yankees, the ones from Albany who in this game used a home run in the 10th inning by Randy Velarde — a real-life damn New York Yankee — to beat the Senators 4-3 before a crowd of 1,767 at Heritage Park.

Velarde, with Albany on an injury rehab assignment, ended the three-hour game when he led off the 10th inning with a shot over the center-field wall off reliever Rafael Diaz (2-3).

MIKE THOMAS

The Senators' loss was their fifth straight against the Yankees, who less than a week ago swept a three-game series on City Island.

Velarde's homer came an inning after the Senators tied the score at 3 on Glenn Murray's homer — his 18th — off Rafael Quirico with one out in the ninth.

Murray's homer followed an outstanding appearance by Mike Thomas. The left-hander allowed only one hit while striking out five in two-plus innings after replacing starter Miguel Batista with two outs in the sixth.

Thomas' work gave the Senators time to rally from an early 3-1 deficit as Tyrone Horne drove in one run with a two-out single in the seventh. Murray tied the score with his homer in the ninth.

Horne, making his second start in left field since Rondell White's promotion to Class AAA Ottawa, accounted for the Senators' first run when he led off the third inning with a homer off the scoreboard in deep right-center.

In what now seemed to be a daily occurrence, the Senators lost shortstop Tim Barker to Ottawa.

All he did was hit .308 in 49 games with a .405 on-base percentage.

EASTERN LEAGUE STANDINGS on July 26			
	Record	Pct.	GB
SENATORS	65 - 33	.663	—
Canton	58 - 41	.586	7 1/2
Bowie	52 - 47	.525	13 1/2
Albany	51 - 47	.520	14
Binghamton	46 - 54	.460	20
London	44 - 54	.449	21
Reading	43 - 54	.443	21 1/2
New Britain	35 - 64	.354	30 1/2

Growing Up Fast

COLONIE, N.Y. — Two games were scheduled, but rain throughout the day made the doubleheader impossible.

The postponement left prized left-hander Gabe White to wait another day to make his long-awaited return to the mound.

JOEY EISCHEN

The rainout also gave Joey Eischen another chance to reflect on a season that so far had gone beyond anyone's realistic expectations for a gifted left-hander who a year ago made the Montreal Expos worry more about his temperament off the field than rejoice in his successes on it.

As the story went, life on a particular night in the summer of '92 was not going especially well for Eischen.

Again.

Something — who knew what this time? — was bothering Eischen while he was pitching for Class A West Palm Beach.

Now, a year later, Eischen only remembered leaving the game and punching the wall next to the clubhouse showers at West Palm Beach's aging Municipal Stadium, leaving behind a softball-size hole in the plaster.

A follow-up forearm shove took care of the rest of the wall. The angry young man who pitched with the mindset of an NFL linebacker had struck again.

EASTERN LEAGUE STANDINGS on July 27		
	Record	Pct.	GB
SENATORS	65 - 33	.663	—
Canton	58 - 42	.580	8
Bowie	53 - 47	.530	13
Albany	51 - 47	.520	14
Binghamton	47 - 54	.465	19 1/2
London	44 - 55	.444	21 1/2
Reading	43 - 55	.439	22
New Britain	36 - 64	.360	30

TUESDAY, JULY 27

"I was having a lot of problems on the field," Eischen said, "and off of it."

Eischen, now 23, had matured since then. So much so that the Senators' clubhouse on City Island sustained no damage a couple of weeks ago when Eischen was told he would skip a start to rest his beleaguered, blistered fingers. There were no fits this time, no gripes, no holes left in the clubhouse wall.

"It's just part of growing up," Eischen said. "I was disappointed to miss the start, but it was not in my best interests."

Finally, after four-plus seasons filled with frustration in the obscurity of Class A baseball, Eischen learned to listen to advice.

At the same time, he became the Eastern League's winningest pitcher with a 13-4 record. The next highest win total was nine.

His 3.41 earned-run average also ranked sixth among active Eastern League starters and second on the Senators only to Gabe White's league-best 2.22 ERA.

The impressive numbers, though, belied Eischen's past, a checkered career that started after the Texas Rangers selected him with their third pick of the 1989 amateur draft.

Eischen struggled in the Rangers' organization, losing 24 of 34 decisions before Texas sent him along with right-handers Jonathan Hurst and Travis Buckley to Montreal in the middle of the 1991 season for Dennis "Oil Can" Boyd, the always entertaining yet equally enigmatic pitcher.

Eischen was the unpolished jewel in the trade, a pitcher who prior to this season was more spectacle than spectacular.

"Each time Joey goes out on the field, he learns," said catcher Rob Fitzpatrick, who was with Eischen in 1992 at Class A West Palm Beach. "He still makes mistakes, like everyone else, but the idea is there. He knows what he needs to do now."

Eischen no longer needed to try to impress batters with fastballs. He was fine with embarrassing them on change-ups.

"He had that mentality (in Class A) of just trying to blow the ball by everybody," said pitching coach Chuck Kniffin, who also was Eischen's pitching coach at West Palm Beach as well as his surrogate father and confidante.

"He really did not know what pitching was all about," Kniffin said. "This year, his velocity has dropped off a little bit, but he's not overthrowing the ball and putting himself into jams."

194

TUESDAY, JULY 27

"Let's give credit where it's due," manager Jim Tracy said. "The kid has grown up a lot."

But not without help. A year ago, when he was staring down teammates on the field before knocking out walls off the field, Eischen was sent by the Expos to see a psychiatrist.

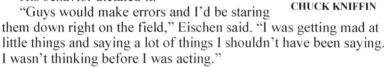

CHUCK KNIFFIN

Not by choice, either

"I didn't want to go," Eischen said.

"I had to go."

His behavior dictated it.

"Guys would make errors and I'd be staring them down right on the field," Eischen said. "I was getting mad at little things and saying a lot of things I shouldn't have been saying. I wasn't thinking before I was acting."

Fitzpatrick said none of his teammates noticed.

"We didn't think it was a problem," Fitzpatrick said with a shrug, "because we knew that was just Joey."

Unfortunately for Eischen, being just Joey was derailing what many expected to be a promising career. He did not have a winning record until the summer of '92, and even that was just 9-8.

Eischen had similar expectations for this season, too.

"My realistic look was to be around .500 now, maybe a game or two over," he said. "I didn't know I would have blossomed like I have."

To make sure his new reality did not change, Eischen embraced part of his rabbit's foot past, saying "I am the most superstitious person you'll ever meet."

Every start, for example, was preceded by a 15-minute shower — no more, no less — that was taken 75 minutes before the game, followed by a quick shave, a couple of Advils and a blaring mini-concert of Metallica through his headphones.

Then he met with Kniffin exactly 35 minutes before the game to go over the opposing hitters he already knew so well.

"I'm trying to get him away from that music," Kniffin said with a parental sigh. "He'll listen to Metallica the day he starts. Then, after the game, you catch him listening to Nat King Cole or Frank Sinatra.

"With him," Kniffin said, "it's one extreme or the other."

WEDNESDAY, JULY 28
Some Normalcy

COLONIE, N.Y. — Gabe White pitched again. Joey Eischen won again. And, for a change, no one was leaving for Ottawa.

Before the night ended here, the Senators had a doubleheader sweep, beating Albany 2-1 and 9-4 in a pair of games played before a crowd of 2,425 at Heritage Park.

In the opener, White — out for nearly four weeks with a badly sprained right ankle — pitched five innings and allowed just one run on four hits before leaving the game trailing 1-0.

Heath Haynes (8-0) picked up the victory after the Senators rallied to tie the score on Shane Andrews' solo homer to start the seventh inning off Ron Frazier before taking the lead on Oreste Marrero's two-out RBI single in the eighth off Rafael Quirico.

Marrero then capped a five-run rally to start the second game with a two-out, three-run homer in the first inning off Brian Faw.

Chris Martin, Cliff Floyd and Tyrone Horne combined for eight of the Senators' 13 hits in the second game with Eischen getting the win.

Eischen (14-4) struck out eight batters in six innings with only two of the four runs off of him earned.

EASTERN LEAGUE STANDINGS on July 28			
	Record	Pct.	GB
SENATORS	67 - 33	.670	—
Canton	59 - 42	.584	8 1/2
Bowie	53 - 48	.525	14 1/2
Albany	51 - 49	.510	16
Binghamton	47 - 55	.461	21
London	45 - 55	.450	22
Reading	44 - 55	.444	22 1/2
New Britain	36 - 65	.356	31 1/2

THURSDAY, JULY 29
Some More Rain

COLONIE, N.Y. — If the Senators still aspired to win 100 games in the regular season, then they would have only 138 games in which to accomplish that as their doubleheader against Albany was rained out. Since the teams were meeting for the final time in the regular season, the games were not rescheduled. With shortstop Tim Barker off to AAA Ottawa, the Senators received infielder Matt Rundels from Class A West Palm Beach.

Darning Some Sox

NEW BRITAIN, Conn. — This time, the Senators scored some runs for Brian Looney against the New Britain Red Sox and, this time, the left-hander picked up his first Eastern League win.

Six days after striking out 13 Red Sox but only receiving a no-decision for his efforts, Looney struck out nine in eight innings of the Senators' 5-1 victory before a crowd of 2,679 at Beehive Field.

Looney (1-1) allowed only three hits before Joe Ausanio pitched a perfect ninth as he continued his comeback from an elbow injury. Looney's eight innings of one-run pitching lowered his ERA from 4.26 to 3.05.

TYRONE HORNE

The victory also was the Senators' 14th in 17 games this season against New Britain.

Looney and Ausanio did not give the Red Sox much of a chance, either, as they combined to hold the top four hitters in New Britain's lineup — Jim Morrison, Alex Delgado, Jim Crowley and Boo Moore — hitless in 16 at-bats.

Meanwhile, Cliff Floyd and Oreste Marrero each had two hits for the Senators with Floyd extending his hitting streak to 11 games, a span over which he was batting .450 with 18 hits, eight RBIs and eight runs scored.

Tyrone Horne, playing in his fifth game for the Senators, had a two-run single in the fifth inning. Since replacing the Ottawa-bound Rondell White on the roster, Horne had seven hits and four walks in 19 plate appearances.

Matt Rundels — the newest Senator after shortstop Tim Barker's promotion to Ottawa — started at second base, batted leadoff and went 1-for-4 with a single in the sixth inning.

EASTERN LEAGUE STANDINGS on July 30			
	Record	Pct.	GB
SENATORS	68 - 33	.673	—
Canton	59 - 43	.578	9 1/2
Bowie	53 - 50	.515	16
Albany	51 - 49	.510	16 1/2
London	47 - 55	.461	21 1/2
Reading	46 - 55	.455	22
Binghamton	47 - 57	.452	22 1/2
New Britain	37 - 66	.359	32

Ripping Some Sox

NEW BRITAIN, Conn. — Mike Hardge sat out the opener of the four-game series here against the New Britain Red Sox.

In part because he already had played in 63 of 65 games since joining the Senators in mid-May. In part, too, because the second baseman had just one hit in 30 at-bats against the Sox.

Hardge, though, found himself back in the lineup for this game and ended up going 3-for-5 with two triples in an 8-4 victory before a crowd of 3,146 at Beehive Field.

MIKE HARDGE

The Senators had 16 hits as they beat New Britain for the 15th time in 18 games to finish July with a four-game winning streak.

The victory also kept the Senators, a team now in constant roster flux, from finishing July with — yikes — a losing record. As it was, they went 14-13 in the month after starting the season with 55 victories in their first 75 games.

Like Hardge, Shane Andrews also had three hits while Cliff Floyd, Tyrone Horne, Rob Fitzpatrick and Chris Martin each had two. Floyd's first hit was a two-run homer in the third inning off Brett Hansen, cutting the Sox's lead to 3-2 and giving the Expos' top prospect 26 homers and 101 runs batted in — both on-going modern-franchise records.

Like Floyd — but with much less fanfare — Fitzpatrick's first hit also was a homer, a three-run drive off Hansen with two outs in the sixth that gave the Senators a 5-3 lead. For Fitzpatrick, the three RBIs matched his total since he drove in six with a pair of three-run homers on June 26 against Reading.

Fitzpatrick's homer, also his first since June 26, made a winner of Reid Cornelius (7-6). Cornelius, who had allowed 13 hits and 16 runs over his last two starts, gave up three runs in the first three innings before settling down.

EASTERN LEAGUE STANDINGS on July 31			
	Record	Pct.	GB
SENATORS	69 - 33	.673	—
Canton	60 - 44	.577	10
Albany	52 - 50	.510	17
Bowie	53 - 51	.510	17
Reading	47 - 55	.461	22
Binghamton	48 - 57	.457	22 1/2
London	47 - 56	.456	22 1/2
New Britain	37 - 67	.356	33

Goodbye Cliff

NEW BRITAIN, Conn. —
Herm Starrette was a nice guy,
always willing to talk, and
always saying something nice
about everybody. Even Earl
Weaver, the Baltimore Orioles'
perpetually cranky manager.

CLIFF FLOYD

Was not all that long ago,
either, when Starrette ran for
sheriff in his hometown of
Statesville, North Carolina. So,
really, just how bad was he?

Yet, nice guy that he was,
Starrette managed to scare the
crap out of the masses every
time he walked into RiverSide
Stadium.

People watched Starrette, wondering what the watcher saw
and pondering which prospect he next would pluck from the
Senators' roster.

They watched Starrette go about his business — partly out of
curiosity and partly out of paranoia.

"It's been that way for 100 years in baseball," said Starrette,
the Expos' minor league field coordinator whose job was to
evaluate the Senators' talent and decide who was ready to move
up or destined to move out.

Starrette finished his latest trip to City Island a week ago.

When he left, he took with him prized center fielder Rondell
White and dropped him off at Class AAA Ottawa.

Shortstop Tim Barker was next.

On earlier visits, he had taken outfielder Curtis Pride, starting
pitcher Kirk Rueter, and relievers Mario Brito and Yorkis Perez.

Barker's promotion pushed to six the number of Senators sent
via Starrette to Ottawa since May 27.

SUNDAY, AUGUST 1

Starrette was both liked and feared by the Senators' players. Liked simply because every player in the minors wanted to be promoted to the next level, to get that one step closer to the majors. Feared, at least by some of the Senators, because not everyone wanted to leave Harrisburg for Ottawa. The majors? Yes, for sure. Class AAA? Uh, not so much. The Class of '93 wanted to stay together as long as possible, preferably through the EL playoffs.

Pride, after all, cried when he was told in mid-June that he would be going to Ottawa. White, too, was apprehensive a few days ago when he was booked on the Starrette Express for Ottawa.

The latest booking on the Starrette Express came in the middle of this game, an 8-6 victory over the New Britain Red Sox in 10 innings before a crowd of 2,383 at Beehive Field.

Not that any of the Senators realized what was going on when Cliff Floyd returned to the dugout after scoring their first run during a four-run rally in the top of the fourth.

Not all of them realized, either, what was happening when manager Jim Tracy pulled aside the Eastern League's best player.

"I just thought Jim was giving him a rest," said Randy Wilstead, the backup first baseman who suddenly became the regular first baseman between the top of the fourth inning and the bottom of it.

"When I found out, I went up and congratulated him and wished him good luck," Wilstead recalled 25 years later of his last dugout exchange with Floyd.

"Cliff was a great guy. He never acted like he was better than anyone else. I never saw him again after that day, though."

Neither did anyone else that summer in Harrisburg, where Floyd had the phone in his apartment disconnected before leaving on the road trip. Apparently, he knew something might be up.

Floyd played in 101 of a possible 103 games, leaving with a .329 batting average, and modern-franchise records with 26 homers and 101 RBIs. He also scored 82 runs, stole 31 bases, posted a stunning .600 slugging percentage and an other-worldly 1.017 on-base slugging percentage.

EASTERN LEAGUE STANDINGS on Aug. 1			
	Record	Pct.	GB
SENATORS	70 - 33	.680	—
Canton	60 - 45	.571	11
Albany	53 - 50	.515	17
Bowie	54 - 51	.514	17
London	49 - 56	.467	22
Binghamton	48 - 58	.453	23 1/2
Reading	47 - 57	.452	23 1/2
New Britain	37 - 68	.352	34

200

SUNDAY, AUGUST 1

Floyd's final hit for the Senators was a single to center to start the fourth inning off Red Sox starter Tim Vanegmond, extending his hitting streak to 13 games. He scored when Glenn Murray followed with a triple to right, a run that cut the Sox's lead to 4-2.

Three more runs followed in the inning on a wild pitch that scored Murray from third and Tyrone Horne's two-run homer.

After the inning, Floyd retreated to the clubhouse with Tracy following him for a final goodbye before the 20-year-old Floyd left for Syracuse, where he was to join Ottawa for its series there.

"Let's just say I gave him one helluva big hug," Tracy said. "There have been several others who have left this team who were tough to say goodbye to, but this guy here ...

"The way he went about his business every day makes him the most special player I have ever managed."

Quite the compliment considering the number of players Tracy helped graduate to the major leagues during his time managing in the Chicago Cubs and Cincinnati Reds systems.

Speculation had intensified near the All-Star break that Floyd soon was heading either to Ottawa or directly to the majors. At the time, Floyd believed he was ready to move up and publicly said so.

The Expos also believed he was ready. They just wanted to give him some more chances to break a few of Harrisburg's records.

"We thought we'd wait until he got 100 RBIs," said Kent Qualls, the Expos' director of minor league operations. "It's a milestone we thought he'd like to achieve at Double-A. It's something that he would remember."

Floyd left the 'Burg as the favorite to join Wes Chamberlain and Matt Stairs as the Senators' third league MVP since 1989.

"This guy came to play day in and day out, whether he was sore or didn't feel well," Tracy said. "It didn't matter; he just played."

Oh, yes, there was the matter of this game, which the Senators eventually won in 10 innings on Tyrone Woods' two-run homer to center off reliever Joe Ciccarella.

Joe Ausanio (1-0) picked up the victory after dodging three hits and two walks over the final two innings.

By then, Cliff Floyd was gone and the Senators lineup that once had Curtis Pride, Rondell White, Tim Barker and, of course, Floyd now had to find other ways to win ballgames.

201

Sweeping The Sox

A Signature Move

Mark Mattern almost never sought autographs for himself. For others, sure. For himself, no. Except one: Cliff Floyd.

"Not only was he the best baseball player we had ever seen to that year, but he was really a grounded, friendly person," Mattern said.

"He was only 20 at the time and was able to handle all the attention. He never refused to help the team out … never refused to give me an interview for the broadcast. I still have a photo of me interviewing Cliff that he signed for me.

"In 21 years as a Senators' broadcaster, he was the only person I asked to do that for me. Over the years, I got a lot of autographed items for a lot of other people and causes, but only one for me."

NEW BRITAIN, Conn. — Just how much Cliff Floyd's promotion hurt the Senators' offense remained to be seen. Now, if the Senators kept getting pitching performances like the one in this game from Gabe White, then they would be just fine.

White, in his second start since coming off the disabled list, held New Britain to one run in six innings of a 5-3 victory that completed a four-game sweep before a crowd of 2,091 at Beehive Field.

White (7-2) walked none and struck out five before leaving with a 3-1 lead, thanks to Tyrone Horne's RBI groundout in the first inning and Glenn Murray's two-run homer in the fourth. Solo runs came in the eighth and ninth. The Red Sox scored twice in the ninth off Rafael Diaz before Heath Haynes recorded the final two outs for his fifth save. The teams met for the final time this season with the Senators winning 17 of 20 games.

EASTERN LEAGUE STANDINGS on Aug. 2			
	Record	Pct.	GB
SENATORS	71 - 33	.683	—
Canton	60 - 46	.566	12
Albany	54 - 50	.519	17
Bowie	54 - 52	.509	18
London	50 - 56	.472	22
Binghamton	49 - 58	.458	23 1/2
Reading	47 - 58	.448	24 1/2
New Britain	37 - 69	.349	35

TUESDAY, AUGUST 3
One Game, Three Losses

HARRISBURG — The Senators lost three times during and after this game

First, they watched Stanton Cameron hit two home runs and drive in seven runs, including two on an eighth-inning homer, before falling 10-9 to Bowie before 3,094 fans on City Island.

GABE WHITE

Then, they lost their top two starting pitchers after the game as Gabe White and Joey Eischen were promoted to Class AAA Ottawa.

Manager Jim Tracy had no trouble finding White after the game. Eischen, well, he was nowhere to be found.

JOEY EISCHEN

Seemed Eischen, who received a no-decision in this start, did not hang around long after giving up five runs on nine hits in only five innings in a game where Mike Thomas (1-1), the third of four relief pitchers, eventually took the loss.

The Senators rallied for six runs in the sixth and three more in the seventh for a brief 9-7 lead that Cameron helped wipe out during Bowie's three-run eighth off Thomas.

Cameron had an RBI single in the first inning, a two-run homer in the fifth and a two-run single in the sixth before his two-run homer in the eighth.

Among the cool stuff Eischen missed were four-hit games by Chris Martin and Matt Rundels. He also missed three RBIs from Tyrone Woods, who had six RBIs in his last three games as he continued to get more at-bats following other recent promotions.

As for Eischen, Tracy eventually found him.

"We tracked him down at the Progress Grille, brought him back here and fined him," Tracy said with a smile.

"And then we sent him to Triple-A."

The amount of the fine was undisclosed. Not that Eischen cared about that.

EASTERN LEAGUE STANDINGS on Aug. 3			
	Record	Pct.	GB
SENATORS	71 - 34	.676	—
Canton	60 - 47	.561	12
Albany	54 - 51	.514	17
Bowie	55 - 52	.514	17
London	51 - 56	.477	21
Binghamton	50 - 58	.463	22 1/2
Reading	48 - 58	.453	23 1/2
New Britain	37 - 70	.346	35

LOOKING BACK
Parting Words

HARRISBURG — Joey Eischen could make you wonder. A sneer from him really could have been a smile. Or not. A stare really could have been an invitation to chat. Or not. A wise-ass retort simply could have been his way of saying, "Hey, how's it going today?" Or, it could have meant get lost.

With Eischen, you never knew for sure.

Some might have attributed the kaleidoscope that was Eischen's personality as being just that of a stereotypically quirky left-handed pitcher.

More likely this simply was Eischen being, well, Eischen.

When he spoke, though, you listened, because he often spoke with raw emotion. Diplomacy never was his forte.

So, no great surprise that when Eischen finally left after the Aug. 3 game for Class AAA Ottawa, he left a clear message for his now-former teammates still loitering in the clubhouse.

"Don't," he said to all within earshot, "f---k up my ring." With that, Eischen was out the door.

"He didn't always use the most tact in getting his point across," manager Jim Tracy remembered a quarter-century later. "But, I'll you what, if you were wearing the same uniform as he was, then he was in the trenches with you."

Exactly for whom Eischen's parting words were meant was anyone's guess.

"That comment was typical Joey," first baseman Randy Wilstead said. "I am sure it was half serious, half joking. I think it was directed at the players he had been playing with all along, not necessarily to the new guys, but with Joey you never know."

Still, no one — the guys still there from April or the replacements arriving ever since — was taking a chance of pissing off Eischen.

"No doubt," said pitcher Rod Henderson, whose arrival from West Palm Beach coincided with Eischen's promotion to AAA. "I wanted to be a part of it and keep things rolling once I got there. You were definitely playing for something bigger than yourself."

WEDNESDAY, AUGUST 4
"The Scrappy Bunch"

HARRISBURG — For those impatient fans who left early, no refunds for you.

ORESTE MARRERO

Should have learned your lesson from Tuesday's series opener against Bowie after the Senators' frantic 10-9 come-from-behind, lose-from ahead game against the Baysox.

This game was just as wild as the Senators rallied for three runs in the 10th inning to beat Bowie 6-5 before the remnants from a crowd of 4,627 on City Island.

"I won't say they don't have faith in us," Glenn Murray said, "but that would be the natural reaction to have, to leave."

What they missed was Bowie tying the score at 3 in the ninth when No. 9 hitter Cesar Devarez followed Jimmy Roso's two-out double to right on an 0-2 pitch with his own RBI bloop single to center off another 0-2 pitch from closer du jour Joe Ausanio.

They also missed Bowie scoring twice in the 10th when Kyle Washington hit a two-run homer halfway to Wormleysburg for a 5-3 lead off Rafael Diaz (3-3).

The Senators tied the score in the bottom of the 10th on Oreste Marrero's two-run homer to right. They then won the game as Mike Hardge, who struck out in his three previous at-bats, singled to center off Rafael Chaves, stole second on the next pitch and scored when Chris Martin bounced Chaves' 2-1 pitch into center.

"That's what we're going to have to be now, the 'Scrappy Bunch,' " Hardge said.

The new-look Senators still were the winning Senators as they picked up their seventh victory in eight games.

The game was a perfect sequel to Bowie's 10-9 win in the series opener with four lead changes and five homers that accounted for eight of the 11 runs and Mylanta for all.

EASTERN LEAGUE STANDINGS on Aug. 4			
	Record	Pct.	GB
SENATORS	72 - 34	.679	—
Canton	61 - 47	.565	12
Albany	55 - 51	.519	17
Bowie	55 - 53	.509	18
London	51 - 57	.472	22
Binghamton	51 - 58	.468	22 1/2
Reading	48 - 59	.449	24 1/2
New Britain	37 - 71	.343	36

THURSDAY, AUGUST 5
Changing Opinions

HARRISBURG — Brian Looney claimed, really, he was not a strikeout pitcher, but his recent numbers would disagree.

BRIAN LOONEY

Utility player Matt Rundels said, really, he was not a gifted outfielder, but his defense in this game certainly belied that notion.

And outfielder Tyrone Woods really was just making up for lost time.

Here were the three lesser-knowns among the Senators' season-long gallery of stars who highlighted a 6-0 shutout of the Bowie Baysox before a crowd of 5,414 at RiverSide Stadium.

The victory was the eighth in nine games for the Senators as they continued to emerge from a July malaise triggered, in part, by a handful of promotions to Class AAA Ottawa.

Looney, the self-admitted contact pitcher, matched the Eastern League's single-game season high with 13 strikeouts, a mark he first reached against New Britain on July 24.

Looney (2-1) scattered four singles, a double and three walks in recording the Senators' fourth complete-game shutout, two of which were against Bowie.

He threw strikes on 86 of his 121 pitches and worked ahead in the count to 27 of the 34 batters he faced.

"I'll say the same thing I've said before: I'm not a strikeout pitcher," Looney said. "I don't throw 98 miles an hour. I'm just hitting spots."

Looney, whose fastball topped out at only 89 mph, had compiled 35 strikeouts over his last 22 innings.

"You can't pitch much better than he has in his last three starts," manager Jim Tracy said. "They weren't picking up his changeup and that made his fastball that much better."

EASTERN LEAGUE STANDINGS on Aug. 5			
	Record	Pct.	GB
SENATORS	73 - 34	.682	—
Canton	61 - 48	.560	13
Albany	56 - 51	.523	17
Bowie	55 - 54	.505	19
Binghamton	52 - 58	.473	22 1/2
London	51 - 58	.468	23
Reading	49 - 59	.454	24 1/2
New Britain	37 - 72	.339	37

THURSDAY, AUGUST 5

Rundels' defense also made Looney that much better.

Having already played second and third in his first week with the Senators, Rundels helped save Looney's shutout with two diving catches in right field — first, off Cesar Devarez's sinking liner to start the sixth inning and, later, Stanton Cameron's drive to open the ninth.

"The kid was the king out there," Looney said of Rundels.

Rundels was not too bad at the plate, either, as he followed Woods' three-run homer to right-center in the fourth with a solo shot to left-center for a 4-0 lead off Bowie starter Terry Farrar.

"We saw him one time and that's all it took," Woods said.

The Senators struck with economy, too, scoring those four runs off the fastball-happy Farrar's first six pitches of the inning.

Chris Martin started the rally by lining Farrar's first-pitch fastball to left for a single and moved to second when Tyrone Horne bunted the next pitch, another fastball, for an infield hit. After Glenn Murray popped up to shortstop Tim Holland on Farrar's third straight fastball, Woods smoked the fourth pitch of the inning — an outside fastball — over the wall in right-center for a 3-0 lead.

"This whole series, they were pitching me outside," Woods said. "I wanted to show them I could drive the ball."

He also wanted to show Jim Tracy he could still drive the ball.

"This is my time to shine for the rest of the season," said Woods, who with the promotions of Cliff Floyd and Rondell White to Class AAA Ottawa was trying to join Murray and Shane Andrews as the Senators' main power threats.

Rundels auditioned for that role, too. He did so with more patience as he waited all of one pitch — an outside changeup — before launching Farrar's 1-0 fastball over the wall in left-center.

"After Woods hit his home run, I thought he'll throw a fastball with me," Rundels said. "When he didn't, and threw the changeup, I thought he'd come back with the fastball."

Looney escaped trouble in every inning from the sixth through the ninth after allowing a hit in each of those innings.

"I was feeling pretty good in the eighth, but got tired in the ninth," Looney said. "I think if I didn't have a shutout going, they would have taken me out."

No need for that.

Long Trip, Bad Start

CANTON, Ohio — The Senators started an 11-game, 10-day road trip. They did not start, well, either, losing 10-3 to the Canton Indians before 5,004 fans at Thurman Munson Memorial Stadium.

The Senators had Tyrone Horne's RBI groundout in the first inning, Matt Rundels' second homer in as many games in the fifth inning and Mitch Simons' sacrifice fly in the seventh.

Canton pounced on Reid Cornelius (7-7) for six runs in less than two innings and Rafael Diaz for four more before the end of the seventh. Harrisburg had won eight of its last nine games, so what's a little hiccup?

EASTERN LEAGUE STANDINGS on Aug. 6			
	Record	Pct.	GB
SENATORS	73 - 35	.676	—
Canton	62 - 48	.564	12
Albany	56 - 52	.519	17
Bowie	55 - 54	.505	18 1/2
Binghamton	53 - 58	.477	21 1/2
London	52 - 58	.473	22
Reading	49 - 59	.454	24
New Britain	37 –73	.336	37

More Of The Same

CANTON, Ohio — Ugueth Urbina, the 19-year-old pitcher who was the latest top prospect assigned to the Senators, finally lost a game. Only took two former major leaguers now pitching for Canton to do it, too. As it was, Urbina (3-1) allowed only three runs on eight singles and two walks in a 3-2 loss before a record crowd of 7,693 at Thurman Munson Memorial Stadium.

Mike Dyer, the onetime Minnesota Twins starter, and Calvin Jones, the onetime Seattle Mariners reliever, held the Senators to one hit after giving up two runs in the second inning on RBI singles from Tyrone Woods and Mike Hardge.

EASTERN LEAGUE STANDINGS on Aug. 7			
	Record	Pct.	GB
SENATORS	73 - 36	.670	—
Canton	63 - 48	.568	11
Albany	57 - 51	.528	15 1/2
Bowie	56 - 55	.505	18
Binghamton	53 - 59	.473	21 1/2
London	53 - 58	.477	21
Reading	50 - 61	.450	24
New Britain	37 –74	.333	37

Still So Dangerous

CANTON, Ohio — Most of the big names had been promoted by now, but the Senators still could put up big numbers.

And the Senators still could put them up in a hurry, just as they did in this game as they used three home runs to help score 10 runs in the seventh inning and break open a 14-3 victory over Canton before a crowd of 4,505 at Thurman Munson Memorial Stadium.

The victory, which followed a pair of losses to open the three-game series, pushed the Senators' lead over second-place Canton to 12 games with only 28 remaining in the regular season. The math was looking good there.

The 10-run seventh — the Senators' most explosive inning in a season of firepower — was highlighted by a pair of three-run homers by Matt Rundels and Chris Martin that bracketed a solo homer by Randy Wilstead.

The first seven runs of the seventh came off Paul Romanoli, who lasted only two-thirds of the inning before being replaced by designated hitter Greg Sparks.

Sparks proceeded to pitch like the infielder he was by trade, allowing a single to No. 9 hitter Rob Fitzpatrick, a double by Mike Hardge and Martin's three-run homer before finally escaping the inning when Tyrone Horne lined out to right fielder Brian Giles.

Watching all of this from the Senators' dugout was pitcher Rod Henderson (1-0), making his Class AA debut after Gabe White and Joey Eischen were promoted a few days earlier to AAA Ottawa.

Henderson allowed just four hits and one earned run over six innings before cooling down during the rally of all rallies in the seventh.

Heath Haynes, Mike Thomas and Joe Ausanio combined for the final three innings, striking out four while allowing only a meaningless run in the eighth inning before the Senators got back on the bus for Reading, where they were to continue their 11-game, 10-day road trip.

EASTERN LEAGUE STANDINGS on Aug. 8			
	Record	Pct.	GB
SENATORS	74 - 36	.673	—
Canton	63 - 49	.563	12
Albany	58 - 52	.527	16
Bowie	57 - 55	.509	18
London	53 - 59	.473	22
Binghamton	53 - 60	.469	22 1/2
Reading	50 - 61	.450	24 1/2
New Britain	38 - 74	.339	37

LOOKING BACK
Watching, Waiting

CANTON, Ohio — The nature of the minor leagues was for teams to serve the next level.

Class AAA Ottawa fed the Montreal Expos with new talent.

Class AA Harrisburg then fed Ottawa. Class A West Palm Beach fed Harrisburg and so on, all the way down to the Expos' team in the neophyte Gulf Coast League.

And players on the level below always took a peek at what was above them.

This was baseball's ultimate carrot-on-the-stick scenario.

Intently following the Senators throughout the season were the players at West Palm Beach in the Class A Florida State League. Those players waited there and watched.

ROD HENDERSON

Who was the latest Senator promoted? Did he play my position? Then again, am I good enough to take his position?

These questions were more important than that day's weather in Florida and the conjecture was just as unreliable.

"Obviously, as a player in the system, you followed what was going on, and especially when teammates were promoted," pitcher Rod Henderson said nearly 25 years after joining the Senators late in Harrisburg's magical season in 1993.

Henderson was one of 12 players promoted during the '93 season from West Palm Beach to the Senators.

Most of those dozen had spent nearly all or part of spring training with the Senators before being sent down to West Palm Beach as others trickled down either from major league camp or Ottawa's spring roster to Harrisburg.

210

LOOKING BACK

"I knew it was going to be a special team before I even arrived in Harrisburg," first baseman Randy Wilstead recalled a quarter-century later, "because of the combination of talent that was in (Class A) Rockford and West Palm Beach the year before, as well as all the No. 1 draft picks that had moved up."

RANDY WILSTEAD

Wilstead came up from West Palm Beach when outfielder Curtis Pride was promoted to Ottawa, getting the word from West Palm Beach manager Rob Leary after batting .333 in 60 games in the Florida State League.

"Rob Leary told me who I was replacing and I knew his stats," Wilstead said of Pride. "I knew that he wasn't going to be an easy person to replace, but I knew I had been playing really well in West Palm Beach, so my confidence level was up."

> *"It was definitely a different mentality with that group. There was a special feeling."*
> *Pitcher Rod Henderson*

Wilstead promptly singled to center in his first at-bat in a 5-0 loss on June 22 at Bowie.

Producing right away was to be expected, not just from Wilstead but from everyone arriving from Class A and joining the Eastern League's most dominant team since the 1983 Reading Phillies.

"Just the confidence and the way the players carried themselves," Henderson said of his new teammates in Harrisburg. "It was definitely a different mentality with that group There was a special feeling."

MONDAY, AUGUST 9
Familiar Territory

READING, Pa. — Joe Ausanio had been in these situations of saving ballgames.

But that was in 1990, in Ausanio's first stop in Harrisburg, back when the Senators were the Pittsburgh Pirates' Class AA team. He saved 15 games that season, at the time a modern-franchise record. He went on to save 15 more games in 1992 for Pittsburgh's Class AAA affiliate in Buffalo.

Then Ausanio's right elbow started to bark at him. Loudly. Painfully. The Pirates put him

JOE AUSANIO

on waivers in the fall of 1992. The Expos claimed him and stashed him in the rookie-level Gulf Coast League to rehab his elbow before sending him back to Harrisburg.

Ausanio, 27 by then, quickly became one of the old heads on a young Senators team. Worked effectively, too, in his first six appearances, winning one game in relief and posting a 1.23 ERA.

He had not, though, saved a game. At least not yet.

Ausanio finally had his chance in this game as Mike Thomas, the Senators' third reliever for starter Miguel Batista, began the ninth inning by walking three straight batters while trying to protect a three-run lead at Reading's aging Municipal Stadium.

Ausanio replaced Thomas and promptly retired leadoff hitter Steve Bieser on a shallow fly to left fielder Tyrone Horne for the first out. Keith Kimberlin then popped out to third baseman Matt Rundels for the second out before Ausanio struck out Phil Geisler to end the game.

The 10-7 lead Ausanio was given to protect turned into a 10-7 victory before a crowd of 7,656 that moved from rabid to silent with each out Ausanio picked up in the ninth.

"Anyone who tells you he's not nervous in that situation," Ausanio said, "is only kidding themselves."

EASTERN LEAGUE STANDINGS on Aug. 9			
	Record	Pct.	GB
SENATORS	75 - 36	.676	—
Canton	63 - 50	.558	13
Albany	58 - 53	.523	17
Bowie	58 - 55	.513	18
London	54 - 59	.478	22
Binghamton	53 - 61	.465	23 1/2
Reading	50 - 62	.446	25 1/2
New Britain	39 - 74	.345	37

MONDAY, AUGUST 9

Maybe the Phillies were kidding themselves, thinking they actually could hit Ausanio's forkball.

They couldn't. Especially Geisler, a dangerous left-handed hitter who easily could have won the game with a long fly ball over Reading's short wall in right field.

Instead, Ausanio jumped ahead in the count before finishing off Geisler with a 1-2 forkball, his third straight to Geisler.

"I've been in this situation before," Ausanio said. "A home run wins the game for them, but in that situation you have to go after them."

Most appreciative was Batista (8-5), who picked up the win despite allowing five runs in five innings on seven hits and four walks. He left four relievers to work the final four innings.

Most impressed was manager Jim Tracy.

"Ausanio was nothing short of awesome," Tracy said. "Not only did he throw strikes, he put them in quality spots. Those forkballs he threw to Geisler, I'm not sure too many major leaguers would do anything with them."

The Senators, as had been their wont this season with the Phillies, seemed to hit everything pitched to them.

Everyone in the starting lineup, including Batista, had at least one hit as the Senators totaled 18 hits with 13 of them coming in the first five innings to give Batista an 8-5 lead. Oreste Marrero had four of the 18 hits, all singles in his first four at-bats. Glenn Murray also had two hits, including his 21st homer, while Mike Hardge drove in three runs with a bases-loaded triple that punctuated the Senators' four-run fourth inning.

New Week, New Faces

READING, Pa. — Hours before Joe Ausanio finished off the R-Phillies, the Expos again tweaked the Senators' roster.

This time, Montreal reassigned struggling reliever Darrin Winston to Class A West Palm Beach, replacing him with two players — Ed Puig, another reliever plucked from the Mexican League, and Marc Griffin, an outfielder from West Palm Beach. Both played in this game with Puig working a scoreless sixth inning and Griffin going 0-for-3 after replacing Tyrone Woods.

TUESDAY, AUGUST 10
"A Little Talk"

READING, Pa. — Jim Tracy watched the first two games of the series his team had just played in Canton and, to be nice, the Senators' manager was not happy. He watched his team score only five runs on 10 hits. Total. For two games. Both losses.

So, he had a 15-minute closed door meeting here and, given the tiny visitors' clubhouse, Tracy could whisper to make his point.

Be aggressive, swing the freakin' bat.

The Senators listened. Actually, they started to listen in Sunday's series finale at Canton, collecting 15 hits in a 14-3 rout.

Eighteen more hits — and another win — came in Monday's series opener here, followed in this game by nine hits and a 7-2 victory over the Reading Phillies before a crowd of 5,522.

"We had a little talk when we got here," cleanup hitter Glenn Murray said. "We were trying to be more aggressive. We got it together in these last couple of games."

Murray had two hits, as did Tyrone Horne, who had 21 hits and 12 walks in his first 16 games with the Senators. Matt Rundels, another recent addition from Class A West Palm Beach, had a homer among his three hits, drove in three and stole two bases.

"We were too passive, looking at too many balls," Tracy said. "We needed to be more aggressive, and that's what we saw."

He also saw another fine start from Brian Looney (3-1), who struck out 11 before leaving after six innings with a 6-2 lead. His third straight win came two days after Rod Henderson had a similar performance — albeit without the strikeouts — during his Class AA debut in Sunday's series-salvaging win at Canton.

"I have been adamant about the strength of our pitching staff," Tracy said. "Looney and Henderson didn't come in here feeling their way around. They are ready.

"And we still have some very good players here who are making a statement that they may have been overshadowed by some very good players who have moved up."

EASTERN LEAGUE STANDINGS on Aug. 10			
	Record	Pct.	GB
SENATORS	76 - 36	.679	—
Canton	63 - 51	.553	14
Albany	59 - 53	.527	17
Bowie	59 - 55	.518	18
London	54 - 60	.474	23
Binghamton	54 - 61	.470	23 1/2
Reading	50 - 63	.442	26 1/2
New Britain	39 - 75	.342	38

214

WEDNESDAY, AUGUST 11
Straight To The Top

READING, Pa. — No batter had been as hot lately as first baseman Oreste Marrero and, conversely, no pitcher had been as cold as Reid Cornelius.

Hard then initially to figure out why Marrero — with eight hits in his last 13 at-bats — was on the bench for this game, especially with Cornelius having lost five of his last seven decisions.

Turned out that Cornelius did not need much help, either from Marrero or the Senators' pinball-like offense, as he shut down the Reading Phillies 4-1 in a rain-shortened, eight-inning game before a soggy crowd of 3,509 at Municipal Stadium.

All he really needed was Marc Griffin's three-run double to right-center in the sixth inning that snapped a 1-1 tie.

As for Marrero, he was given the night off after being told before the game he was being promoted the next day to Montreal.

Not Class AAA Ottawa, but directly to the major leagues — the first Senator this season to take that in-your-wildest-dreams direct route to the majors.

Not Cliff Floyd. Not Rondell White. Not Kirk Rueter.

No, the winner of that office pool was the unheralded Marrero, who despite his .333 batting average in 85 games constantly struggled for playing time on a team loaded with top prospects.

Marrero swapped roster spots with Derrick White, the Senators' hard-hitting first baseman in 1992 whose stubbornness over his approach at the plate so irked the Expos' coaching staff that the decision was made to exile him from the majors to Class AA.

As for Cornelius (8-7), he gave up just one run in the first inning, and allowed only six hits and a walk while striking out seven in his truncated complete game.

Far different results than five days earlier, when Cornelius gave up six runs on seven hits and three walks, and did not survive the second inning of a 10-3 loss at Canton.

EASTERN LEAGUE STANDINGS on Aug. 11			
	Record	Pct.	GB
SENATORS	77 - 36	.681	—
Canton	63 - 52	.548	15
Albany	60 - 53	.531	17
Bowie	60 - 55	.522	18
Binghamton	55 - 61	.474	23 1/2
London	54 - 61	.470	24
Reading	50 - 64	.439	27 1/2
New Britain	39 -76	.339	39

THURSDAY, AUGUST 12
Scoreboard Watching

BALTIMORE — There was the small matter of taking batting practice before a twilight doubleheader against the Bowie Baysox.

But no one on the Senators seemed to care about BP. Not with updates coming in from Philadelphia, where Oreste Marrero, their teammate just 24 hours earlier, was making his major league debut in the Expos' afternoon game against the Phillies.

Not only did Marrero start at first base and bat seventh in the order, Kirk Rueter, who opened the season as the Senators' No. 4 starter, was making his seventh start for Montreal since his July promotion from Class AAA Ottawa. Unlike Rueter, Marrero made his debut coming right from Class AA, the first in the Senators' Class of 1993 to reach the majors in such a direct route.

Marrero did just fine, going 2-for-5 with an RBI double off Tommy Greene in the third and a single off Roger Mason in the seventh. Rueter's day was not so fine as he lasted only two innings, giving up three runs in a game the Phillies eventually won 7-4.

For the Senators, their doubleheader against Bowie was more akin to Rueter's day, losing the first game 7-2 and then giving up two runs in the ninth to fall 4-3 in the second game before a crowd of 1,719 at Memorial Stadium. Despite the losses, the Senators clinched a playoff spot as Binghamton fell 4-2 at New Britain.

Ugueth Urbina (3-2) lasted just one inning in the opener, giving up three runs on four hits and three walks. Rafael Diaz, making a spot start, pitched well in the second game, allowing just one run on two hits in six innings before Bowie scored twice in the ninth off Mike Thomas (1-2) for the walk-off win.

Even though playoff rosters already were frozen, the Senators made an addition after the deadline with today's arrival of Kristen Blix Vander Woude, the 7-pound, 11-ounce baby girl born to general manager Todd Vander Woude and his wife, Kathy.

"She was 2 1/2 weeks early," Vander Woude said. "She was due on Lunch Bag Night."

EASTERN LEAGUE STANDINGS on Aug. 12			
	Record	Pct.	GB
SENATORS	77 - 38	.670	—
Canton	63 - 53	.543	14 1/2
Albany	61 - 53	.535	15 1/2
Bowie	62 - 55	.530	16
Binghamton	55 - 62	.470	23
London	54 - 62	.466	23 1/2
Reading	51 - 64	.443	26
New Britain	40 - 76	.345	37 1/2

FRIDAY, AUGUST 13
Free Willy

BALTIMORE — In his first three pro seasons, Randy Wilstead showed he could hit and he showed he could field. This season, he showed he could quietly sit on the Senators' bench.

Top prospect Cliff Floyd put him there. So did the hot-hitting Oreste Marrero. In between, a flaming pain of a shoulder injury kept him there.

Patience was one word to describe Wilstead's season.

Frustration was another.

Surprise was a word added to the list in this game as the struggling first baseman unexpectedly found himself batting cleanup in the Senators' revamped offense.

All Wilstead did was drive in three runs with three hits and a sacrifice fly during a 6-3 victory over the Bowie Baysox before a crowd of 5,051 at Memorial Stadium.

> *"I had to be patient ... but, I'll be the first to tell you that this whole year has been frustrating."*
> *Randy Wilstead*

Wilstead's three hits pushed his batting average from .188 to .221. The three RBIs nearly doubled his total to seven in 28 games since arriving from West Palm Beach following Curtis Pride's promotion in mid-June.

"To tell you the truth, it was a confidence builder," Wilstead said of hitting fourth for the first time since leaving the Class A Florida State League. "And ... I was a little surprised."

So were the Baysox, who fell behind 1-0 on Wilstead's first-inning single to right that scored Mike Hardge and 3-0 on Wilstead's opposite-field sacrifice fly to left that scored Glenn Murray in the third inning.

Wilstead pushed that lead to 4-0 off Jose Mercedes when he led off the sixth inning a towering homer to right — the kind that long-ago first baseman Boog Powell used to hit for the Orioles in this stadium.

EASTERN LEAGUE STANDINGS on Aug. 13			
	Record	Pct.	GB
SENATORS	78 - 38	.672	—
Canton	64 - 53	.547	14 1/2
Albany	61 - 54	.530	16 1/2
Bowie	62 - 56	.525	17
Binghamton	55 - 62	.470	23 1/2
London	55 - 62	.470	23 1/2
Reading	51 - 65	.440	27
New Britain	40 - 76	.345	38

FRIDAY, AUGUST 13

"He looked like a genius tonight, by all means," Bowie manager Don Buford said of Jim Tracy, who batted Wilstead fourth rather than using Murray in his customary spot.

ROD HENDERSON

Tracy said he simply wanted to space out his left-handed hitters with Marc Griffin batting second and Wilstead fourth.

The move allowed Wilstead to momentarily push aside a frustrating season that started in spring training when Marrero beat him out for the Senators' final roster spot and continued when Floyd returned from left field to first base just as Wilstead was promoted to Harrisburg in June.

"Cliff is Cliff and Oreste was hitting .330, so I couldn't argue," Wilstead said. "I had to be patient … but I'll be the first to tell you that this whole year has been frustrating."

"I told him he had to hang in there," Tracy said. "It boils down to opportunity, and now Randy Wilstead has the opportunity to get some at-bats."

Opportunity was a tangible that Rod Henderson appreciated.

After pitching only three innings in 1992 when an auto accident left him with a cracked right wrist and two fractured vertebrae, Henderson turned in his second straight impressive start for the Senators after going 12-7 at West Palm Beach.

Against Bowie, Henderson (2-0) took a shutout into the eighth inning before a pair of errors led to three unearned runs.

Henderson lasted for 111 pitches before Heath Haynes recorded the final out of the eighth and Ed Puig pitched a perfect ninth for his first save since joining the Senators earlier in the week.

"I was trying to stay ahead and get them to swing at the first pitch," Henderson said, "but I was getting tired."

Despite his newfound role as cleanup hitter, Wilstead may not have the chance to get as tired. Not with the normally hard-hitting and now somewhat ticked Derrick White — the Senators' first baseman in 1992 — expected to join the Senators at any moment after the Expos reassigned him from the majors to Class AA.

"Derrick White is going to get his at-bats," Tracy said, "but so is Randy Wilstead."

Batista, The Pitcher

BALTIMORE — There had been plenty of
games this season when Miguel Batista could
frustrate everyone associated with the Expos.
The decision makers in Montreal. The
Senators' coaching staff. His teammates.
And, on occasion, opposing batters.
Depending on the game, Batista either was
a thrower or a pitcher. Semantically speaking,
Batista always considered himself a pitcher
first and foremost, never a thrower.

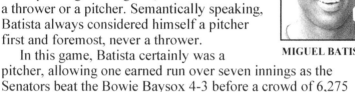

MIGUEL BATISTA

In this game, Batista certainly was a
pitcher, allowing one earned run over seven innings as the
Senators beat the Bowie Baysox 4-3 before a crowd of 6,275
at Baltimore's old Memorial Stadium.

The Senators gave Batista an early 4-0 lead on an RBI single
from Rob Fitzpatrick in the second inning and a three-run homer
from Glenn Murray in the third off Bowie starter Chuck Ricci.
Murray's homer was his 22nd; the RBIs his 78th, 79th and 80th.

"I didn't get all of it," Murray said of Ricci's 1-1 slider that he
launched over deep over the wall in left.

"I thought I got just enough to get it out, but the ball was
carrying well. It was a slider that stayed up. He had gotten me out
with it earlier and I guess he thought he could get me out again."

Ricci guessed wrong with Murray.

His teammates guessed wrong most of the game with Batista
(9-5), who gave up just four hits before leaving after seven innings
and 109 pitches with a 4-2 lead. Mike Thomas dodged an eighth-
inning homer by Stanton Cameron to finish with his second save.

"Batista was great,"
manager Jim Tracy said.
"We've been working
with him, getting him to
use his breaking ball
more. He was throwing
it for strikes, and he also
pitched inside."

EASTERN LEAGUE STANDINGS on Aug. 14			
	Record	Pct.	GB
SENATORS	79 - 38	.675	—
Canton	65 - 53	.551	14 1/2
Albany	62 - 54	.534	16 1/2
Bowie	62 - 57	.521	18
Binghamton	56 - 63	.471	24
London	55 - 63	.466	24 1/2
Reading	51 - 66	.436	28
New Britain	41 - 77	.347	38 1/2

SUNDAY, AUGUST 15
The Other Guy

BALTIMORE — The first guy did well. The other guy, though, gave up a gift-wrapped double that cost him one run and a two-run grounder that came tantalizingly close to being a no-run out.

The result left Brian Looney as the other guy in the Mike Mussina Spectacle with a 3-1 loss as the Senators managed only one hit off the Baltimore Orioles' rehabbing All-Star and then just two more off Bowie's bullpen before a crowd of 12,247.

"Pitch for pitch," manager Jim Tracy said, "our guy was as good as their guy."

Looney (3-2) allowed only five hits in seven innings. He left trailing 3-0 after Bowie scored once in the first inning and twice in the sixth. The first run came with two outs as Ed Alfonzo walked and scored when Stanton Cameron was credited with a double that nearly drilled sun-blinded right fielder Glenn Murray in the head.

"I just lost it in the sun," said Murray, whose sunglasses were on top of his cap rather than in front of his eyes.

"I couldn't see out of them."

All part of a 24-pitch ordeal that was Looney's first inning.

"I couldn't get my curveball over and I couldn't get my changeup over," Looney said.

Looney recovered to retire 14 straight Bowie batters between Cameron's sun-aided double and T.R. Lewis' bunt single that started Bowie's two-run sixth. That rally ended on Jim Wawruck's two-out, two-run grounder just past second baseman Mike Hardge.

Mussina was nearly perfect, retiring the first five batters before Shane Andrews' two-out single in the second and the next 13 to then leave after six innings with a 3-0 lead. The Senators' lone run came in the ninth as Murray deposited Rafael Chaves' 2-0 pitch halfway up the left-field bleachers.

Looney said he gave no thought to competing against Mussina.

"I might have if I had to hit against him," Looney said. "He did have some nasty stuff."

EASTERN LEAGUE STANDINGS on Aug. 15			
	Record	Pct.	GB
SENATORS	79 - 39	.669	—
Canton	66 - 53	.555	13 1/2
Albany	62 - 55	.530	16 1/2
Bowie	63 - 57	.525	17
Binghamton	57 - 63	.475	23
London	56 - 63	.471	23 1/2
Reading	51 - 67	.432	28
New Britain	41 - 78	.345	38 1/2

LOOKING BACK
The All-Star

BALTIMORE — He seemed more ice than man with frozen packs strapped across his back, along his shoulder and around his right elbow.

His eyes, well, at least they were not sore as they darted back and forth between the reporters asking about his injury rehab assignment and the clubhouse TV that was showing the waning moments of the Baltimore Orioles' sixth straight loss.

Mike Mussina unenthusiastically answered all of the questions about cutting down the Senators as if he had just pitched in a simulated game. His thoughts really were on when and where he would rejoin the Orioles.

Understandable. No need anymore for the All-Star pitcher to remain with the Class AA Bowie Baysox, not after beating the Senators 3-1 on Aug. 15 in a second and final rehab start to test his ailing back and shoulder.

Mussina's line for the game: six innings, one hit, no runs, no walks, nine strikeouts, no doubt.

Mussina threw 83 pitches. He left to a strong ovation from the crowd of 12,247 — 8,000 more than what the Baysox averaged for home games at old Memorial Stadium, but far less than the 18,000 they projected for this game.

Against the Senators, Mussina looked like the pitcher who won 18 games for the Orioles in 1992 and who started the '93 season at 11-4. He threw 58 of his 83 pitches for strikes, struck out the first four batters he faced and did not fall behind in the count to a batter until he went 2-1 to Derrick White with two outs in the fourth.

"I thought I did exactly what you saw," the 24-year-old Mussina said. "I threw good. I felt good."

He looked even better to the Senators.

"You get a feel for what you're going to face one day (in the majors)," said Shane Andrews, whose two-out single in the second inning was Harrisburg's lone hit off Mussina.

"He was painting out there," Andrews said. "He didn't throw any pitches over the plate. He was inside, outside, inside, outside."

LOOKING BACK

The At-Bat

BALTIMORE — Of the 41 players on the Senators' roster during the 1993 season, 22 of them reached the majors. Alas, Randy Wilstead was not one of them.

RANDY WILSTEAD

He was an excellent hitter, an excellent fielder. But as a 16th-round draft choice, he was not quite excellent enough to get the same chances given to higher draft choices.

Wilstead, though, did what few in the majors, let alone the minors, had ever done.

He stared down Mike Mussina, a five-time All-Star pitcher who during his Hall of Fame-caliber career won 270 games. Before most of those 270 wins came along, Wilstead nearly bagged the pitcher called "Moose" with a head-high line drive on Aug. 15 in Mussina's injury rehab start here.

Mussina pitched six innings in this game, his second and final injury rehab start before returning to the Baltimore Orioles. He allowed only a single to Shane Andrews while striking out nine in a game Bowie won 3-1.

After the game, the always self-assured Mussina said only one batter in the Senators' lineup gave him a reason to pause.

The batter was Randy Wilstead.

The moment came in the second inning after Mussina recorded his fourth straight strikeout to open the game.

Wilstead was next. He quickly fell behind and eventually worked the count to 3-2 before ripping Mussina's ninth pitch to him back up the middle. Somehow, Mussina raised his left hand fast enough for the liner to go into his glove instead of his face.

"I'm lucky I didn't get hit in the head," Mussina said.

The moment, albeit one that at the time resulted in an out, had remained with Wilstead for more than 20 years after his own career ended in the obscurity of the minors.

His memory was just as clear in 2018 as it was in 1993.

"None of us was nervous," Wilstead remembered. "We were just excited to see what we could do against the best of the best.

LOOKING BACK

"Mussina was amazing, and we knew it. We were a strong team that was just arrogant enough to think we could beat him.

"I remember (Glenn Murray) passing me after he struck out and saying, 'Good luck.' ... After his comment, I knew I needed to take a two-strike approach right from the start."

Turned out that Wilstead's at-bat started with two strikes, both called by umpire Doug Eddings. Eddings, then in his sixth season in the minors, was calling balls and strikes for a major league All-Star in an old major league ballpark that once housed the Baltimore Orioles, who a year earlier moved into Camden Yards

"I stepped in the box and the first pitch was two, three inches off the outside corner," Wilstead remembered. "The second pitch was two, three inches off the inside corner. I remember turning to the umpire and saying, 'I'm OK with you giving him one side of the plate, but you can't give him that much on both.'

"He said, 'Him, I can give both sides of the plate. Now, shut up and get back in the box and hit.' I knew after that I was going to have to hit anything that wasn't in the dirt or above my shoulders.

"I remember fighting off a bunch of pitches and bantering with the umpire. In fact, we bantered so much that (Bowie catcher Jimmy Roso) told us both to shut up at one point.

"Between fouling pitches off and obvious balls, I got to the 3-2 count. The last pitch was the only one I remember being anywhere near the middle of the plate and I just barely missed hitting it on the barrel, and lined it right back at Mike's face. I remember the Bowie coach running out there to make sure Mike was OK. As he was running out, he was actually yelling at me, saying, 'You better not have hurt him.' In my arrogant and youthful way, I yelled back, 'Tell him not to throw it down the middle of the plate!' Like I said, I was too young and dumb to realize what I was saying.

"I know the umpire was the main reason I even hit the ball, because he had made me so mad, and I wasn't going to let him win and call me out on strikes. To this day, I think umpires' strike zones are garbage.

"Later, as I was walking out to the bus, the Bowie reporter found me and told me that Mike Mussina said I was a tougher out than a lot of big leaguers. I don't know if that was true ... I can always hope he said it. What a compliment, if he did."

MONDAY, AUGUST 16
No Doubting Thomas

HARRISBURG — There was no rout of the other team, a frequent occurrence this season.

ED PUIG

Nor was there much offense. Just one of those grind-it-out nights on City Island.

The Senators scored all of their runs in the third inning, bolting to a four-run lead before giving up three in the fifth and then coasting to a 4-3 victory over the Reading Phillies before a crowd of 5,481. The victory — the 80th in 119 games — put the Senators a full two weeks ahead of any other team in the Eastern League.

For a change, the storyline was not the Senators' offense as no one had more than one hit, scored more than one run or drove in more than one run.

Now pitching, well, there was plenty of that, especially in relief of starter Reid Cornelius (9-7).

Cornelius worked an eventful five innings over which he allowed three runs on four hits, three walks, a wild pitch and a balk before relievers Ed Puig, Joe Ausanio and Mike Thomas combined for four shutout innings.

In that time, the trio allowed only two singles while walking none and striking out just as few.

Thomas worked a perfect ninth for his third save after Ausanio, a closer throughout his pro career, allowed a mere single in the eighth. Before that, Puig was Puig, stymying the Phillies in the sixth and seventh to give him seven shutout innings in seven appearances since joining the Senators from the Mexican League.

"I'm really beginning to like what I see in our relievers," said manager Jim Tracy. "I know it seems like a role reversal to have Ausanio set up Mike, but we know what Joe can do with his arm coming around. If we are going to see if Thomas can be a closer, this is the time of the season to find out."

EASTERN LEAGUE STANDINGS on Aug. 16			
	Record	Pct.	GB
SENATORS	80 - 39	.672	—
Canton	66 - 53	.555	14
Albany	62 - 55	.530	17
Bowie	63 - 57	.525	17 1/2
Binghamton	57 - 63	.475	23 1/2
London	56 - 63	.471	24
Reading	51 - 68	.429	29
New Britain	41 - 78	.345	39

224

One Costly Pitch

HARRISBURG — The game report headed back to Montreal showed a loss in the standings for the Senators, but carried only glowing words for the story behind that defeat.

UGUETH URBINA

Ultimately, the Expos' talent evaluators cared nothing of the Senators' 4-3 loss in this game to the Reading Phillies. What interested them was the postgame report filed by manager Jim Tracy and pitching coach Chuck Kniffin.

That report showed Ugueth Urbina, the Eastern League's youngest player at just 19, pitched like the prospect the Expos envisioned when they signed him out of Venezuela in the summer of 1990.

Urbina (3-3) was brilliant through six innings in a game played before 3,684 rain-soaked fans at RiverSide Stadium. He allowed just two singles before giving up a grand slam in the seventh to onetime first-round pick and now fading prospect Jeff Jackson.

"How can you fault that kind of pitching?" Tracy rhetorically asked. "That wasn't even a bad pitch he threw him. He threw it down and on the corner. Jackson just made a heck of an effort to go and get it."

Urbina's fastball sat between 93 and 96 mph, numbers that brightened any postgame report.

"He was keeping the ball down, and he stayed ahead in the count," Tracy said. "He was done in by one pitch. He showed me that he is going to be important to this pitching staff."

Mike Hardge had given Urbina an early 2-0 lead with a homer to left-center in the third inning and an RBI single in the fourth before the Phillies rallied.

"We haven't been able to relax at home with them," Tracy said. "They have a 4-4 record with us here. Nobody else has played us that tough at RiverSide."

EASTERN LEAGUE STANDINGS on Aug. 17			
	Record	Pct.	GB
SENATORS	80 - 40	.667	—
Canton	68 - 53	.562	12 1/2
Albany	62 - 57	.521	17 1/2
Bowie	63 - 59	.516	18
Binghamton	59 - 63	.484	22
London	57 - 63	.475	23
Reading	52 - 68	.433	28
New Britain	41 - 79	.342	39

"Hello My Name Is ..."

HARRISBURG — As practical jokes go in the minor leagues, this was fairly standard stuff.

Distract a teammate, switch game jerseys, get a good laugh when he goes on the field wearing somebody else's name across his back.

The unknowing fool du jour here was Matt Rundels, the utility player extraordinaire who strolled onto the field to warm up for this game wearing Ugueth Urbina's jersey.

Embarrassed, Rundels quickly exited the field, wanting to distance himself from Urbina, the up-and-coming pitcher who was a down-and-out bad hitter with seven strikeouts in his eight at-bats.

MATT RUNDELS

Almost as fast, Rundels — one of the Senators' best hitters since arriving in late July from Class A West Palm Beach — reemerged from the clubhouse, found himself back in left field, drove in two runs with a solo homer in his first at-bat and a bases-loaded walk in his final at-bat.

By the end of the night, the Senators had two more solo homers from Derrick White and Shane Andrews as they beat the Reading Phillies 6-2 before a crowd of 4,715 at RiverSide Stadium.

"I didn't know," Rundels said of the jersey switch. "I just went out there and started throwing. Well, at least I did better than (Urbina) in my first at-bat."

That at-bat tied the score at 1 with one out in the second inning as Rundels drove a 1-2 slider from Darrell Goedhart over the wall in left-center for his fifth homer in 21 games.

"I was looking for an off-speed pitch," Rundels said, "and he hung a slider."

The hit was Rundels' 11th in only 21 at-bats against the Phillies, who while playing the Senators tough on City Island lost to them for the 14th time in 19 games overall.

EASTERN LEAGUE STANDINGS on Aug. 18			
	Record	Pct.	GB
SENATORS	81 - 40	.669	—
Canton	69 - 53	.566	12 1/2
Albany	62 - 58	.517	18 1/2
Bowie	63 - 60	.512	19
Binghamton	60 - 63	.488	22
London	57 - 65	.467	24 1/2
Reading	52 - 69	.430	29
New Britain	43 - 79	.342	38 1/2

WEDNESDAY, AUGUST 18

"It's nothing in particular," Rundels said of his penchant for punishing Reading. "Lately, I've been hitting the ball well."

And looking at it, too. His bases-loaded walk in the eighth against Toby Borland forced home Chris Martin with a fourth run before Andrews followed with a two-run double to clinch Rod Henderson's third victory in as many Class AA starts. Henderson worked the first five innings with Rafael Diaz, Joe Ausanio and Mike Thomas combining for the final four.

SHANE ANDREWS

Diaz gave Henderson immediate help, retiring seven of eight batters before Phil Geisler singled to center with one out in the eighth, stole second and moved to third on Rob Grable's groundout.

Ausanio replaced Diaz to protect a 3-2 lead and struck out Jeff Jackson on three pitches, the last being a nasty sidearm breaking ball to end the inning.

"That was a major key in the game," manager Jim Tracy said of Ausanio's work in the eighth. "It kept us with a one-run lead."

Rundels and Andrews then helped break open the game off the normally reliable Borland in the bottom of the eighth.

In between, Diaz allowed just the one hit to Geisler while recording eight outs before Ausanio replaced him to finish off the eighth.

"I know it's the end of the season," Diaz said, "but at least I know I can finish strong."

RAFAEL DIAZ

Unfit To Be Ty

Matt Rundels, an infielder by trade, started his eighth straight game either in left or right field, and he would start the next four in the outfield, too. In part because he was hitting so well. In part, too, because Tyrone Woods and Tyrone Horne, a pair outfielders by trade, were continuing to spend quality time with trainer Jim Young. Woods (groin) had not played in 10 games, while Horne (hamstring) had missed six straight.

A Little Pep Talk

HARRISBURG — Jim Essian, the former major league catcher and manager, remained a major league motivator when he spoke with pitcher Miguel Batista moments before his start against the Reading Phillies.

MIGUEL BATISTA

"I just told Mike they thought he was horseshit," Essian said, adding with a smile. "I told him I thought he should know that."

Not that Batista needed much motivation against Reading, a team he already had beaten four times this season in as many starts.

Batista soon became 5-for-5 against the Phillies, holding them hitless through the first five innings en route to a 3-0 victory before a crowd of 4,088 at RiverSide Stadium.

The game was Reading's last of the season against the Senators and that was just fine with the Phillies, who lost 15 of those 20 games and 29 of 40 to Harrisburg since the start of the '92 season.

"He told me what they said before the game," Batista said of Essian, the onetime Chicago Cubs manager who now was a roving minor league instructor for Montreal.

"What do they want? I was 4-0 against them. What did I have to do? Throw a no-hitter?"

Batista (10-5) did for a bit, allowing only a two-out walk to Rob Grable in the second inning. Reading finally picked up a hit in the sixth as Casey Waller led off the inning by grounding Batista's first pitch into center field for a single.

Batista ran into trouble with two outs in the seventh, loading the bases on a single and two walks. Heath Haynes deftly worked out of the jam by striking out Jeff Jackson before Joe Ausanio handled the last two innings to earn his second save.

"I was trying to be too fine there," Batista said of his final inning. "but I didn't want to give them anything they can hit."

EASTERN LEAGUE STANDINGS on Aug. 19			
	Record	Pct.	GB
SENATORS	82 - 40	.672	—
Canton	70 - 53	.569	12 1/2
Albany	63 - 58	.521	18 1/2
Bowie	63 - 61	.508	20
Binghamton	60 - 64	.484	23
London	57 - 66	.463	25 1/2
Reading	52 - 70	.426	30
New Britain	44 - 79	.358	38 1/2

FRIDAY, AUGUST 20
"We Deserved to Lose"

HARRISBURG — The thunderstorms before the game did nothing for the mood. Nor did the aggressiveness, or lack thereof, at the plate. Same with the slipshod effort on slippery conditions in the soggy outfield.

Jim Tracy watched all of this during a 5-3 loss to Canton before a crowd of 3,834 on City Island and even the ever-optimistic Tracy was left with one dreary thought.

"All in all," Tracy said, "I just feel like we deserved to lose tonight. We didn't do a whole lot tonight as a ballclub to create anything for ourselves. We created it, but we didn't finish it.

"We left too many people stranded on base and didn't get it done that way, and when you do things like that, when you don't execute when you've got runners in scoring position, you make it that much easier for the opposition."

> "We didn't do a whole lot ... to create anything for ourselves."
> Manager Jim Tracy

The opposition here, the Canton Indians, began the night facing a Harrisburg team with a magic number of four — any combination of four wins or four Canton losses — to clinch the Eastern League's regular-season title.

The Senators needed to wait to celebrate that fait accompli after wasting a 10-strikeout effort by Brian Looney, who left after six innings with the score tied at 3.

The Senators stranded eight runners on base, including leaving the bases loaded in the third inning after back-to-back homers by Randy Wilstead and Rob Fitzpatrick to start the inning gave them a 2-0 lead.

Canton snapped the 3-3 tie against reliever Rafael Diaz (3-4) with two runs in the seventh on a wild pitch and RBI groundout.

"We were a very unaggressive offensive club," Tracy said. "We had a very aggressive inning when we hit two home runs ... from that point on, we lost our aggressiveness."

EASTERN LEAGUE STANDINGS on Aug. 20		
	Record	Pct.	GB
SENATORS	82 - 41	.667	—
Canton	71 - 53	.573	11 1/2
Albany	63 - 59	.516	18 1/2
Bowie	63 - 61	.508	19 1/2
Binghamton	61 - 64	.488	22
London	57 - 67	.460	25 1/2
Reading	52 - 70	.426	29 1/2
New Britain	45 - 79	.363	37 1/2

Major League Help

HARRISBURG — Always nice when the major leaguers down on injury rehab assignments helped out with a victory.

GLENN MURRAY

Not that the Senators had the rehabbing major leaguer. The Montreal Expos had yet to send one to City Island since starting their Class AA affiliation here in 1991. Hey, those airplane tickets cost money, you know.

No, the injured big leaguer helping out here was Joel Skinner, who just two years earlier was Cleveland's regular catcher. Now, he was trying to work his way back to the majors.

So, naturally, in his first game for Canton in Friday's series opener, Skinner went 0-for-4 with two strikeouts. In this game, he was even worse, going 0-for-5 with three strikeouts and a costly passed ball in the ninth inning to help the Senators rally for a 9-8 victory before a record crowd of 5,724 at RiverSide Stadium.

The offenses took turns smacking around a couple of pitchers as Canton scored seven runs in five innings off starter Reid Cornelius before the Senators scored seven runs — all in the sixth — off reliever Nap Robinson to cut the Indians' lead to 8-7.

The Senators won the game with one out in the ninth on Glenn Murray's two-run single off Calvin Jones, another former big leaguer who like Skinner was trying to get back to the majors.

Jones did nothing to help himself as Mike Hardge started the inning with an infield single to short and promptly stole second. Jones then walked Chris Martin before striking out Derrick White. Along the way, both Hardge and Martin advanced a base on a passed ball by the normally sure-handed Skinner.

Murray followed with a game-winning, walk-off single to right, scoring both Hardge and Martin.

Murray finished with three RBIs, as did Tyrone Horne and Matt Rundels.

EASTERN LEAGUE STANDINGS on Aug. 21			
	Record	Pct.	GB
SENATORS	83 - 41	.669	—
Canton	71 - 54	.568	12 1/2
Albany	63 - 60	.512	19 1/2
Bowie	63 - 63	.508	21
Binghamton	62 - 64	.492	22
London	57 - 68	.456	26 1/2
Reading	54 - 70	.435	29
New Britain	46 - 79	.368	37 1/2

SUNDAY, AUGUST 22

One Down, One To Go

HARRISBURG — There would be no more waiting for the Senators to formally clinch a regular-season title that, really, had belonged to them for weeks, if not months.

JIM TRACY

And, there was no doubt, not after the second inning of this game as they bolted to a 6-0 lead on their way to an 11-3 rout of Canton before a crowd of 3,708 at RiverSide Stadium.

The victory — their 84th in only 125 games — eliminated any chance for the Senators to be caught by second-place Canton for the Eastern League's regular-season title.

Not that Canton ever was going to catch them. Maybe later in the playoffs, but not now. For now, the Senators received the honor of winning the EL title — for the regular season.

> *"They have a mission and they know that they have half of it."*
>
> Manager Jim Tracy

Not quite all of the hardware the Senators had wanted since the start of training camp in Lantana, Florida

"They have a mission and they know that they have half of it," manager Jim Tracy said, "but they're going to make every attempt to come out here and finish the job, because there's a championship ring that somebody could possibly take away from them. We want the big victory. That's what we're looking for.

"For me, to have an opportunity one more time to reach out, hand them a championship ring and tell them 'Thank you' one more time, that's what I'm looking forward to."

First, there was the little matter of this game, of finishing out the regular season and of course, the playoffs.

EASTERN LEAGUE STANDINGS on Aug. 22			
	Record	Pct.	GB
SENATORS	84 - 41	.672	—
Canton	71 - 55	.563	13 1/2
Albany	63 - 61	.508	20 1/2
Bowie	64 - 63	.504	21
Binghamton	63 - 64	.496	22
London	57 - 69	.452	27 1/2
Reading	54 - 71	.432	30
New Britain	47 - 79	.373	37 1/2

231

SUNDAY, AUGUST 22

The Senators' late finish Saturday to win that game in the bottom of the ninth and their fast start today were too much for Canton. At least, thought second baseman Mike Hardge, that was how the Indians carried themselves in the series finale.

DERRICK WHITE

"It looked like they didn't even want to show up today," Hardge said. "We saw it, took advantage and never let up."

Derrick White's RBI single to center field accounted for the first two runs in the Senators' three-run first inning. White also accounted for the other run when he hustled from first to home after Canton second baseman Miguel Flores

> *"It looked like they didn't even want to show up today. We saw it, took advantage and never let up."*
>
> *Second baseman Mike Hardge*

meandered into shallow right field to retrieve Shane Andrews' two-out bloop single.

Three more runs came in the second inning on Lance Rice's RBI single to center field, Chris Martin's sacrifice fly to right and Tyrone Horne's RBI double to right.

Five more runs followed in the fourth off Canton starter Mike Dyer and, well, nothing in this game mattered much after that.

Actually, with Ugueth Urbina pitching, the Senators could have stopped after the second inning as Urbina (4-3) allowed just one run on five hits before leaving after six innings with an 11-1 lead.

"When you have that big lead, you just want to go out there and get a nice inning and go back, sit down and go back out again," Urbina said.

UGUETH URBINA

"I was really uncomfortable just sitting down there and waiting to be out there again."

Letdown? Hardly

LONDON, Ont. — Clinch the regular-season title and a gaudy trophy on Sunday and then make a seven-hour bus ride to the Eastern League's northern-most outpost.

ROD HENDERSON

No one would have blamed the Senators for giving themselves a night off, even though the schedule required them to play this game against the London Tigers.

Naturally, the Senators won, and won big, as they beat the Tigers 10-2 before a crowd of 2,003 at Labatt Memorial Park.

No real surprise, either, as the victory was their 12th in 16 games against London.

Winning again in just his fourth Class AA start, Rod Henderson (4-0) allowed two runs on five hits and four walks over five innings before Ed Puig and Mike Thomas split the final four innings, holding the Tigers to just one more hit while striking out five of them.

Hardly sleep deprived, the Senators totaled 13 hits and built a 5-1 lead by the middle of the fourth inning.

Chris Martin and Matt Rundels each had three hits, while Martin, Tyrone Woods and Lance Rice each had two RBIs.

Woods' RBIs came on a two-run single in the fourth as he was making his first start after missing two weeks with a strained groin muscle.

Rice's RBIs came in the sixth on a two-run homer — his first of the season — over the right-field wall.

Oh, yeah, Derrick White picked up another single to push his hitting streak to six games after going just 1-for-17 immediately following his demotion from the Expos to Harrisburg in a move that sent Oreste Marrero to the majors.

EASTERN LEAGUE STANDINGS on Aug. 23			
	Record	Pct.	GB
SENATORS	85 - 41	.675	—
Canton	71 - 56	.559	14 1/2
Albany	64 - 62	.508	21
Bowie	65 - 63	.508	21
Binghamton	64 - 64	.500	22
London	57 - 70	.449	28 1/2
Reading	55 - 72	.433	30 1/2
New Britain	47 - 80	.370	38 1/2

Fixing A Couple Of Pieces

LONDON, Ont. — With most of the headline-making prospects promoted to Class AAA and beyond and the Eastern League's regular-season title clinched, the Senators were getting extra work for a few players who had struggled at times.

They used another victory here — 9-5 over London before a crowd of 1,617 at Labatt Memorial Park — to help tweak Tyrone Woods and Rob Fitzpatrick.

Woods, the outfielder whose playing time early in the season was limited by the glut of prospects in front of him and of late by a groin pull, had two homers and three runs batted in.

Fitzpatrick, the catcher who entered the game hitting just .221, launched a grand slam in the sixth inning that turned a 3-2 deficit into a suddenly comfortable 6-3 lead.

Not bad production from the No. 8 and 9 hitters in the lineup to go along with Miguel Batista (11-5), who allowed two earned runs in five innings before Heath Haynes, Ed Puig and Joe Ausanio combined for the final 12 outs.

A couple of hitting streaks were extended, too, as Tyrone Horne reached 10 games with Derrick White at seven.

All-Stars Announced, Floyd MVP

In a surprise to absolutely no one, Cliff Floyd before the game was named the Eastern League's most valuable player after he batted .329 in 101 games with 26 homers and 101 RBIs. The homers and RBIs still led the league as of Aug. 24, even though Floyd was promoted Aug. 2 to Class AAA Ottawa.

Floyd also was voted the league's rookie of the year. He joined center fielder Rondell White, and pitchers Joey Eischen and Gabe White on the league's postseason All-Star team. Eischen also was selected the EL's pitcher of the year, while Jim Tracy was named the EL's manager of the year.

EASTERN LEAGUE STANDINGS on Aug. 24			
	Record	Pct.	GB
SENATORS	86 - 41	.677	—
Canton	72 - 56	.563	14 1/2
Bowie	66 - 63	.512	21
Albany	64 - 63	.504	22
Binghamton	64 - 65	.496	23
London	57 - 71	.445	29 1/2
Reading	56 - 72	.438	30 1/2
New Britain	47 - 81	.367	39 1/2

87 And Climbing

LONDON, Ont. — In an afternoon game in which everyone in the Senators' starting lineup had at least one hit, an RBI or a run scored, the Senators tied a modern-franchise record for wins in a season with their 87th.

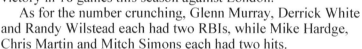

CHRIS MARTIN

In beating London 7-3 in front of crowd of 739 — really, can you call that a crowd? — the Senators moved the Tigers closer to missing the playoffs in what would be their last season in Ontario.

The Senators needed only 128 games to reach 87 wins, matching the total compiled by the 1991 team in a full 140-game season. The three-game sweep also gave the Senators their 14th victory in 18 games this season against London.

As for the number crunching, Glenn Murray, Derrick White and Randy Wilstead each had two RBIs, while Mike Hardge, Chris Martin and Mitch Simons each had two hits.

The RBIs gave Murray eight in the last four games and 92 for the season.

The hits gave Martin 101 for the season, becoming the fifth Senator after Cliff Floyd, Rondell White, Murray and Shane Andrews to reach the 100-hit plateau.

Tyrone Horne also pushed his hitting streak to 11 games with Derrick White extending his streak to eight, a span over which he was batting .323 after collecting just one hit in his first 17 at-bats after his demotion from the majors.

The biggest boost in this game, though, came from Rafael Diaz, the middle reliever who in making a spot start for Brian Looney held the Tigers to six hits before leaving with two outs in the sixth and the Senators up 2-0. Diaz (4-4) had allowed just one run in his last 11 2/3 innings as a starter.

EASTERN LEAGUE STANDINGS on Aug. 25			
	Record	Pct.	GB
SENATORS	87 - 41	.680	—
Canton	73 - 56	.566	14 1/2
Bowie	67 - 63	.515	21
Albany	65 - 63	.508	22
Binghamton	64 - 66	.492	24
London	57 - 72	.442	30 1/2
Reading	56 - 73	.434	31 1/2
New Britain	47 - 82	.364	40 1/2

Going Hollywood

HARRISBURG — While the Senators once again were pounding the London Tigers in an afternoon game on Aug. 25 in Ontario, Harrisburg Mayor Stephen Reed was discussing plans for the team's quaint little ballpark on City Island.

The Cleveland Indians were coming to the 'Burg, Reed announced. The wannabe thespian in Reed never just said anything, he always *announced* it.

And not quite the real Cleveland Indians, either, but rather the  fictional ones from the 1989 movie "Major League."

Seemed Reed struck a deal to have RiverSide Stadium used to film the spring training scenes for the upcoming, brilliantly titled sequel, "Major League 2."

Good luck camouflaging those dark green, oversized, hardly southern Florida shade trees beyond the outfield walls.

To give the place a spring training feel, the Hollywood folks were planning to tweak the billboards in the outfield to include products from Florida, repaint the dugouts with the Indians' logo and place palm trees around the stadium.

That makeover was expected to start on Sept. 8, the day after the Senators' final home game in the first round of the playoffs.

Reed said filming on the island would be done over a week, beginning on Sept. 18, a few days after the playoffs finished.

The core of actors from the first movie — Charlie Sheen, Tom Berenger, Corbin Bernsen, Dennis Haysbert and James Gammon — were expected on the island to film the spring training scenes on the same field that this season was home to Cliff Floyd, Rondell White, Kirk Rueter, Curtis Pride, Gabe White, Ugueth Urbina, Miguel Batista, Joey Eischen and Glenn Murray.

Your call as to which group had the bigger stars.

Lots Of Talk, But No Deal

HARRISBURG — There was no game on the schedule. Just another off day, the last one in the regular season.

TODD VANDER WOUDE

In 24 hours, the Senators would be back on City Island, playing in front of fans clad in red. Somewhere in the crowd, likely adorned in a Senators cap and matching sports shirt, would be Van Farber, the New York real estate developer who placed a bid to buy the Senators from Jerry Mileur.

Farber had been a staple at the ballpark ever since word came out he was planning to buy the team for $4 million.

He was in the stands, schmoozing fans.

He was in the clubhouse, chatting up players.

He talked of the team using "we" and "us." He did that a lot.

"At this point," he said, "I expect to be the next owner of the Harrisburg Senators."

He first needed the OK from the Eastern League's other seven teams, followed by approvals from the National Association that governed the minors and Major League Baseball that governed, well, everything.

"It's my hope that everything can be finalized in the next 60 to 90 days," Farber said, "if they pump

VAN FARBER   it through.

So far, nobody had primed anything, let alone pumped. No approvals had come and none seemed forthcoming.

While both Farber and Mileur were optimistic, Senators general manager Todd Vander Woude — the walking, talking definition of optimism — was more far more cautious.

"That whole transaction seemed to be a problem from the start," Vander Woude remembered a quarter-century later.

"From the paperwork (left) incomplete by Van to how we were going to operate in the future," Vander Woude said. "I sensed many problems because the sale was taking way too long, especially as we were planning for the 1994 season."

237

Looking The Other Way

HARRISBURG — Most of the crowd already had left City Island. Manager Jim Tracy was gone, too, having been ejected for the first time this season. And Glenn Murray, with a little prodding from Derrick White, changed his approach at the plate. Murray normally feasted on inside fastballs. Liked to pull them toward left field. He scared a lot of third basemen that way.

So, when the Senators had two runners — Tyrone Horne and Chris Martin — on first and second and no one out in the bottom of the 11th, Murray instinctively thought about looking for an inside pitch from Binghamton reliever Jim McCready.

Until White made a suggestion: Look elsewhere, look away.

Murray listened and then slapped McCready's 0-1 slider into right field to score Martin and lift the Senators over the Mets 7-6 before the remnants of the original crowd of 3,513.

"I was thinking fastball over the plate, but I knew he didn't want to come in and miss inside," Murray said. "(White) told me to look outside and go the other way."

Murray's 93rd RBI gave the Senators their sixth straight victory, as well as passing the 1991 team for the most wins since pro baseball returned to City Island in 1987.

Joe Ausanio (2-0), the Senators' sixth pitcher, picked up the victory. He struck out both batters he faced in the top of the 11th after inheriting two runners from Mike Thomas.

A few minutes later, Martin started the bottom of the 11th with a single to center, moved to second on Horne's walk and easily scored on Murray's opposite-field single.

For a moment, though, there was another option for Murray being considered by third-base coach Greg Fulton, who took over when Tracy was ejected in the fifth by plate umpire Bob Ashley for his scathing review of Ashley's strike zone.

"I thought about bunting," Fulton said. "Then I thought, 'No, I'm going to let a man with 92 RBIs hit his way there.' "

EASTERN LEAGUE STANDINGS on Aug. 27			
	Record	Pct.	GB
SENATORS	88 - 41	.682	—
Canton	73 - 58	.557	16
Bowie	68 - 64	.515	21 1/2
Albany	66 - 64	.508	22 1/2
Binghamton	64 - 67	.489	25
London	59 - 72	.450	30
Reading	56 - 76	.424	33 1/2
New Britain	50 - 82	.379	39 1/2

238

SATURDAY, AUGUST 28
Wasting Woods' Work

HARRISBURG — There were some games in 1993 when the negatives simply outnumbered the positives.

And not by much, either.

This was one of those games as Tyrone Horne and Derrick White saw their hitting streaks end at 12 and nine games apiece, while previously perfect Ed Puig gave up two runs after Ugueth Urbina gave up the first five in a 7-6 loss to the Binghamton Mets on City Island.

So went the Senators' six-game winning streak that included two walk-offs.

TYRONE WOODS

The positives were a pair of home runs by Tyrone Woods, who drove in four of the Senators' six runs with a three-run homer in the second inning for a 3-0 lead and a solo homer in the ninth for the final run.

Marc Griffin also picked up a pinch-hit single in the seventh, snapping an 0-for-16 slump. Griffin's single also gave the Senators their 17th pinch hit in 55 attempts.

The crowd of 4,786 pushed the Senators' attendance to 236,361 in 65 home games, setting the all-time Harrisburg single-season record since pro baseball was first played on the island in 1890.

MARC GRIFFIN

As for Urbina (4-4), he started when Rod Henderson was held out, just as Brian Looney was a few days ago. He was tagged for five runs on six hits and seven walks before leaving the game with two outs in the sixth.

"They were getting a little bit tired," pitching coach Chuck Kniffin said of Henderson and Looney. "We want them strong for the playoffs."

EASTERN LEAGUE STANDINGS on Aug. 28			
	Record	Pct.	GB
SENATORS	88 - 42	.677	—
Canton	73 - 59	.553	16
Albany	67 - 64	.511	21 1/2
Bowie	68 - 65	.511	21 1/2
Binghamton	65 - 67	.492	24
London	60 - 72	.455	29
Reading	57 - 76	.429	32 1/2
New Britain	50 - 83	.376	39 1/2

"Still Kicking Butts"

HARRISBURG — August afforded luxuries for some; manic, desperate chases for others.

RANDY WILSTEAD

The Senators, long the runaway leaders in the Eastern League, continued to juggle their lineup to rest regulars before the playoffs. Not so fortunate were the Binghamton Mets, the defending EL champions who had played at a .600 clip over the last three weeks in a mad rush to reach the postseason.

That rush was slowed in this game as the Senators beat the Mets 8-3 in front of 3,790 fans on City Island. Slowing the Mets, in particular, were Randy Wilstead and Tyrone Woods, who were 7-for-7 with five RBIs.

"We clinched — what? — a week ago, and we're still kicking people's butts," Wilstead said. "That says something about the character of this team."

Wilstead, starting at first base for the first time since Derrick White arrived on Aug. 14, had two doubles and two singles among his four hits. Woods, who missed 13 games earlier this month with a pulled groin, drove in three runs on three singles and a sacrifice fly.

Their work came after a shaky, 41-pitch first inning from Miguel Batista (12-5), who eventually pitched into the seventh before Mike Thomas recorded the final eight outs.

"Coming into this series, I didn't expect to play at all," Wilstead said. "I mostly prepared to be a pinch-hitter."

Wilstead did just that less than 24 hours ago in a 7-6 loss to the Mets, picking up a double for his first pinch-hit in 11 tries. The five hits in two games raised his average 38 points to .267 in 101 at-bats since arriving June 23 from Class A West Palm Beach.

"And, tomorrow," Wilstead said with a faint smile, "I expect to be back as a pinch-hitter."

EASTERN LEAGUE STANDINGS on Aug. 29			
	Record	Pct.	GB
SENATORS	89 - 42	.679	—
Canton	74 - 59	.556	16
Bowie	69 - 65	.515	21 1/2
Albany	67 - 65	.508	22 1/2
Binghamton	65 - 68	.489	25
London	60 - 73	.451	30
Reading	58 - 76	.433	32 1/2
New Britain	50 - 84	.373	40 1/2

Diaz Delivers, Again

HARRISBURG — Give Rafael Diaz the choice and he would rather be a starting pitcher. Every time, all the time. Who was to argue? Especially after this game as Diaz turned in his third straight impressive start with a 4-2 victory over the Binghamton Mets before a crowd of 2,933 on City Island.

RAFAEL DIAZ

Unfortunately for Diaz, a strong argument for him to stay in the bullpen came from manager Jim Tracy, who saw Diaz's path to the major leagues dotted with signposts that read: middle relief, spot starting.

"The way he pitches, the way his arm bounces back, his versatility," Tracy said. "There's an eighth or ninth man on a major league pitching staff," Tracy said. "Ralph Diaz can be used several ways and that, to me, increases his marketability."

So did Diaz's latest performance: six innings of six-hit pitching that all but eliminated the Mets — the defending EL champions — from the playoff race.

HEATH HAYNES

"I basically do whatever they tell me," Diaz said, "but I'm a lot more comfortable starting, but I know my role here is out of the bullpen."

In this last three spots starts, Diaz (5-4) allowed only three runs over 17 2/3 innings. Diaz was followed in this game by Heath Haynes, who used only 18 pitches to work two perfect innings. Haynes' appearance was his 55th, a modern-franchise record for pitchers.

"This is good now," Diaz, the loyal soldier, said of his role, "because this gives some time for the (regular) starters to get their rest."

EASTERN LEAGUE STANDINGS on Aug. 30			
	Record	Pct.	GB
SENATORS	90 - 42	.682	—
Canton	74 - 59	.556	16 1/2
Albany	68 - 65	.511	22 1/2
Bowie	69 - 66	.511	22 1/2
Binghamton	65 - 69	.485	26
London	60 - 73	.451	30 1/2
Reading	58 - 77	.430	33 1/2
New Britain	51 - 84	.378	40 1/2

LOOKING BACK
Murray's Time

HARRISBURG — The patterns of Glenn Murray's career were easy to read.

GLENN MURRAY

Sizzling starts, fizzling finishes; wonders of April and May that dissolved into the woes of July and August.

Murray earned the reputation of being Aesop's fabled hare, a stigma that in the winter of 1992-93 nearly drove the Montreal Expos to trade him to the California Angels.

"I was just too impatient," Murray said of his past. "I always wanted to do too much."

This season, the 22-year-old outfielder wanted to blend into the clubhouse walls and disappear.

Actually, he wanted to blend more into a Cliff than a wall as Murray — like so many of the other Senators — was putting together his best season playing alongside Cliff Floyd, the can't-miss prospect.

No coincidence between Murray's growth as a player and Floyd's presence in a lineup that has ripped through the Eastern League.

Floyd commanded the spotlight. Highly touted teammates like Murray settled for a residual flicker, and they were OK with that.

"Nobody really noticed me, because of Cliff," Murray said. "And nobody noticed Shane (Andrews) or Rondell (White), either, because everything was Cliff.

"I'm not saying Cliff didn't deserve it; just we weren't feeling any pressure." Murray said. "I don't think they notice me now, but that doesn't bother me. As long as the right people, the people who pay me, notice."

LOOKING BACK

Those people were the Expos, who have waited for this type of season from Murray since selecting him with their second pick in the 1989 amateur draft.

Murray launched his 25th homer on Aug. 30 during a 4-2 victory over the Binghamton Mets on City Island.

Those 25 homers, as well as his 95 RBIs, easily eclipsed his career highs of 13 homers for Class A West Palm Beach in 1992 and 60 RBIs for Class A Rockford in 1991.

In the four weeks after Floyd's Aug. 2 promotion to Class AAA Ottawa, Murray hit seven homers while driving in 25 runs.

Now, he had six games left in the regular season to hit one homer to match Floyd's modern-franchise record and six RBIs to match Floyd's league lead.

Murray admitted he occasionally thought of Floyd's records. Well, maybe a little more than occasionally.

> *"Nobody really noticed me, because of Cliff. And nobody noticed Shane or Rondell, either, because everything was Cliff."*
>
> Glenn Murray

"Every day," Murray said with a smile. *"Every day."*

August's upswing in production came after a horrid July, a month in which Murray's cousin was murdered in their hometown of Manning, South Carolina.

"Glenn's matured so much this season," second baseman Mike Hardge said. "He doesn't go out there anymore saying, 'I don't care what happens today.' He's more determined than ever to prove himself to everybody."

Murray learned to put perspective before potential, given his perspective forever was altered in December 1992, when he was shot above his left knee in a nightclub incident in his hometown.

Whatever lessons Murray did not learn then when a stray bullet nearly ended his career were reinforced in July, when his cousin, Claude, was murdered in Manning during an argument over a Walkman.

"When we're between batters, I sometimes think about it and I wonder," Murray said. "It's strange. I know I could be sitting at home right now watching baseball on TV.

"I know I was lucky."

243

Looney Strong In Loss

HARRISBURG — The result was not important, the preparation was. Given that, the Senators came out winners in a game they actually lost 3-1 to the London Tigers before a crowd of 2,841 on City Island.

After skipping over Brian Looney in his previously scheduled start, manager Jim Tracy watched with great appreciation as Looney pitched eight shutout innings, allowing just two singles and two walks while striking out seven.

That London scored three runs in the ninth to beat reliever Ed Puig (0-1) mattered little to Tracy, who already had Looney lined up to start the first game of the EL playoffs.

"The positive thing is Brian will start for us in the playoffs Monday," Tracy said. "His effort tonight was nothing short of spectacular. The rest obviously did Brian a world of good."

EASTERN LEAGUE STANDINGS on Aug. 31			
	Record	Pct.	GB
SENATORS	90 - 43	.677	—
Canton	74 - 59	.556	16
Bowie	70 - 66	.515	21 1/2
Albany	68 - 66	.507	22 1/2
Binghamton	65 - 69	.485	25 1/2
London	61 - 73	.455	29 1/2
Reading	59 - 77	.434	32 1/2
New Britain	51 - 85	.375	40 1/2

Bound For The Majors

The phone rang at 2 a.m., which Rondell White thought was an odd hour to hear from minor league ops director Kent Qualls.

"I kind of thought it was something about winter ball," White said. "Then he told me about going to the big leagues, and I couldn't sleep. The only sleep I got was on the plane."

That would be the one headed to Denver, where White joined the Expos in time for their series against the Colorado Rockies.

White batted .328 in 90 games for the Senators before his promotion July 24 to Class AAA Ottawa, where in 37 games he was hitting .380 with seven homers, 32 RBIs and 11 steals.

"He's a leader," Expos manager Felipe Alou said. "He's scared of nothing and he's got all the tools."

Reid, Rob Re-emerge

HARRISBURG — How appropriate that on a night when a clear, hauntingly full moon hung over RiverSide Stadium, a couple of specters reappeared for the Senators.

First, there was Reid Cornelius, who in his three previous starts had allowed 15 earned runs over 14 innings. All he did in this game was pitch eight sparkling innings in a 5-4 victory over London before a crowd of 4,551 in the regular-season home finale.

The crowd pushed the Senators' season attendance at RiverSide Stadium to 250,476, marking the first time that a quarter-million people watched games on the island in any year since pro baseball arrived there in 1890.

Cornelius (10-7) allowed just one run on six hits before leaving with a 5-1 lead and then watched as Mike Thomas gave up three runs in the ninth before Joe Ausanio closed out the Tigers for his fifth save.

The other apparition to re-emerge was Rob Fitzpatrick as the light-hitting catcher capped a 4-for-4 game with a two-run single in the eighth for a 5-1 lead.

"I'll tell you what was even bigger," manager Jim Tracy said, "and that was Fitzpatrick's play behind the plate."

That would be the two pitchouts Fitzpatrick used to snuff out London rallies in the third inning, when he threw out Shannon Penn trying to steal second base with one out, and then in the fifth inning, when he caught Brian Saltzgaber napping off third base with one out.

"You can go to any ballpark in America," Tracy said of Fitzpatrick, "and you won't see two stronger throws than you did tonight."

REID CORNELIUS

ROB FITZPATRICK

EASTERN LEAGUE STANDINGS on Sept. 1			
	Record	Pct.	GB
SENATORS	91 - 43	.679	—
Canton	74 - 61	.548	17 1/2
Bowie	71 - 65	.522	21
Albany	68 - 67	.504	23 1/2
Binghamton	67 - 69	.493	25
London	61 - 74	.452	30 1/2
Reading	60 - 77	.438	32 1/2
New Britain	50 - 86	.368	42

A Little Rest, Another W

BINGHAMTON, N.Y. — First, they fine-tuned Brian Looney for the start of the postseason. That was a couple of days ago.

ROD HENDERSON

The Senators did the same in this game with Rod Henderson as he held Binghamton to two hits over six innings in a 5-2 victory before a crowd of 2,778 at Municipal Stadium.

The victory was Henderson's fifth in as many starts since, like Looney, joining the Senators from Class A West Palm Beach. He also lined up behind Looney as the Senators' first two starters for the upcoming Eastern League playoffs.

Henderson in this game was part of a three-run rally in the fourth inning with an RBI double down the right-field line as the Senators turned an early 1-0 deficit into a 3-1 lead.

MITCH SIMONS

Henderson left after six innings with that same 3-1 lead, which grew to 5-1 with a pair of runs in the top of the ninth on RBI singles from Rob Fitzpatrick and Mitch Simons.

Mike Thomas, who worked out of a jam in the eighth, allowed a run in the bottom of the ninth but finished with his fifth save.

Simons finished with two hits after replacing Mike Hardge, who was ejected in the fourth for expressing his view of Jeff Nelson's strike zone.

Like Looney before him, Henderson's last regular-season start was pushed back a few days after working 166 innings between Harrisburg and West Palm Beach.

"It was a combination of a lot of innings and me starting to tire at the end of my first full season," Henderson remembered a quarter-century later.

"I skipped a start ... hoping to be a little stronger for the playoffs."

EASTERN LEAGUE STANDINGS on Sept. 2			
	Record	Pct.	GB
SENATORS	92 - 43	.681	—
Canton	74 - 61	.548	18
Bowie	71 - 65	.522	21 1/2
Albany	68 - 67	.504	24
Binghamton	67 - 70	.489	26
London	61 - 74	.452	31
Reading	60 - 77	.438	33
New Britain	50 - 86	.368	42 1/2

Ugh for Urbina

BINGHAMTON, N.Y. — Ugueth Urbina did well against most of the Eastern League in his 11 starts after joining the Senators.

Most, though, did not include the Binghamton Mets, who once again frustrated the 19-year-old Urbina, beating him 4-2 before a crowd of 5,871 at Municipal Stadium.

In his final start before the playoffs, where he would pitch Game 3 of the EL semifinals, Urbina gave up three runs on six hits and two walks before leaving after six innings with the Mets ahead 3-2.

UGUETH URBINA

Against the Mets, Urbina was 1-2 in four starts with a 4.74 ERA. Against the rest of the EL, he was 3-3 with a 3.38 ERA.

This game, of course, meant little to the Senators, who weeks ago wrapped up the regular-season title, even though they needed to wait until Aug. 22 to formally clinch that title.

While Urbina's final line, which included six strikeouts in six innings, was not bad, the Senators' offense was not good as they managed only eight singles and a double off three Binghamton pitchers.

Even then, their offense mostly was limited to Derrick White, Shane Andrews and Lance Rice, each of whom had two singles off starter Denny Harriger, and relievers Bryan Rogers and Pete Walker. Rice accounted for both of the runs off Harriger with RBI singles in the second and fourth innings. While he had the Senators' only extra-base

LANCE RICE

hit with a double, Glenn Murray remained one homer shy of tying the modern-franchise record of 26 set by Cliff Floyd before his promotion Aug. 2 to Class AAA Ottawa.

EASTERN LEAGUE STANDINGS on Sept. 3		
	Record Pct.	GB
SENATORS	92 - 44 .676	—
Canton	74 - 61 .548	17 1/2
Bowie	71 - 66 .518	21 1/2
Albany	69 - 67 .507	23
Binghamton	68 - 70 .493	25
London	61 - 74 .452	30 1/2
Reading	60 - 77 .438	32 1/2
New Britain	50 - 86 .368	42

A Win With A Purpose

BINGHAMTON, N.Y. — You might have thought the message already had made its way around the Eastern League after the Senators demolished the London Tigers in a bench-clearing brawl back in May on City Island.

Don't mess with the boys from the 'Burg.

Apparently, the word did not reach here as the Binghamton Mets instigated another bench clearer in the middle of this game against the Senators.

The Mets lost both the fight and the game. The former came in the sixth inning, the latter MIGUEL BATISTA later with a 5-3 final before 3,369 fans with ring-side seats at Municipal Stadium.

First, the brawl, which officially started when Miguel Batista aimed his first pitch in the bottom of the sixth at Binghamton Butch Huskey, who like Glenn Murray was one homer shy of matching Cliff Floyd's league-leading 26.

Not that Huskey was thinking about Floyd at the moment.

Nanoseconds later, the benches emptied. Among those ejected were Batista, Murray, Tyrone Woods and manager Jim Tracy.

Now, the reason for Batista's purpose pitch came an inning earlier when Mets starter Juan Castillo walked Batista with one out, gave up a two-run homer to the next hitter, Chris Martin, and then drilled Marc Griffin with his next pitch.

Tyrone Horne followed with another two-run homer off Castillo, giving the Senators a 4-3 lead and erasing the lead the Mets took on David Howard's three-run homer in the first inning.

Batista (13-5) lasted just long enough — five innings and one well-aimed purpose pitch at Huskey — to pick up his sixth straight win.

Ed Puig and Joe Ausanio combined for the final 12 outs with Ausanio picking up his sixth save.

EASTERN LEAGUE STANDINGS on Sept. 4			
	Record	Pct.	GB
SENATORS	93 - 44	.679	—
Canton	75 - 62	.547	18
Bowie	72 - 66	.522	21 1/2
Albany	69 - 68	.504	24
Binghamton	68 - 71	.489	26
London	62 - 75	.453	31
Reading	62 - 77	.446	32
New Britain	50 - 88	.362	43 1/2

248

Corbin's Moment

BINGHAMTON, N.Y. — The season had been both promising and brutal for Archie Corbin, the Senators' soft-spoken relief pitcher from Beaumont, Texas.

While Corbin was often brilliant in his first 41 appearances for the Senators, nothing ever would ease the grief following the midseason death of his newborn son.

For one game, there was some solace.

In this game, the regular-season finale, Corbin simply was brilliant, getting the start and working six shutout innings in a 3-0 win over the B-Mets before a crowd of 3,433.

ARCHIE CORBIN

GLENN MURRAY

Corbin (5-3) allowed just two hits and two walks while striking out 10 before Heath Haynes, Rafael Diaz and Mike Thomas each worked an inning as the Senators prepared to open the Eastern League playoffs against Albany in just over 24 hours on City Island.

Glenn Murray gave Corbin the only run he needed in the second as he led off the inning with a homer off Joe Roa.

The homer was Murray's 26th, tying Cliff Floyd both for the league lead, as well as tying him for the most homers in Harrisburg history since Joe Munson hit 33 in 1925 for a previous incarnation of the Senators.

Corbin knew he would not start again in the playoffs and, like the rest of the relievers, his role would be dictated by the success of the five starters who all would pitch in the majors.

"It doesn't matter if I pitch now or not," Corbin said. "I just want to get a championship and go home with a ring."

FINAL EASTERN LEAGUE STANDINGS		
	Record Pct.	GB
SENATORS	94 - 44 .681	—
Canton	75 - 63 .543	19
Bowie	72 - 67 .518	22 1/2
Albany	70 - 68 .507	24
Binghamton	68 - 72 .486	27
London	63 - 75 .457	31
Reading	62 - 78 .443	33
New Britain	51 - 88 .367	43 1/2

Regular Season Stats

BATTING

Player	Avg.	G	AB	R	H	2B	3B	HR	RBI	BB	SO	SB
Curtis Pride	.356	50	180	51	64	6	3	15	38	12	36	21
Tyrone Horne	.352	35	128	22	45	8	1	4	22	22	37	3
Matt Rundels	.342	34	117	27	40	5	0	6	17	14	31	8
Oreste Marrero	.333	85	255	39	85	18	1	10	49	22	46	3
Mike Daniel	.333	3	6	1	2	0	1	0	1	0	3	0
Rod Henderson	.333	2	3	0	1	1	0	0	1	0	2	0
Cliff Floyd	.329	101	380	82	125	17	4	26	101	54	71	31
Rondell White	.328	90	372	72	122	16	10	12	52	22	72	21
Miah Bradbury	.313	9	32	4	10	5	0	1	6	0	1	0
Tim Barker	.308	49	185	40	57	10	1	4	16	30	32	7
Chris Martin	.294	116	395	68	116	23	1	7	54	40	48	16
Ron Krause	.288	17	59	12	17	5	1	1	8	7	15	2
Edgar Tovar	.262	12	42	5	11	0	0	0	3	1	4	0
Shane Andrews	.260	124	442	77	115	29	1	18	70	64	118	10
Randy Wilstead	.259	45	108	10	28	7	0	4	15	12	21	1
Glenn Murray	.253	127	475	82	120	21	4	26	96	56	111	16
Tyrone Woods	.252	106	318	51	80	15	1	16	59	35	77	4
Miguel Batista	.250	9	20	2	5	1	0	0	2	3	9	0
Kirk Rueter	.250	3	8	1	2	0	0	0	0	0	0	0
Heath Haynes	.250	13	4	0	1	0	0	0	0	0	1	0
Mike Thomas	.250	8	4	1	1	1	0	0	1	1	3	0
Mike Hardge	.244	99	386	70	94	14	10	6	35	37	97	27
Lance Rice	.235	46	136	12	32	10	0	1	20	16	22	0
Mitch Simons	.234	29	77	5	18	1	1	0	5	7	14	2
Derrick White	.228	21	79	14	18	1	0	2	12	5	17	2
Rob Fitzpatrick	.226	99	341	44	77	10	1	11	46	36	82	6
Joey Eischen	.200	7	15	2	3	2	0	0	1	0	0	0
Reid Cornelius	.154	6	13	2	2	0	0	0	0	0	6	0
Marc Griffin	.151	24	53	5	8	2	0	0	6	7	9	5
Gabe White	.125	3	8	1	1	1	0	0	0	0	1	0
Ugueth Urbina	.000	5	10	0	0	0	0	0	0	1	7	0
Rick DeHart	.000	5	4	0	0	0	0	0	0	1	3	0
Greg Fulton	.000	1	4	0	0	0	0	0	0	0	3	0
Archie Corbin	.000	12	3	0	0	0	0	0	0	0	1	0
Rafael Diaz	.000	11	3	0	0	0	0	0	0	1	2	2
Brian Looney	.000	1	3	0	0	0	0	0	0	0	3	0
Mario Brito	.000	7	2	0	0	0	0	0	0	0	0	0
Yorkis Perez	.000	11	1	0	0	0	0	0	0	0	1	0
Joe Ausanio	.000	7	1	0	0	0	0	0	0	0	0	0
Darrin Winston	.000	4	0	0	0	0	0	0	0	1	0	0
Ed Puig	.000	4	0	0	0	0	0	0	0	0	0	0
Chris Johnson	.000	0	0	0	0	0	0	0	0	0	0	0
TOTALS	**.278**	**138**	**4672**	**802**	**1301**	**229**	**41**	**170**	**738**	**507**	**1006**	**187**

Regular Season Stats

PITCHING

Pitcher	G	W	L	SV	ERA	IP	H	R	ER	BB	SO
Joe Ausanio	19	2	0	6	1.21	22.1	16	3	3	4	30
Kirk Rueter	9	5	0	0	1.36	59.2	47	10	9	7	36
Rod Henderson	5	5	0	0	1.82	29.2	20	10	6	15	25
Gabe White	16	7	2	0	2.16	100.0	80	30	24	28	79
Brian Looney	8	3	2	0	2.38	56.2	36	15	15	17	76
Ed Puig	14	0	1	1	2.45	18.1	16	5	5	7	10
Heath Haynes	57	8	0	5	2.59	66.0	46	27	19	19	78
Mario Brito	36	4	3	10	2.68	50.1	41	17	15	11	52
Yorkis Perez	34	4	2	3	3.45	44.1	49	26	17	20	58
Rafael Diaz	31	5	4	0	3.56	91.0	86	46	36	31	62
Joey Eischen	20	14	4	0	3.62	119.1	122	62	48	60	110
Archie Corbin	42	5	3	4	3.68	73.1	43	31	30	59	91
Ugueth Urbina	11	4	5	0	3.99	70.0	66	32	31	32	45
Reid Cornelius	27	10	7	0	4.17	157.2	146	95	73	82	119
Miguel Batista	26	13	5	0	4.34	141.0	139	79	68	86	91
Darrin Winston	24	1	0	1	4.63	44.2	53	30	23	19	36
Mike Thomas	25	2	2	6	4.73	32.1	34	18	17	19	40
Rick DeHart	12	2	4	0	7.68	34.0	45	31	29	19	18
Chris Johnson	1	0	0	0	13.53	1.1	1	2	2	3	0
TOTALS	**138**	**94**	**44**	**36**	**3.49**	**1212.0**	**1086**	**569**	**470**	**538**	**1056**

REGULAR SEASON VS. THE EASTERN LEAGUE

	Home Games		Road Games	
	W	L	W	L
Albany Yankees	5	5	4	4
Binghamton Mets	6	4	7	3
Bowie Baysox	8	2	4	6
Canton Indians	7	3	6	4
London Tigers	7	3	8	2
New Britain Red Sox	8	2	9	1
Reading Phillies	6	4	9	1
TOTALS	**47**	**23**	**47**	**21**

KIRK RUETER

A RARE MOMENT DURING THE 1993 SEASON WHEN GREG FULTON AND THE SENATORS FOUND THEMSELVES LOOKING UP TO ANYTHING ASSOCIATED WITH THE PHILLIES.

"It's like Colin Powell said during the Gulf War, 'We came with a big tool box.' And we came out of spring training using all our tools."

Coach Greg Fulton

252

THE POSTSEASON

"*I remember some words that I had with (the players) before our opening series against Albany to begin the season. ... I told them how good they were and, if they stayed together and worked collectively, there was no telling what they could accomplish as a group. I encouraged them to focus on getting better as individual players and strive to do something as a group that would never be forgotten.*"

Manager Jim Tracy

BRIAN LOONEY

So It Begins, Again ...

HARRISBURG — Brian Looney had been compared to Kirk Rueter, who had been compared to All-Star Bob Tewksbury, whom batters in the major leagues compared to Scrooge.

Not just for how they pitched — sneaky quick and freakishly accurate — but for how they lifted themselves from obscurity to prominence.

Brien Taylor needed no such comparison. He was born with a golden left arm, a gift from God that made him baseball's top pitching prospect.

Seemingly, there was no comparison between Looney, often an afterthought as an amateur, and Taylor, who earlier in the season conceded he did not need a good pickoff move because so few batters ever reached base against him.

But this was the postseason, and playoffs always brought comparisons.

Both Looney and Taylor were among the EL's best pitchers over last seven weeks. Looney struck out batters with nasty

MONDAY, SEPTEMBER 6

changeups; Taylor with fastballs and curveballs. Both were left-handers doing all the right things to get to the majors.

The comparisons would continue at 4:05 this afternoon as Looney faced Taylor and the Albany Yankees in Game 1 of the best-of-5 Eastern League semifinals at RiverSide Stadium.

Looney was 3-2 in eight starts for a team that posted the league's best record since Reading went 96-44 in 1983.

Ironically — or, perhaps, ominously — Looney's only shaky start came in a 6-4 loss to Albany on July 19 on City Island, where after five shutout innings the Yankees ruined his Class AA debut with a six-run sixth inning. Since then, Looney allowed only 10 earned runs in 51 innings.

Taylor, whose Class AA debut came Opening Night at RiverSide, was even more impressive, allowing one earned run over his last 35 innings to finish at 13-7. That stretch was Taylor's best since the New York Yankees took him first overall in the 1991 amateur draft and gave him $1 million to sign.

While Taylor, 21, had been scrutinized since his early high school days in Beaufort, North Carolina, Looney, 23, largely was unknown when the Montreal Expos selected him out of Boston College in the 10th round of the same 1991 draft.

"The scout who signed me told me one of the reasons they drafted me was because I had a hockey mentality," Looney said. "I guess they liked that."

Since leaving college, where he also played hockey, Looney was 20-12 with a 2.42 ERA in 65 pro games. Yet, on his Class A teams, Looney always was stuck behind higher draft choices.

"I think if I was a first-round pick, I'd be in the major leagues right now," Looney said. "It's frustrating, but if you keep putting up the numbers, then somebody's bound to notice."

The Expos already had.

"I'll go beyond his pitching in the Eastern League and say he's pitching as good as anybody in baseball," manager Jim Tracy at the time.

"I had to hit against that stuff for two years in the big leagues," Tracy said, "and I'm telling you that this guy has stuff that can get big league hitters out."

255

MONDAY, SEPTEMBER 6

Found In The Woods

HARRISBURG — The marathon of the regular season now gave way to the mad dash of the short-season playoffs. This was when the unexpected was expected, when the afterthoughts of a given story during the summer became postseason headliners.

The Senators on this day had their headliner in Tyrone Woods, the oft-forgotten outfielder at the start of the season who now was unexpectedly filling the role of clean-up hitter for the start of the Eastern League playoffs on City Island.

All Woods did was pick up three hits and become the focal point of two rallies as the Senators beat the Albany Yankees and Brien Taylor 8-1 in Game 1 of the best-of-5 semifinals before a late afternoon crowd of 3,716 at RiverSide Stadium.

"Yeah, I was surprised to see myself hitting fourth," Woods said. "But when I saw that, I got pumped up."

Woods' surprise was understandable. He finished the regular season hitless in his last 10 at-bats. Against the much-heralded Taylor, he was only 1-for-8 with four strikeouts.

Hardly the numbers you wanted for a clean-up hitter on a team continuing its season-long, Sherman-like March to the Sea or, in this case, the Eastern League title.

"That's something I gave serious thought to last night, just who I was going to hit No. 4," manager Jim Tracy said.

He settled on Woods for a couple of reasons.

MONDAY, SEPTEMBER 6

"Number one," Tracy said, "Tyrone Woods has the ability to hit left-handers. And with the way he's been swinging the bat in the last eight, 10 days … it worked out very well."

Real well for Woods, whose first-inning single scored Glenn Murray for a 2-1 lead off Taylor and whose sixth-inning double off the chest of Albany third baseman Andy Fox scored Mike Hardge for a 7-1 lead.

More than enough for

GLENN MURRAY SCORES IN 6th AS ALBANY'S JORGE POSADA LOOKS ON

Brian Looney, who over the last seven weeks emerged as the Senators' top starter. After Jalal Leach's two-out homer gave Albany a 1-0 lead in the first inning, Looney held Albany to three singles over the next seven before leaving with an 8-1 lead.

"I wanted to treat this as any other game, but I think I was a little too psyched up," Looney said afterward. "I was getting the ball up. I wasn't myself until the later innings."

Taylor struggled. His struggles may have been self-inflicted.

"He was tipping his pitches," one Senator said with a smile.

Taylor, who allowed only one earned run in his previous 35 innings, allowed two runs in the first inning on a wild pitch that scored Chris Martin and on Woods' RBI single.

"If you have two good pitchers throwing against each other, you'll have a 1-1 game maybe 10 percent of the time," Murray said. "Somebody's going to break through. Maybe it's because you see one guy more. We've seen Brien three times this year."

The Senators all but ended the game in the sixth, scoring three runs on one hit — Woods' double — three walks and two errors.

"We were outpitched, outhit, outplayed, outdefensed," Albany manager Bill Evers said. "I don't think we were intimidated by them. All the pressure is on them. They won 94 games. Everybody expects them to win. Nobody expects us to win."

And they didn't.

LOOKING BACK

JIM TRACY AND HIS TEAM WITH THEIR "APPETIZER" TROPHY

"Not The One We Want"

HARRISBURG — Manager Jim Tracy made certain his players took part in the pregame ceremony on Sept. 6 to receive the Joe Buzas Trophy for winning the EL's regular-season title.

Looking on from their dugout along the third-base line were the Albany Yankees, a team that finished 24 games behind the Senators during the regular season and now were their first-round playoff opponent.

The Yankees saw the Senators, and they saw a target.

"I don't care what kind of bull's-eye they put on our back," Tracy said. "You know what I was impressed with? The comments I heard (from the Senators) on the way back to our dugout. They were saying, 'Hey, that's not the one we want.' "

What they want is something the Senators have not had since 1987, when pro baseball returned to City Island and the Senators beat Vermont in the finals. Since then, the Senators have been to two finals — 1989 and 1991 — and lost both times to Albany.

"Today," Mike Hardge said, "is only a token."

"An appetizer," Tyrone Woods said. "Just an appetizer."

Not Your Average Joe

HARRISBURG — Joe Ausanio was done for the night, his right arm spent after 4 1/3 innings.

JOE AUSANIO

In fact, so protective of his tender right elbow, Ausanio was busy icing it down when Glenn Murray doubled to left field with one out in the 12th inning.

Ausanio, though, made sure he did not miss another pitch.

He quickly returned to the dugout, just in time to watch Derrick White drill Brian Faw's 3-1 pitch into center field to score Murray with the winning run as the Senators beat Albany 7-6 in Game 2 of the Eastern League semifinals.

The victory, which took 4 hours and 5 minutes to complete before a crowd of 2,549 on City Island, followed Monday's 8-1 rout in Game 1 and gave the Senators a commanding 2-0 lead in the best-of-5 series now headed to Albany.

"I nearly missed the end of the game," Ausanio said.

Without Ausanio, the Senators never would have reached the 12th inning as he struck out seven of the 14 batters he faced and retired the final 13 in a row.

Ausanio's performance on this night simply was the greatest by a relief pitcher in the Senators' modern era.

White's hit was his biggest of the game that saw the Senators fritter away a 4-1 lead, only to rally for a 6-6 tie in the seventh inning when Yankees center fielder Jason Robertson misplayed a couple of fly balls and those gaffes turned into two runs.

Murray started the final rally in the 12th inning with a one-out double to left off Rich Polak, the Yankees' fourth pitcher.

Faw then replaced Polak, giving Ausanio some extra time to go from the clubhouse to the dugout as White came to the plate.

Faw gave Ausanio another few seconds to settle in as he fired his first pitch past catcher Jorge Posada, allowing Murray to move to third base.

TUESDAY, SEPTEMBER 7

"When he threw that one over the catcher, I thought they'd walk me," White said.

The Yankees did not, which was bizarre since walking White would have set up a potential inning-ending double play with the struggling Shane Andrews on deck.

Instead, White worked the count to 3-0 before fouling off a pitch. Then, with the infield and outfield playing in, White laced Faw's next pitch into center to win the game, end the marathon and make Ausanio's Herculean effort worth the extra ice bags.

"This is big," Murray said. "The first game was big, but now it's 2-0 and they have to beat us three in a row."

Nobody with a functioning cerebellum envisioned Albany doing that.

"With the way they got beat yesterday, to come back and lose a squeaker like this, it's worse than getting beat 8-1 again," White said. "Now, we can only lose the series."

Ausanio distanced the Senators from that unlikely scenario as he worked a career-high 4 1/3 innings, in great part because relievers Archie Corbin and Mike Thomas were unavailable. Corbin was only two days removed from starting the regular-season finale at Binghamton, while Thomas was sent home before the game after arriving on the island with flu-like symptoms.

> *"I told Trace that if I'm not going to pitch tomorrow, then I wanted to keep going out there."*
> *Reliever Joe Ausanio*

Ausanio needed only 52 pitches to retire 13 of the 14 batters he faced.

He combined with starter Rod Henderson, as well as relievers Benny Puig and Heath Haynes, to strike out 20 batters.

"We were monitoring his pitch count very closely," manager Jim Tracy said of Ausanio. "He had a couple of innings out there of good morning, good afternoon, good night."

Ausanio hardly noticed.

"I think that was a little adrenaline going out there," he said.

"I've never pitched that many innings in my career. I told Trace that if I'm not going to pitch tomorrow, then I wanted to keep going out there."

260

Rain? Albany? Shocking

COLONIE, N.Y. — Chris Martin tugged at his coffee, took a peek out of the visitors' clubhouse door for the umpteenth time to check the rain and repeated the same question.

Rhetorical as it was.

"What are they waiting for?" Martin asked at 6 p.m., just an hour away from the scheduled first pitch.

"What," the Senators shortstop and resident team weather geek asked again a few minutes later, "… are *they* waiting for?"

They were the Albany Yankees, and they were waiting for the rain to stop. They also were waiting on a miracle.

After two stunning losses on City Island — one an 8-1 rout, the other a 7-6 marathon that took 12 innings — the Yankees now were one loss away from being swept by the Senators in the best-of-5 Eastern League semifinals.

Game 3 eventually was — to answer Martin's repeated questions — rained out.

The rainout was the seventh this season for the Senators at Heritage Park.

"I've been up here four times," manager Jim Tracy said, "and I've seen the sun for about 20 minutes."

The latest rainout gave the Yankees and their manager, Bill Evers, another 24 hours to ponder their predicament: How to win three straight games from a team that this season lost three straight on only three occasions.

"I think it's going to be very, very difficult to beat my club three games in a row," Tracy said. "If they do, I'll be the first one over in their dugout to congratulate them."

While Martin and others sipped coffee while waiting for the rainout to become official, Tracy played Mr. Fix It as he repaired an audio glitch with the VCR unit aboard the team's chartered bus.

"Got the job done," Tracy said after reviving the VCR and allowing half of his team to finish watching "Tango and Cash" without having to guess what syllable actor Sylvester Stallone was trying to utter next.

THURSDAY, SEPTEMBER 9

Caught Looking Ahead

COLONIE, N.Y. — Tyrone Woods admitted the Senators were doing some scoreboard watching, just not the right one.

Instead of paying attention to their game here against Albany, the Senators were sneaking peeks to check the score on the EL's other semifinal, the one between Canton and Bowie.

They learned, too, that the other best-of-5 series was tied at 2.

The Senators also learned that their own series against Albany was still quite alive as the Yankees beat them 3-1 in Game 3 before a smattering of 739 fans at Heritage Park to prevent a sweep in their own best-of-5 series.

"We were thinking about Bowie and Canton," Woods said, "and taking these guys lightly."

The Yankees had no such luxury.

"We're not out of it," Albany pitcher Ron Frazier said, "and I think we wanted to show people that."

Frazier, who allowed only one earned run against the Senators during the regular season, struck out 11 in this game and left with a 3-1 lead after walking Tyrone Horne to lead off the eighth.

Brian Faw replaced Fraizer after Horne's walk and worked out of one of the Senators' myriad scoring chances.

The final chance came in the ninth inning when Woods singled off Faw with one out before Rich Polak ended the game by retiring Rob Fitzpatrick on a fly to deep left field and striking out Mike Hardge.

The Yankees scored all of their runs off Ugueth Urbina on a two-run homer in the second inning by Lyle Mouton and a solo homer in the fifth by Andy Fox. Coming into this game, Mouton and Fox, two of Albany's most dangerous hitters, were a combined 2-for-15 in the series.

"We had a lot of big swings tonight that meant nothing," said manager Jim Tracy.

Most of those empty swings came against Frazier.

"I was trying to keep the fastballs in, because they all looked like clones to me," Frazier said. "They all can hit the ball hard."

FRIDAY, SEPTEMBER 10
On To The Finals

COLONIE, N.Y. — The pregame talk lasted 90 seconds. By Jim Tracy's STT, that would be Standard Talking Time, it was a millisecond, but one in which he had plenty of time to make his point.

Get the job done, get it done now, the bus has been packed for three days and, really, we're running out of clean clothes.

Just as they had all season, the Senators understood their manager.

After Wednesday's rainout here, Thursday's 3-1 loss in Game 3 and yet another seemingly endless rain delay before this game, the Senators had grown weary of all things Albany.

JIM TRACY

OK, really, they came to hate being here, and a potential Game 5 here was looming.

So, the Senators did what they did best, and that was score early and often, building a fast 5-2 lead en route to beating Albany 8-4 in Game 4 and clinching their best-of-5 Eastern League semifinal series.

Next up: Canton, which beat Bowie in five games of the other semifinal.

"It was very brief," Tracy said of his pregame talk, which deviated from his usual power-of-positive-thinking approach.

DALE CARNEGIE

"I prefaced it by telling them this is no time for me to stand up and do my best Dale Carnegie. I just wanted to get them refocused."

The Senators did that following an afternoon thunderstorm, coupled with a leaky tarp, that left the infield unplayable until 8:41 p.m. — 96 minutes after the scheduled first pitch.

When the game finally started, Tyrone Woods jump-started the Senators with a two-run homer in second to tie the score at 2.

263

FRIDAY, SEPTEMBER 10

Wood's game-tying homer came when he launched Darren Hodges' 1-0 pitch deep over the left-field wall, a drive that took only one bounce before hitting the roof of the Senators' clubhouse.

REID CORNELIUS

Derrick White's RBI single punctuated a three-run rally in the fifth inning that gave the Senators a 5-2 lead.

The Senators all but clinched the series with two more runs in the eighth off a Class AA neophyte pitcher named Andy Pettitte.

After White and Woods opened the inning by harmlessly bouncing pitches back to Pettitte for easy outs, Andrews singled to center and scored on Matt Rundels' pinch-hit double to left with Rundels then scoring on Rob Fitzpatrick's single to center.

The Senators' final run came in the ninth on Marc Grffin's sacrifice fly, adding to the lead as temperatures dipped into the mid-50s and chasing away what remained of the family-and-friends gathering of 509 from Heritage Park.

Watching this from the Senators' dugout was starter Reid Cornelius, who allowed four runs on nine hits before leaving with two outs in the sixth.

From there, Tracy and pitching coach Chuck Kniffin mixed and matched relievers as Mike Thomas, Rafael Diaz, Ed Puig and Heath Haynes combined for the final 10 outs.

Cornelius and Co. also combined for 11 strikeouts with three of those coming against Albany catcher Jorge Posada, who like Pettitte was a Class AA newbie.

Posada, who like Pettitte eventually would become an All-Star in the majors, ended up striking out nine times in the four-game series.

After Cornelius left the game, the Yankees managed one hit and that came on Jalal Leach's two-out single in the ninth.

By then, Albany's early lead was a distant memory, just as it was in Games 1 and 2 when the Yankees scored first only to lose.

Nothing Left To Give

HARRISBURG — This simply did not happen often.
Like almost never.

Joe Ausanio had been that good as the Senators' closer.

But the almost-never became a duck-and-cover reality in this game as Ausanio failed to retire any of the four batters he faced in the ninth inning with all four scoring as the Canton Indians posted a stunning 4-3 victory in Game 1 of Eastern League finals.

After Canton closer Calvin Jones struck out Glenn Murray to end the game, the crowd of 1,655 quietly filed out of RiverSide Stadium.

The Senators, just as quietly, retreated to their clubhouse, knowing they were one loss away in Game 2 of having Canton take a 2-0 lead in the best-of-5 finals.

Canton put itself in that enviable position with only one inning of effectiveness after eight innings of futility against starter Brian Looney, who allowed only two hits, struck out nine and left a seemingly safe 2-0 lead for Ausanio to protect.

> *"Physically, I felt fine out there. Maybe, I wasn't mentally prepared to go into that game. Unfortunately the team had to pay for it."*
> *Reliever Joe Ausanio*

Only Ausanio had nothing left in his right arm four days after he pitched an otherworldly, career-high 4 1/3 innings of relief in Game 2 of the semifinals against Albany.

Ausanio walked Brian Giles and Omar Ramirez to start the ninth with Miguel Flores reaching on an infield single to load the bases. Ausanio sailed his next pitch past Rob Fitzpatrick for his only wild pitch of the season, one that allowed Giles to score.

David Bell then worked the count to 2-1 before grounding a single past Ausanio and into center field, scoring both Ramirez and Flores to give Canton a 3-2 lead.

"Physically, I felt fine out there," Ausanio said.

"Maybe, I wasn't mentally prepared to go into that game. Unfortunately, the team had to pay for it."

SATURDAY, SEPTEMBER 11

Manager Jim Tracy had no regrets going with Ausanio. "The man has done it for us since the day he showed up," Tracy said of Ausanio, who was 2-0 with six saves and a 1.21 earned-run average in 19 games during the regular season.

"He just didn't have it tonight. He's a human being, too."

Ed Puig replaced Ausanio and retired Patrick Lennon and Mike Sarbaugh before Hector Vargas doubled to right to score Bell for a 4-2 lead.

The Senators, who built an early 2-0 lead on Tyrone Woods' RBI single in the first inning and Derrick White's sacrifice fly in the third, tried to rally in the ninth against closer Calvin Jones.

Mike Hardge walked with one out, stole second — his third steal of the game — and scored on Chris Martin's two-out single to left. Martin then stole second, but Jones struck out Murray on a 2-2 pitch in the dirt to end the game.

Martin was the ninth and final baserunner stranded by the Senators, who managed only two runs despite getting eight hits and four walks off Canton's Shawn Bryant.

"We took a tough half-inning there in the ninth, but we dominated that game," Tracy said. "They didn't get a runner to second base until the ninth inning. That's dominating."

Bryant, constantly pitching out of trouble, left runners on base in every inning through the sixth before leaving after eight.

While Bryant was fortunate, Looney was fantastic.

Six of his nine strikeouts came in a row between the fourth and sixth innings. He also retired 15 straight batters between Mike Sarbaugh's single to lead off the second and Bell's single to begin the seventh.

"After seven innings, I was getting behind in the counts," Looney said. "(Tracy) asked me after that how I felt. I didn't want to tell him I was tired, but I think he kind of knew."

So, after eight innings and 115 pitches, Looney was done with Tracy replacing him with one of the Eastern League's most experienced closers in Ausanio.

No-brainer of a move, given Ausanio's resume.

"Jim made the right move," Canton manager Brian Graham said. "You have to go with your closer there."

SUNDAY, SEPTEMBER 12
And A Hush Fell …

HARRISBURG — Less than 17 hours had passed since the ninth-inning meltdown that cost the Senators in Game 1 of the Eastern League finals against Canton.

Now, in a best-of-5 series, the Senators needed to win three of the next four games to finish what they started. Three of those games, if the series went that far, were scheduled for Canton's drab, monochromatic Thurman Munson Memorial Stadium.

No worries. Not in Game 2. Not with Rod Henderson pitching for the Senators, who had yet to lose in any of the first six games the right-hander had started for them since arriving in early August from Class A West Palm Beach.

Turned out that Henderson was done before the end of the fifth inning in this game, leaving after Greg Sparks' three-run homer gave the Indians a 5-2 lead.

The lead grew to 6-2 before the

ROD HENDERSON

Senators batted in the bottom of the fifth and, four innings later, Canton had won 7-5 to take a commanding 2-0 lead in the series.

The time was 5:20 in the afternoon as the crowd of 1,744 slowly, quietly and dejectedly walked out of RiverSide Stadium. The Senators were doing much the same as they returned to their clubhouse.

Just as everyone did after Game 1.

There was no sign of the swagger the Senators had been carrying since the season opened on April 9.

267

SUNDAY, SEPTEMBER 12

"I don't know if it's a state of shock," manager Jim Tracy said after losing for the second time in 20 hours to a Canton team that finished 19 games behind the Senators during the regular season.

"Did they beat us? Yes. Did we help them? Yes," Tracy said. "We now have to play three error-free ballgames."

While Sparks' homer punctuated the four-run rally in the fifth inning for a 6-2 lead, Canton actually may have won the game in the bottom of the sixth.

After the Senators rallied for two runs off Dave Mlicki to cut their deficit to 6-4, they had two runners on and two outs with Lance Rice facing reliever Apolinar Garcia.

Rice promptly drilled Garcia's 0-1 pitch to deep right field only to lower his head as Brian Giles raced back to the wall to make a leaping, crashing, rally-killing, inning-ending and, quite possibly, game-saving catch.

"The turning point," Tracy said.

"You could just see their heads drop," Giles said. "If that ball gets through, it's two runs."

The Senators also managed to bring the tying run to the plate in both the eighth and ninth innings. Garcia wriggled out of the jam in the eighth with a double-play grounder and strikeout before Calvin Jones retired Derrick White on a line drive to second baseman Miguel Flores to end the game.

"When you get behind, you have to press to get back," White said, "and the later it gets, the harder you press. ... We'd catch up and then we'd relax. Trying to get the lead is the tough part."

The tough part now waited for them 300 miles away at Munson Memorial, where the Senators needed to win three straight for a title they first envisioned for themselves in spring training.

A quarter-century later, Tracy remembered what he said to his players as they waited to board the team bus for Canton.

"I told them I'm not going to Canton to play one f----ing game and then turn around to come home," Tracy said.

"I told them if you don't think we're going there to win three straight, then don't get on the bus."

When the bus finally left City Island for Ohio, everyone was aboard.

DERRICK WHITE

A Change Of Attitude

HARRISBURG — He was using Kirk Rueter's old No. 37, Rondell White's old locker and Cliff Floyd's old batting helmet.

As the Eastern League playoffs approached, this was as close as Derrick White found himself to the major leagues.

A month earlier, Derrick White was the one in the majors, where Rueter and Rondell White now were playing for the Montreal Expos and where Floyd would join them in a few days.

Now Derrick White was using equipment that once belonged to the same players who started the season with the Class AA Senators and who since passed him on their way to the majors.

Derrick White had no intention of playing this season in Harrisburg, where he starred in 1992 before starting the '93 season at Class AAA Ottawa on his way to a midseason promotion to the Expos.

So when the 23-year-old White was demoted to Harrisburg in mid-August, he was stunned. And perplexed. And frustrated.

All of which was understandable. The man had his pride.

LOOKING BACK

He had simmered, albeit reluctantly, since rejoining the Senators in a move that saw Oreste Marrero replace him on the Expos' roster. He now had re-emerged as an offensive force in the Eastern League playoffs, batting .400 through the Senators' first six postseason games.

"They wanted me to get some work," White said of the Expos, "but what's the sense of coming back here? What was there to prove here?"

Seemingly not much after he batted .277 in 134 games for the Senators in 1992 with 13 homers and 81 runs batted in.

Seemingly not much unless, of course, the Expos wanted to send him a message, like don't piss off the major league coaching staff with your stubbornness.

"If one thing I've learned, this is a business," White said. "I've also learned people can tell you one thing one minute and then another thing the next. ... It's been a good experience for me."

Really, it's been a nightmare for the Expos' sixth-round choice in the 1991 amateur draft.

He had reached the majors in just over two years. He hardly had arrived there when Expos manager Felipe Alou began praising his new first baseman for his ability to catch the ball.

And then came the advice from the coaching staff.

Derrick, change your swing. Derrick, move your hips. Derrick, don't raise your hands when you're batting. Derrick, lose that hitch. Derrick, are you even listening? Derrick ...

"It's like if you take a new job and you're where you want to be, and the boss tells you he wants you to do this, this and this. You're going to do it, because you want the job," White said.

"That's what happened there."

Too much advice led to too many 0-for games. White's batting average dipped to .224 with two homers in 17 games.

"Felipe told me I'd be back in two weeks, to come down here and get my confidence back," White said. "I took it to heart, but I haven't heard anything."

He was not going to hear back, either, at least not for a while.

Alou and the Expos had noticed that White returned to City Island with a different attitude, and not with a good one, either.

LOOKING BACK

One of the nicest of guys ever to play on City Island had returned there with nastiest of scowls.

Derrick White had become a 6-foot-1, 220-pound mass of anger.

All by design, White insisted.

"I didn't want people to think I was going to come down here with a smile on my face for being in the big leagues for three weeks and that I was satisfied with that," he said.

"Hey, I believe I belong up there. Don't think I came down here to show everybody the new pair of cleats I got in the big leagues."

Alas, the shiny new cleats could not help White at the plate. He batted just .228 in 79 at-bats over 21 games to end the regular season, which ended with him still in Harrisburg and still waiting on that call back from the Expos.

The scowl that White said was by design had been perceived differently by others.

"Early on, I don't think his mental disposition was where it should have been," manager and master motivator Jim Tracy said, ever so tactfully, at the time.

"Yes, it got to the point where I had to talk to him."

Words worked. Since the EL playoffs started, White was 10-for-25 with six RBIs and three stolen bases in six games, all away from the scrutiny of the major league staff.

"D was a strong player," catcher Lance Rice remembered a quarter-century later. "Once he got over his anger, he played great."

"Everything I did was under a microscope," White said. "That never happened before.

"Mentally, it made me feel like I couldn't relax anymore. I had to be mechanical," White said. "I was just so mixed up on what I was supposed to be working on. It seemed like after every swing I was looking down at Trace and seeing if I was holding my hands right, if my feet were right.

"Now I'm just at the point of playing and letting everything else take care of itself."

271

LOOKING BACK

New Team In Town

ACTORS TOM BERENGER
AND CHARLIE SHEEN AS
"INDIANS" ON CITY ISLAND

HARRISBURG — Within minutes after the Senators' Game 2 loss in the finals to Canton on Sept. 12, the workers moved in.

There were temporary palm trees to reposition, billboard signs to replace and dugouts to paint with new colors.

RiverSide Stadium was getting its final makeover before being used to film spring training scenes for the movie "Major League 2."

The Hollywood folks — director, producers, actors, cameramen and assorted minions — were biding their time until the end of Game 2.

They did not care about the Senators losing another game to the future, wannabe Cleveland Indians. They were busying themselves with bringing back to life the fictitious Cleveland Indians of movie fame.

Workers already were moving palm trees into the players' parking lot beyond the right-field line when the Senators boarded their bus late Sunday afternoon for a 300-mile ride to Canton.

Canton was where the future, wannabe Montreal Expos knew they now needed to sweep three games of the best-of-5 finals if they hoped to win an Eastern League title they had predicted for themselves back in spring training.

"It was a little strange to see palm trees in Harrisburg," said first baseman and Utah native Randy Wilstead. "We knew they were going to film there, but we didn't realize it would happen before the season was over."

Only over in Harrisburg, but not for the Senators.

The season still had some games left.

MIGUEL BATISTA

Rested, Armed, Ready

CANTON, Ohio — For eight days, the Senators rested pitcher Miguel Batista.

With good reason.

They were hiding him from an Albany team that during the regular season routinely torched him and saving him for a Canton team that had not come close to figuring out the right-hander.

Now, Batista was trying to keep alive Harrisburg's flickering championship hopes, and he did that quite nicely for six-plus innings before the Senators rallied late to beat Canton 5-2 in a must-win Game 3 of the Eastern League finals at Thurman Munson Memorial Stadium.

This game was played in sharp contrast to the first games of the series at RiverSide Stadium, where the Senators lost both after blowing a 2-0 lead in the ninth inning of Game 1 before making three errors less than 20 hours later in losing Game 2.

Now there was to be a Game 4, another must-win, of course, and one made possible by Batista.

Batista pitched well into the seventh and threw better than 94 mph on 43 of his 98 pitches against a Canton offense that scored only two runs off him in 13 innings during the regular season.

MONDAY, SEPTEMBER 13

"They told me they wanted to pitch me against Canton," Batista said. "I wanted to be in the last game here, to kill them, but in the situation we're in …"

That was one of desperation.

Batista gave up two runs on Ryan Martindale's leadoff homer in the fifth and Mike Sarbaugh's game-tying sacrifice fly that followed Greg Sparks' one-out triple in the sixth.

Sparks, though, was counterproductive as his two errors at first base led to two unearned runs for the Senators. Two more gift runs came on a pair of errors by third baseman David Bell.

Bell's first error led to two eighth-inning runs that made a winner of reliever Ed Puig, who replaced Batista in the midst of a seventh-inning jam. Heath Haynes eventually worked a perfect ninth for the save.

With the score at 2 in the eighth, Glenn Murray started the go-ahead rally off Paul Abbott with a one-out grounder to Bell, who threw the ball past Sparks for a two-base error.

> "Don't let us win Game 4, because then the momentum is on our side and I don't care if we're playing them on the 'Field of Dreams.' "
>
> Manager Jim Tracy

Tyrone Horne drove Abbott's next pitch into right field for a single to score Murray for a 3-2 lead. A fourth run eventually scored on Tyrone Woods' RBI single that brought home Derrick White. The lead grew to 5-2 in the ninth as Shane Andrews led off with a walk before scoring when Sparks dropped Murray's two-out, pop-up.

Canton's sloppiness came after two brilliant defensive plays by the Senators, starting with Murray's leaping catch at the center-field wall off Pat Lennon's drive to open the sixth and ending with second baseman Mike Hardge's throw to the plate to catch Omar Ramirez for the second out of the seventh.

From there, a change in momentum seemed inevitable.

"The advantage still is in their dugout," manager Jim Tracy said, "but don't let us win Game 4, because then the momentum is on our side and I don't care if we're playing them on the 'Field of Dreams.' "

LOOKING BACK
Another Hit For Floyd

CANTON, Ohio — Cliff Floyd, whom
the Senators could have used right about
now being down 0-2 in the best-of-5 finals,
earned another reward for his record-
breaking, four-month stay with Harrisburg.

Floyd, the Expos' top prospect who had
not played for the Senators since his Aug. 2
promotion to Class AAA Ottawa, was
being named the minor league player of the
year by USA Today's Baseball Weekly.

The official announcement had not yet
been made, but the Senators already had
received the news before Game 3 of the
best-of-5 Eastern League finals on Sept. 13.

"Who was his competition?" manager
Jim Tracy rhetorically asked.

"Who? Manny Ramirez?"

Actually, nobody.

In 101 games for the Senators, Floyd
batted .329 with 26 homers and 101 RBIs.

CLIFF FLOYD

The homers and RBIs not only represented modern-day records
for the Senators, but also remained the best in the Class AA
Eastern League despite Floyd spending the final four-plus weeks
of the season in Ottawa.

The numbers already were enough to make the 20-year-old
Floyd the runaway choice as the Eastern League's MVP.

The first baseman-left fielder also had 17 doubles, four triples
and 31 stolen bases in Harrisburg before moving up to Ottawa.

His closest competition may well have been the 21-year-old
Ramirez, Canton's sometimes-hustling-sometimes-not right
fielder who led the EL with a .340 batting average. He also had
17 homers and 79 RBIs in 89 games before his promotion to
AAA Charlotte.

"Manny didn't drive in 101 runs in 101 games," Tracy said.
"Manny's a good player, but he's no Cliff Floyd."

275

TYRONE HORNE   GLENN MURRAY   DERRICK WHITE   TYRONE WOODS

The Four Musketeers

CANTON, Ohio — Through the first week of the postseason, the Big Four had carried the Senators.

In the four games of the semifinals against Albany and the first three games of the finals against Canton, the quartet of Tyrone Horne, Glenn Murray, Derrick White and Tyrone Woods combined to hit .398.

Stunning numbers that actually got even better in Game 4 of the finals, another must-win game, as the Big Four combined for nine hits to lead the Senators over Canton 10-2, tie the best-of-5 series, and force a fifth and deciding game at Thurman Munson Memorial Stadium.

"They had 15 hits and we had six," Canton manager Brian Graham said of the Senators. "I'd bet on the team that had 15. I hope we're the ones with 15 (in Game 5)."

Not that the Indians ever expected to play a Game 5, not after winning the first two games of the series on City Island and certainly not after they had been chilling a couple of cases of champagne for the last 48 hours.

"The advantage they had, they lost," Senators manager Jim Tracy said. "We have momentum, but there are nine innings left for the championship."

But first Game 4, a rout that featured the revival of a vaunted, but heretofore dormant, power game.

Solo homers by Murray and Horne, homers that gave the Senators leads of 1-0 and 6-2, matched the team's total in the

TUESDAY, SEPTEMBER 14

first seven games of the playoffs. The homers also were the first allowed by the Indians in their nine postseason games.

While Woods and White did not homer like Murray and Horne, they did their best to have Canton change its postgame beverage from champagne to Maalox.

Woods, the power hitter sometimes forgotten on a team full of prospects, had three more hits to raise his postseason batting average to .500, while White — the defrocked major leaguer — had both a hit and an RBI for the eighth straight playoff game.

"We want to step up and lead the team," Horne said after the game. "Glenn started us off and then, all of a sudden, boom."

"That's what we got to do," Murray said. "They're looking for us to carry them."

Lots of heavy lifting in this game also came from 19-year-old starter Ugueth Urbina, a winner in only one of his previous six starts. He held Canton to six hits before leaving after eight innings and 119 pitches. Mike Thomas pitched an uneventful ninth to set up yet another — and final — game in the series.

For the second time in as many games, but only for the third time in the playoffs, the league's best offense scored first.

This early lead came when Murray drilled Mike Dyer's 2-2 pitch over the left-field wall with two outs in the first inning for a 1-0 lead. Murray doubled the lead in the third with an RBI double before eventually scoring on White's sacrifice fly.

The lead grew to 5-0 in the fourth on Rob Fitzpatrick's RBI single and David Bell's run-scoring error.

After Bell's two-run homer off Urbina in the fourth, the Senators broke open the game with a three-run rally in the fifth off reliever Nap Robinson.

Horne started this rally by launching Robinson's fourth pitch of the inning over the scoreboard in deep left-center. Shane Andrews then drove in two runs with a double off Robinson before Matt Rundels accounted for the Senators' final two runs with an RBI single in the seventh and a fielder's choice groundout in the ninth.

"We want this bad now," Horne said.

"Our pride," he said, "is on the line."

LOOKING BACK
Poking the Bear

CANTON, Ohio — The Senators first noticed when their team bus pulled into the parking lot at perpetually cheerless Thurman Munson Memorial Stadium.

Really, they could not help but notice.

"I remember the Canton players showing up with their cars packed," pitcher Rod Henderson recalled a quarter-century later. "Like we were going to just tap out and go home,"

That was before Game 3 on Sept. 13, when the Canton Indians had a commanding and seemingly safe 2-0 lead in the best-of-5 Eastern League finals.

Youthful exuberance, but some of the Canton's older heads, older heads like Indians manager Brian Graham, knew better. Just a year earlier, he watched Canton fritter away a similar advantage in the finals before losing to Binghamton.

A quarter-century later, Canton radio announcer Jim Clark cringed as he remembered Graham's cautionary words to his players before Game 3 as they tried to sweep the Senators after winning the first two games of the finals in Harrisburg.

"I remember Brian telling them that nobody should be looking ahead," Clark said, "because that's a pretty good ballclub over there."

The giddiness in thinking of sweeping one of the most dominant teams in the history of the minors spread beyond Canton's clubhouse, where the champagne already was on ice.

There was the man with the broom, the one who positioned himself above the Senators' dugout before Game 3, the one who taunted a team he thought was done.

Jack Hibbard, the man with the broom, was the 60-year-old president of the Canton Indians' booster club. He had suffered through the Indians' collapse in the 1992 EL finals.

With each passing sweep of his broom, the postal carrier from Canton let the Senators know that he would suffer no more.

LOOKING BACK

"I'm superstitious," Clark said of seeing the broom from his spot in Canton's radio booth. "I was like, 'Get *that* out of here.'"

Senators radio broadcaster Mark Mattern admitted he was remarkably unenthused as he arrived at Munson Memorial to call Game 3, a game he thought might be the final one for a team that had run the perfect marathon only to be nine bad innings away from collapsing just yards shy of the finish line.

"I was thinking that this would be a huge waste of time," Mattern remembered of making the 300-mile trip to Canton.

"The odds were not in our favor," Mattern said. "I didn't really get back into the proper frame of mind until I saw the first of several brooms in the stands. There were not a lot of fans there, but some sat right above the Senators' dugout. I am pretty sure our players saw the brooms, as well."

Oh, yes, they did, and, predictably, they were not amused.

> *"I remember seeing it and saying to Fitzy that I would like to grab that broom and stick it somewhere."*
>
> *First baseman Randy Wilstead*

Among the first of the Senators to notice were first baseman Randy Wilstead and catcher Rob Fitzpatrick.

"I remember seeing it and saying to Fitzy that I would like to grab that broom and stick it somewhere," Wilstead recalled a couple of decades later. "It was definitely a motivator for us."

The new, improved and now mellowed Derrick White even tried diplomacy to placate the broom-waving Jack Hibbard.

Before Game 3, the power-hitting first baseman offered Hibbard free tickets for Games 4 and 5 that the Senators confidently believed would follow.

The mailman from Canton, though, never took the offer, never believing there would be a need for Game 4, let alone Game 5.

"He never came back," White said with a laugh after the Senators beat the Indians 5-2 in the must-win Game 3 and 10-2 in another must-win in Game 4.

White never saw Hibbard for Game 5.

"I told him I'd leave tickets," White said. "That guy was confident, but Canton wasn't. You could see it in their faces."

WEDNESDAY, SEPTEMBER 15

MANAGER JIM TRACY IN HIS FINAL PREGAME MEDIA SESSION IN 1993

... And So It Ends

CANTON, Ohio — The time was shortly after 3 p.m. when manager Jim Tracy took a seat in the visitors' dugout at Thurman Munson Memorial Stadium. His red batting practice jersey, the one with white letters and numbers, added some much needed contrast to a dugout and stadium that seemed forever bathed in the color of battleship gray.

Outside of the green grass on the field, the place simply was devoid of color — much like the home team it housed, the suddenly ashen-faced Canton Indians, who 48 hours earlier had a 2-0 lead over the Senators in the best-of-5 Eastern League finals.

All that had changed.

The Indians had blown their two-game lead, having followed up their two stunning victories over the weekend on City Island with two dismal losses at home to the Senators. Now, instead of popping the corks on the champagne they had been chilling for two days and nights, the Indians were on the verge of going from upsetting one of the greatest teams in the history of the minors to becoming just another chump to be steamrolled by that team.

WEDNESDAY, SEPTEMBER 15

In the dugout, Tracy talked of the preceding six months, from the start of spring training through the first four games of the finals and of the rain in the area that threatened to postpone Game 5 for another 24 hours.

He talked of the 41 players he had on his roster since Opening Day on April 9, the ones who moved on, the ones who came in to replace them and the ones who stayed all season.

He talked of how each contributed to each of the Senators' 99 victories — the 94 during the regular season and the five so far in the playoffs against Albany in the semifinals and Canton in the finals.

He talked of where he was going to manage in winter ball, and which of his players could join him there in Mexico.

He talked of what the Montreal Expos might have planned for him in 1994.

He talked about a lot of things, because Jim Tracy always had a lot of things to say.

But there was one thought he kept to himself, and that was the thought of failure, of enduring a loss in Game 5 after watching his team masterfully survive two must-win games.

"I never said this to anybody," Tracy said a quarter-century later. "As proud as I was of this team, I kept asking myself this question, 'Am I going to get back on the bus with these kids and ride back to Harrisburg, saying this is the second-best team in the league?'

"I don't know if I could have dealt with that heartbreak. People would call us the second-best team and we'd be 99 and 48. Think about that, *99 and 48*. ... This kept going through my mind, but I didn't say anything to anybody."

As Tracy held one last media bull session in the dugout before Game 5, Senators general manager Todd Vander Woude was meeting with his counterpart in Canton's front office.

Vander Woude was busy negotiating the deal of the season.

Like everyone else, Vander Woude noticed the 48 bottles of champagne the Indians were chilling since Monday afternoon.

The Indians were planning to open those bottles after Game 3.

That didn't happen as the Senators won that game 5-2.

The Indians then planned to open the bottles after Game 4.

That didn't happen, either, as the Senators again won 10-2.

281

WEDNESDAY, SEPTEMBER 15

Now, four hours before Game 5, Vander Woude told his counterparts from Canton that he was prepared to buy the bottles, all 48 of them, because the Senators were hoping themselves — no, really, planning — to open the bottles in their clubhouse in, oh, seven hours or nine innings, whichever came first.

"I forget the cost," Vander Woude said 25 years later, "and, yes, the bottles were still chilled."

None of Harrisburg's players knew of Vander Woude's negotiations, although the Senators' players knew the Indians spent two days planning to party at their expense.

"I do remember Canton being ready to celebrate each day when we showed up to the park," pitcher Rod Henderson said.

Of course, there was another not-so-small matter for each team, and that was playing Game 5, a game that would be played in cool, damp conditions following rain in the morning.

Just as they did before Games 3 and 4, the Senators did not deviate from their routine for their third straight must-win game.

"I just remember us approaching each game like we did in the regular season," Henderson said. "We took BP and did our pregame work like it was another day. I credit Trace for that. There was no panic."

Meanwhile, the Indians were looking for a psychological edge, something — anything, really — that would give them a boost after losing Games 3 and 4 by a combined score of 15-4.

They already were planning to start former major league pitcher Randy Veres in Game 5 with another former major leaguer, Calvin Jones, ready to come out of the bullpen.

Then, too, the Indians started former major leaguers Paul Abbott and Mike Dyer in Games 3 and 4, and that did not turn out well for them.

The edge they settled on: Throwback uniforms.

As they had earlier in the season to commemorate the 45th anniversary of the Cleveland Indians' last World Series winner in 1948, the Canton Indians decided to wear retro, 1948 jerseys for Game 5.

"When we saw this, we laughed," catcher Lance Rice remembered years later. "It seemed so desperate."

Meanwhile, Tracy prepared his lineup with the Senators donning the same road grays they had been wearing all season.

WEDNESDAY, SEPTEMBER 15

expos
LINEUP CARD

DATE 9/15/9

EXPOS	OPPONENTS
1 — A HARDCE - 4● B D	7 R A RAMIREZ - 8● B D
2 — A MARTIN - 6● B D	2 R A FLORES - 4● B D
3 — A MURRAY - 8 ● B D	3 L A GILES - 9● C B D
4 — A HORNE - 7● B D	4 R A BELL - 6 ● C B D
5 — A D. WHITE - 3 C B D	5 R A LENNON - DH ● B D
6 — A WOODS - DH ●●● B D	6 L A SPARKS - 3●● B D
7 — A RUNDELS - 9●● B D	7 S A PEGUERO - 7 ● B D
8 — A ANDREWS - 5 B D	8 R A SARBAUGH - 5● B D
9 — A FITZPATRICK - 2 B D	9 R A MARTINDALE - 2 B D
10 — A CORNELIUS C S.P. B D	10 A ~~VERES~~ - S.P. C B ~~GARCIA~~ ~~VALDEZ~~ ~~JONES~~

LH	EXTRA	RH
GRIFFIN	SIMONS	
WILSTEAD		
	RICE	

LH	EXTRA	RH
		ODOR
		SUED
		VARGAS

PITCHERS

THOMAS	CORBIN
PUIG	DIAZ
LOONEY	HAYNES

PITCHERS

THE LINEUP CARD POSTED BY JIM TRACY IN THE DUGOUT FOR GAME 5

283

WEDNESDAY, SEPTEMBER 15

Right on time, Randy Veres — clad in his retro 1948 uni — delivered his first pitch at 7:05 p.m. to Mike Hardge.

REID CORNELIUS

A moment later, Hardge grounded out to shortstop David Bell. Chris Martin then flied out to left fielder and onetime Senator Julio Peguero before Glenn Murray bounced out to first baseman Greg Sparks.

Veres was just as perfect in the second inning, retiring Tyrone Horne on a grounder to Miguel Flores at second and Derrick White on a flyout to right fielder Brian Giles before striking out Tyrone Woods.

To that point, Randy Veres may just as well have been freakin' Bob Feller, circa 1948.

He was that good, that dominant.

And, turns out, that much of an illusion as he started the third by hitting Matt Rundels with his first pitch of the inning before the previously struggling Shane Andrews singled to left.

With two on and none out, Tracy sent Rundels and Andrews on a double steal that turned into a run as Canton catcher Ryan Martindale bounced his throw into left field as he tried to get Rundels at third. Rundels quickly lifted himself off the grass in front of Tracy in the third-base coach's box and ran home for a 1-0 lead.

Not much of a lead, but a lead nonetheless for Reid Cornelius, who almost assuredly would have been bumped from this start in favor of emerging prospect Brian Looney had a potential rainout turned into a reality and pushed Game 5 to the next day.

Cornelius, the onetime front-line prospect whose career had been slowed by injuries, was coming off a vexing season in which he had a 10-7 record in 27 starts but a rather crummy 4.17 ERA to go with it. He was his typical sporadically brilliant self in winning the deciding Game 4 of the semifinals, beating Albany 8-4 but giving up four runs on nine hits and leaving in the sixth.

Now, with no rainout coming for this game and Looney not available for much more than an inning, the Senators' season depended on Cornelius being more brilliant than sporadic.

WEDNESDAY, SEPTEMBER 15

Given what had happened with Cornelius during the regular season, that 1-0 lead likely was not going to hold up.

How could it? No way, not after the Indians scored 27 runs in only 25 2/3 innings off Cornelius during the season.

TYRONE HORNE

"I just wanted to go as hard as I could for as long as I could," Cornelius said.

"I know those guys hit me pretty well all year."

The oh-no moment for Cornelius, or so it seemed, came in the fifth inning.

With the Senators clinging to their precarious 1-0 lead, Cornelius gave up a one-out single to Mike Sarbaugh before Martindale, the Indians' No. 9 hitter, followed with a high drive to deep left field.

Really high and really deep, and really ready to turn that 1-0 lead for the Senators into a 2-1 deficit.

Didn't happen, though.

Just as Martindale's drive was going out, left fielder Tyrone Horne — who as a fielder was a helluva hitter — climbed the wall, stretched out all 5-foot-9 of his body and caught the ball at the top of the wall.

"It was gone," Horne said.

Disbelief followed from all over the stadium, starting with Jim Tracy in the Senators' dugout.

A quarter-century later, he still could see the play develop and remember what he said to pitching coach Chuck Kniffin as they watched Horne race back to the fence.

"When the ball was first hit and he was retreating to the wall, I said to Kniff, 'Does he have a depth perception problem, because that ball is in Massillon,' " Tracy said.

"He scales the wall and he comes running back to the infield," Tracy recalled. "I still don't see the ball, but he's running in and smiling, and then he holds up the ball. I said to Kniff, 'Are you effing kidding me?' "

Randy Wilstead, also watching from the dugout, recalled seeing the catch of Horne's career and of the Senators' season, and then looking across the field at the Indians' bench.

WEDNESDAY, SEPTEMBER 15

"I remember their demeanor changing from them being in command of the series to them fighting to stay alive," Wilstead said. "Tyrone wasn't really known for his outstanding defense, so it was huge for us. He was a good outfielder, but a much better hitter."

And, at that moment, Horne was the ultimate game changer.

"If that kid doesn't make that catch," Canton manager Brian Graham said, "it changes the whole momentum in the game."

Two batters later, Cornelius retired Miguel Flores on a fly ball to right fielder Matt Rundels, ending the threat and the inning.

From the Senators' bullpen, reliever Ed Puig saw Horne's catch and needed only six words to assess the Indians' chances over the final four innings.

"They," Puig said, "were done for the night."

"I think that play sealed the deal," Mark Mattern, the Senators' radio broadcaster, remembered a quarter-century later.

Even more certain was Jim Clark, Mattern's counterpart in the Canton radio booth.

"You could see it slipping away," Clark said of the Indians. "Their jaws were so tight. You could seem them clinching. My color guy was ready to hang himself."

All over a 1-0 lead. Seemed like much more and, soon enough, it was.

While Horne was still being congratulated in the dugout, Martin led off the top of the sixth with a single to left off Veres.

Murray then grounded into a fielder's choice, replacing Martin at first and starting his own tour around the bases as he stole second before scoring on White's two-out single to center.

The RBI was White's ninth in as many postseason games.

Three more runs for a 5-0 lead followed in the seventh off reliever Apolinar Garcia. The runs came on a mix of hustle, alertness and situational hitting.

First, Rundels led off the inning with a single to center and scored when Shane Andrews followed with a double to left-center.

Garcia, as if his inning was not already off to a lousy start, then hit Rob Fitzpatrick with a pitch before Martin loaded the bases with a one-out single to right.

286

WEDNESDAY, SEPTEMBER 15

Andrews pushed that lead to 4-0 when he scored on Murray's sacrifice fly to center fielder Omar Ramirez.

ED PUIG

Fitzpatrick then scored on a passed ball by Martindale, capping a truly awful night for Martindale with a throwing error in the second that gave the Senators their 1-0 lead that was followed by Horne's miraculous catch off his would-be homer in fifth.

A few minutes later, Ramirez flied out to Murray in center to end the bottom of the seventh, Cornelius' final inning.

His final line: seven innings, four singles, four walks and 10 strikeouts.

"It probably was as good of a performance as Reid Cornelius has had all year," Tracy said, "and he had some pretty good performances for us."

As Cornelius sat down in the dugout, Puig stood up in the bullpen, grabbed a baseball and started to play catch with backup catcher Lance Rice.

None of the Senators' relievers had more experience than Puig, then a month shy of his 28th birthday and now only six outs away from completing his ninth pro season.

And none of the Senators' relievers had the same success of Puig in the postseason after Joe Ausanio's brilliant 4 1/3 innings of near-perfect work against Albany in Game 2 of the semifinals.

That extended outing, though, turned out to be Ausanio's last effective moment of the postseason. After that, Puig took over Ausanio's high-leverage spots and worked 6 1/3 scoreless innings, a span covering four playoff games.

Puig faced only four batters in the bottom of the eighth inning before the Senators scored three more runs in the ninth on run-scoring doubles by Fitzpatrick and Murray off onetime Seattle Mariners reliever Calvin Jones.

Murray's double to left field was his 10th hit in the five-game series.

Puig watched from the dugout as the lead grew from 5-0 to 8-0. The size of the lead mattered little to him.

287

WEDNESDAY, SEPTEMBER 15

FINALLY, HOLDING THE HARDWARE THEY HAD PURSUED SINCE DAY 1

"At that time," Puig remembered 25 years later, "I was feeling invincible. There was no chance for them to get me."

The time was 9:45 when Puig took the mound for the bottom of the ninth. He struck out Greg Sparks to start the inning and then retired Julio Peguero on a tapper in front of the plate.

All that remained was Mike Sarbaugh, the Indians' third baseman who grew up in Mt. Joy, Pa., a 40-minute car ride from City Island.

Sarbaugh sent Puig's final pitch back up the middle, off of Puig's body and right to Mike Hardge at second base. Hardge's flick of a throw to Derrick White at first base ended the game.

The time was 9:49.

The Senators had their championship.

And they had Canton's champagne. All 48 bottles.

"You go over there and sweep them in their own ballpark," Jim Tracy remembered a quarter-century later, "and then to get permission to purchase their champagne they had on ice for two or three days … realizing what we had just accomplished, there were tears of joy."

WEDNESDAY, SEPTEMBER 15

All the Senators did during the final three days of their season was outscore Canton in Canton 23-4.

Against a Canton offense that, even with Manny Ramirez already in Cleveland, had four of the Eastern League's best hitters in Brian Giles, Omar Ramirez, David Bell and Miguel Flores, as well as two other players — outfielders Patrick Lennon and Julio Peguero — who already had time in the majors.

Against Canton starters Paul Abbott, Mike Dyer and Randy Veres, who had combined for 78 appearances in the majors before finding their way to Canton in their hopes of one day returning to the majors.

The Senators did not help them with that.

Instead, the Senators drank.

First, the champagne. Then, the beer Todd Vander Woude picked up, knowing the 48 bottles of champagne he purchased seven hours earlier from Canton would last only so long.

"Just to know," Ed Puig said, "that the champagne was theirs, it tasted even better when we drank it."

Almost everybody drank.

Randy Wilstead — the Senators' sometimes first baseman, sometimes designated hitter and fulltime Mormon — did not drink.

Well, at least not the champagne.

One of his teammates ducked into the clubhouse toward the end of the game to make sure those charged with handing out the champagne also took care of Wilstead.

"The guys knew I was a devout Mormon," Wilstead said a quarter-century later.

"They protected me. One of them — I don't know who — went to the clubby before the final out and told him I was a Mormon and I didn't drink.

"So, when we went in the clubhouse to celebrate, there was a Sprite in my locker and not champagne. I thought that was cool."

WEDNESDAY, SEPTEMBER 15

The celebration in the clubhouse carried on toward midnight, when the Senators finally boarded the team bus and pointed it toward Harrisburg for the final 300-mile leg of a journey that started six months earlier in Lantana, Florida.

During the trip home, the Eastern League trophy made its way through the bus, up and down the aisles, being grabbed, embraced, caressed and, in Tracy's case, cried over.

Eventually, Jim Tracy left the trophy on the inside seat of the front row of the bus, next to the seat he normally occupied. He now allowed himself some time to wander to the back of the bus where the older players traditionally sat on road trips.

This was where Derrick White held court, along with Mike Hardge, Tyrone Woods, Shane Andrews and infielder-turned-clubhouse-comedian Mitch Simons.

"I finally had a chance to let my guard down with them," Tracy recalled years later, "so now I was hearing all the stories about what really was going on in the clubhouse that they didn't want Skip to know about during the season."

The BS session went on for two hours before Tracy finally returned to the front of the bus, again taking his seat next to the trophy. The same trophy that back in spring training the Senators fully expected to hold on this day, but the same trophy that only hours earlier Tracy privately thought could slip away.

"I sat there for the longest period of time," Tracy said of the quiet that overcame him despite the din of the ongoing celebration around him.

"Then, I cried," he said. "I was thankful. I thanked God that I was blessed being around this group of kids who did anything I asked of them. For them to play as unselfishly as they did with the talent they had … I was just overwhelmed.

"Of all that we went through during the year, there was a finality to it, a sadness to it."

Only temporarily.

The finality of that one moment simply represented the culmination to all of the astounding moments — their moments — that made for the story of the Class of '93.

Nothing can ever change that.

290

Postseason Stats

BATTING

Player	Avg.	G	AB	R	H	2B	3B	HR	RBI	BB	SO	SB
Mitch Simons	1.000	1	1	0	1	0	0	0	0	0	0	0
Tyrone Woods	.457	8	35	4	16	3	0	1	6	5	8	0
Derrick White	.421	9	38	5	16	1	0	0	9	3	6	5
Glenn Murray	.372	9	43	11	16	5	0	1	7	1	8	2
Tyrone Horne	.355	9	31	7	11	1	0	1	3	9	8	2
Chris Martin	.286	9	42	4	12	2	0	0	5	2	6	2
Shane Andrews	.200	9	30	6	6	2	0	0	3	7	13	1
Lance Rice	.200	2	5	0	1	0	0	0	0	0	1	0
Matt Rundels	.190	8	21	4	4	1	0	0	4	3	4	1
Mike Hardge	.171	9	35	8	6	0	1	0	2	9	10	6
Rob Fitzpatrick	.161	8	31	4	5	2	0	1	5	1	11	0
Randy Wilstead	.063	6	16	2	1	0	1	0	2	3	5	0
Marc Griffin	.000	5	1	0	0	0	0	0	1	0	0	0
TOTALS	**.289**	**9**	**329**	**55**	**95**	**17**	**2**	**4**	**47**	**43**	**80**	**19**

PITCHING

Pitcher	G	W	L	SV	ERA	IP	H	R	ER	BB	SO
Mike Thomas	3	0	0	0	0.00	3.0	0	0	0	4	4
Heath Haynes	3	0	0	1	0.00	2.1	2	0	0	1	3
Archie Corbin	1	0	0	0	0.00	2.0	0	0	0	3	0
Brian Looney	2	1	0	0	0.57	15.2	6	1	1	3	16
Ed Puig	6	1	0	0	0.79	11.1	7	1	1	0	11
Rafael Diaz	2	0	0	0	2.70	3.1	3	2	1	1	2
Reid Cornelius	2	2	0	0	2.84	12.2	13	4	4	4	18
Miguel Batista	1	0	0	0	2.84	6.1	9	2	2	2	3
Ugueth Urbina	2	1	1	0	3.29	13.2	12	5	5	6	14
Joe Ausano	2	1	1	0	8.31	4.1	2	4	4	3	7
Rod Henderson	2	0	1	0	9.72	8.1	15	10	9	5	15
TOTALS	**9**	**6**	**3**	**1**	**2.93**	**83.0**	**69**	**29**	**27**	**32**	**93**

POSTSEASON VS. THE EASTERN LEAGUE

	Home Games		Road Games	
	W	L	W	L
Albany Yankees	2	0	1	1
Canton Indians	0	2	3	0
TOTALS	**2**	**2**	**4**	**1**

DERRICK WHITE

REID CORNELIUS

Comings And Goings

By their nature, minor league teams constantly have rosters in flux. Players always are moving up a level, down a level or just going home to pursue whatever fate has planned for them.

The 1993 Senators were no different with more than 50 roster moves, beginning with pitcher Bob Baxter being placed on the disabled list on Opening Day and ending with first baseman Derrick White being reassigned from the Montreal Expos to the Senators with three weeks remaining in the regular season.

Here they are, the roster moves that made, broke up and remade the Class of '93.

APRIL

9 — Pitcher Bob Baxter (elbow) placed on disabled list
15 — Pitcher Chris Johnson traded to Chicago Cubs
16 — Pitcher Darrin Winston added from extended spring training
26 — Shortstop Edgar Tovar reassigned to Class A West Palm Beach
26 — Shortstop Tim Barker added from AAA Ottawa
30 — Catcher Miah Bradbury promoted to AAA Ottawa
30 — Coach Greg Fulton activated as backup catcher

MAY

1 — Catcher Miah Bradbury refused AAA promotion and retired
7 — Catcher Lance Rice added as free agent
7 — Catcher Greg Fulton deactivated, returned to coaching staff
18 — Infielder Ron Krause retired
18 — Second baseman Mike Hardge added from West Palm Beach
22 — Catcher Rob Fitzpatrick (left ankle) placed on disabled list
22 — Catcher Mike Daniel added from West Palm Beach
22 — Pitcher Bob Baxter activated from DL, sent to West Palm Beach
25 — Pitcher Rafael Diaz (right shoulder) placed on disabled list
27 — Pitcher Kirk Rueter promoted to Ottawa
27 — Pitcher Rick DeHart added from Class A San Bernadino
29 — Catcher Rob Fitzpatrick activated from disabled list
29 — Catcher Mike Daniel reassigned to West Palm Beach
29 — Shortstop Tim Barker (right thumb) placed on disabled list
29 — Infielder Mitch Simons added from West Palm Beach

JUNE

8 — Pitcher Rafael Diaz activated from disabled list
21 — Outfielder Curtis Pride promoted to Ottawa
21 — First baseman Randy Wilstead added from West Palm Beach
26 — Shortstop Tim Barker activated from disabled list
26 — Infielder Mitch Simons deactivated
30 — Infielder Mitch Simons reassigned to West Palm Beach

JULY

2 — Pitcher Gabe White (right ankle) placed on disabled list
5 — Pitcher Mario Brito promoted to Ottawa
5 — Pitcher Ugueth Urbina added from Class A Burlington
6 — Pitcher Yorkis Perez promoted to Ottawa
7 — Pitcher Mike Thomas added from West Palm Beach
13 — Pitcher Archie Corbin (family) placed on temporary inactive list
16 — Pitcher Brian Looney added from West Palm Beach
20 — Pitcher Rick DeHart reassigned to West Palm Beach
20 — Pitcher Joe Ausanio added from Class A Gulf Coast League
24 — Outfielder Rondell White promoted to Ottawa
24 — Outfielder Tyrone Horne added from West Palm Beach
26 — Infielder Tim Barker promoted to Ottawa
28 — Pitcher Gabe White activated from disabled list
29 — Infielder Matt Rundels added from West Palm Beach

AUGUST

2 — First baseman-left fielder Cliff Floyd promoted to Ottawa
2 — Pitcher Archie Corbin activated from temporary inactive list
4 — Pitcher Gabe White promoted to Ottawa
4 — Pitcher Joey Eischen promoted to Ottawa
4 — Pitcher Rod Henderson added from West Palm Beach
4 — Third baseman Shane Andrews (left shoulder) placed on DL
4 — Infielder Mitch Simons added from West Palm Beach
9 — Pitcher Darrin Winston reassigned to West Palm Beach
9 — Pitcher Benny Puig added from Saltillo of Mexican League
9 — Outfielder Marc Griffin added from West Palm Beach
11 — Third baseman Shane Andrews activated from disabled list
12 — First baseman-DH Oreste Marrero promoted to Montreal Expos
12 — First baseman Derrick White added from Montreal Expos

PERFECT ATTENDANCE

While relief pitchers Archie Corbin and Rafael Diaz, as well as catcher Rob Fitzpatrick and third baseman Shane Andrews, were on Harrisburg's roster from start to finish, only six other members of the Class of '93 — three pitchers and three position players — spent the entire season in Harrisburg without spending a day on the disabled list.
They were:
Miguel Batista, starting pitcher
Reid Cornelius, starting pitcher
Heath Haynes, relief pitcher
Chris Martin, infielder
Glenn Murray, outfielder
Tyrone Woods, outfielder

HAYNES **WOODS**

293

1993: By The Numbers

RECORD BY GAMES	
Home	47 - 23
Road	47 - 21
Night games	72 - 33
Day games	22 - 11
One-run games	23 - 11
Extra-inning games	9 - 4
Shutouts	10 - 2
Doubleheaders	6 - 4

RECORD BY DAYS	
Monday	11 - 6
Tuesday	13 - 8
Wednesday	16 - 4
Thursday	9 - 6
Friday	17 - 5
Saturday	14 - 5
Sunday	14 - 10

RECORD BY MONTHS	
April	13 - 4
May	23 - 6
June	19 - 10
July	14 - 13
August	21 - 10
September	4 - 1

WHEN LEADING	
After 1st inning	31 - 7
After 2nd inning	42 - 8
After 3rd inning	56 - 8
After 4th inning	68 - 7
After 5th inning	74 - 7
After 6th inning	80 - 5
After 7th inning	75 - 3
After 8th inning	74 - 2

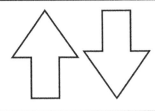

WHEN TRAILING	
After 1st inning	17 - 14
After 2nd inning	20 - 18
After 3rd inning	19 - 24
After 4th inning	17 - 28
After 5th inning	14 - 31
After 6th inning	11 - 32
After 7th inning	9 - 34
After 8th inning	3 - 32

HOW TO SCORE 802 RUNS	
Homers	271
Singles	226
Doubles	110
Groundouts	53
Errors	36
Sacrifice flies	32
Triples	31
Wild pitches	15
Walks	14
Squeeze bunts	6
Balks	4
Stolen bases	3
Passed balls	1

WHEN THOSE 802 SCORED	
With none out	186
With one out	269
With two outs	347
1st inning	90
2nd inning	67
3rd inning	88
4th inning	114
5th inning	89
6th inning	99
7th inning	95
8th inning	96
9th inning	52
Extra innings	12

PRODUCTION LINE	
Top third of order	331
Middle of order	269
Bottom third of order	202

AGAINST THE LEAGUE

	Against	Allowed
Albany	90	86
Binghamton	103	80
Bowie	98	88
Canton	133	105
London	141	78
New Britain	109	65
Reading	128	67

**MANAGER JIM TRACY GREETS
CLIFF FLOYD ROUNDING THIRD
AFTER ONE OF FLOYD'S 26 HOMERS**

RECORD AGAINST EL	
Albany	9 - 9
Binghamton	13 - 7
Bowie	12 - 8
Canton	13 - 7
London	15 - 5
New Britain	17 - 3
Reading	15 - 5

NOTE: Two rainouts on the Senators' final trip to Albany in late July were not rescheduled, leaving them with 138 games instead of 140.

ALL-STAR BREAK	
Before break	60 - 26
After break	34 - 18

THE FLOYD FACTOR	
With Cliff Floyd	70 - 33
Without Cliff Floyd	24 - 11

295

RONDELL WHITE **CLIFF FLOYD** **TIM BARKER** **ORESTE MARRERO**

LONGEST HITTING STREAKS

24 games	Rondell White	June 4-July 4
17	Cliff Floyd	June 4-June 19
15	Tim Barker	May 1-May 20
15	Oreste Marrero	June 12-June 28
13	Cliff Floyd	July 19-Aug. 1
12	Tyrone Horne	Aug. 9-Aug. 27
12	Mike Hardge	Aug. 16-Aug. 29
11	Rondell White	May 10-May 20
10	Cliff Floyd	April 21-May 3
10	Curtis Pride	May 14-May 23
10	Rondell White	July 6-July 18

LEFTY-RIGHT BATTING SPLITS

	Against left-handers		Against right-handers	
Team average	**.291**		**.274**	
Individuals	Cliff Floyd	.353	Curtis Pride	.371
(50 at-bats)	Chris Martin	.333	Tyrone Horne	.360
	Tim Barker	.316	Matt Rundels	.344
	Rondell White	.311	Rondell White	.332
	Rob Fitzpatrick	.301	Cliff Floyd	.316
	Mike Hardge	.300	Oreste Marrero	.316
	Tyrone Woods	.254	Tim Barker	.305
Team homers	**53**		**117**	
Individuals	Cliff Floyd	10	Glenn Murray	18
	Glenn Murray	8	Cliff Floyd	16
	Tyrone Woods	8	Curtis Pride	15
	Shane Andrews	6	Shane Andrews	12

CURTIS PRIDE **CHRIS MARTIN** **GLENN MURRAY** **SHANE ANDREWS**

HITTING LIKE NIGHT AND DAY

	Night Games		Day Games	
Team average	**.274**		**.290**	
Individuals	Curtis Pride	.388	Oreste Marrero	.382
(50 at-bats)	Tyrone Horne	.384	Chris Martin	.361
	Matt Rundels	.355	Glenn Murray	.327
	Cliff Floyd	.344	Shane Andrews	.306
	Rondell White	.338	Rondell White	.302
	Oreste Marrero	.317	Curtis Pride	.297
	Tim Barker	.309	Cliff Floyd	.284
Team homers	**120**		**50**	
Individuals	Cliff Floyd	21	Glenn Murray	11
	Glenn Murray	15	Cliff Floyd	5
	Tyrone Woods	15	Oreste Marrero	5

FUTURE MLB ALL-STARS VS. THE '93 SENATORS
(Regular season only)

	Against Senators	Against rest of EL
Brian Giles, Canton	.400	.316
Manny Ramirez, Canton	.345	.339
Jose Lima, London	1-1, 3.21 ERA	7-12-0, 4.14
Ricky Bottalico, Reading	0-0, 2 saves, 0.00	3-3-18, 2.53

MLB ALL-STARS ON REHAB VS. THE '93 SENATORS

Mike Mussina, Bowie (Baltimore)	1 start, 6 innings, 0 runs
Charles Nagy, Canton (Cleveland)	1 start, 5 innings, 0 runs

SECOND BASEMAN
MIKE HARDGE

HOW THE '93 SENATORS COMPARED TO REST OF EL

HITTING

Batting average	.278	1st
Runs scored	802	1
Runs per game	5.81	1
Hits	1,301	1
Doubles	229	1
Triples	41	4
Home runs	170	1
RBIs	738	1
Total bases	2,122	1
Stolen bases	187	1
Walks	507	3
Intentional walks	23	3
Strikeouts	1,006	1
Slugging percentage	.455	1
On-base percentage	.353	1
Fewest hit in DP	76	1
Hit by pitch	47	4
Sacrifice bunts	44	3
Sacrifice flies	32	6

PITCHING

Earned-run average	3.49	1st
Shutouts	10	3
Complete games	8	5
Saves	36	4
Fewest hits	1,086	1
Most strikeouts	1,056	1
Fewest walks	538	8
Fewest home runs	75	1
Fewest hit batters	48	4
Wild pitches allowed	66	4
Walks-hits per 9 innings	1.34	1

FIELDING

Fielding percentage	.971	3rd
Fewest chances	5,093	1
Most double plays	108	7
Fewest errors	147	3
Fewest passed balls	22	5

BIRTHDAY CANDLES IN '93	
SOMETHING OLD	
Ed Puig	27
Joe Ausanio	27
Mario Brito	27
Darrin Winston	27
Lance Rice	26
SOMETHING NEW	
Ugueth Urbina	19
Edgar Tovar	19
Cliff Floyd	20
Rondell White	21
Mike Hardge	21
Gabe White	21

UGUETH URBINA

LEAGUE AVERAGE AGE BATTERS IN 1993	
Harrisburg	22.7
Binghamton	23.3
Canton	23.4
Bowie	23.5
London	23.6
Albany	23.7
New Britain	23.9
Reading	24.5
PITCHERS IN 1993	
London	22.7
Harrisburg	23.2
Binghamton	23.4
Bowie	23.7
Albany	23.8
New Britain	23.9
Reading	24.0
Canton	25.1

EL'S YOUNGEST IN '93	
Ugueth Urbina, Harrisburg	19
Edgar Tovar, Harrisburg	19
Julian Tavarez, Canton	20
Justin Thompson, London	20
Brian Edmondson, London	20

WEIGHTS & MEASURES	
HEAVIEST SENATORS	
Glenn Murray	225
Cliff Floyd	220
Derrick White	220
Shane Andrews	215
Chris Johnson	215
LIGHTEST	
Marc Griffin	170
Chris Martin	170
Edgar Tovar	170
Mitch Simons	172
TALLEST	
Chris Johnson	6-8
Cliff Floyd	6-5
SHORTEST	
Tyrone Horne	5- 9
Mitch Simons	5- 9
Brian Looney	5-10
Ed Puig	5-10

299

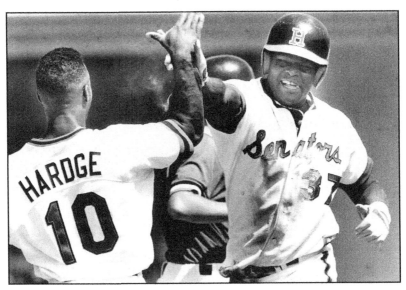

MIKE HARDGE WELCOMES HOME DERRICK WHITE

Just How Dominant?

MARGINS OF VICTORY BY RUNS

One run	22
Two runs	20
Three runs	10
Four runs	8
Five runs	11
Six runs	4
Seven runs	6
Eight runs	5
Nine runs	1
Ten or more	7

CATCH 'EM IF YOU CAN RECORDS

Scoring seven runs	12-3
Scoring eight runs	11-0
Scoring nine runs	6-2
Scoring 10 or more	16-0

TRACKING HOMERS

April (17 games)	22
May (29 games)	48
June (29 games)	37
July (27 games)	24
August (31 games)	36
September (5 games)	3
Postseason (9 games)	4
TOTAL	**174**

Note: The Senators hit at least one home run in 103 of their 138 games in the regular season and only once went as long as four games without a home run.

THE SAMSON EFFECT

When homering	77-26
Without homering	17-18

Breaking Records

As you might expect, a team that won 100 games from Opening
Night through the end of the playoffs and had 22 future major
leaguers on its roster might set some franchise records along the
way. The Class of '93 had plenty.

REGULAR SEASON TEAM RECORDS

MOST WINS

Overall	94
At home	47
On road	47*
At midseason	52
In one month (May)	23

FEWEST LOSSES

Overall	44
At home	23
On road	21
At midseason	18
In one month (May)	6

BATTING

Runs scored	802
Home runs	170
Runs batted in	738
Doubles	229*
Stolen bases	187*
On-base percentage	.353
Slugging percentage	.455
On-base & slugging	.808
Total bases	2,122

PITCHING

Strikeouts	1,056*
Strikeouts per 9 innings	7.8*
Walks allowed	538*

WINNING STREAKS

Overall	12
At home	10
Non-consecutive games	17 of 18

HOME RUNS

Consecutive games	14

ATTENDANCE 250,476*

* Record since broken

REGULAR SEASON INDIVIDUAL RECORDS
BATTING

Batting average, right-handed batter	.328, Rondell White*
Slugging percentage, overall	.600, Cliff Floyd*
Slugging percentage, left-handed batter	.600, Cliff Floyd
On-base, slugging, overall	1.017, Cliff Floyd*
On-base, slugging, right-handed batter	.892, Rondell White*
On-base, slugging, left-handed batter	1.017, Cliff Floyd
Home runs, overall	26, Cliff Floyd*
	26, Glenn Murray*
Home runs, right-handed batter	26, Glenn Murray*
Home runs, left-handed batter	26, Cliff Floyd*
Doubles, right-handed batter	29, Shane Andrews*
Triples, overall	10, Rondell White*
	10, Mike Hardge*
Triples, right-handed batter	10, Rondell White
	10, Mike Hardge
Runs batted in, overall	101, Cliff Floyd*
Runs batted in, right-handed batter	96, Glenn Murray
Runs batted in, left-handed batter	101, Cliff Floyd*
Walks, right-handed batter	64, Shane Andrews*
Strikeouts, overall	118, Shane Andrews*

PITCHING

Wins, overall	14, Joey Eischen
ERA, left-hander (75+ innings)	2.16, Gabe White*
Appearances	57, Heath Haynes*
Starts, overall	27, Reid Cornelius*
Runs allowed	95, Reid Cornelius*
Walks, right-hander	86, Miguel Batista
Wild pitches, overall	10, Miguel Batista*
Wild pitches, left-hander	9, Joey Eischen*
Hit batters, overall	13, Reid Cornelius*

FIELDING

Errors by catcher	18, Rob Fitzpatrick
Errors by first baseman	16, Cliff Floyd*

* Record since broken

302

SINGLE-GAME TEAM RECORDS
ATTENDANCE
Largest home crowd   5,724, Aug. 21 vs. Canton*
Largest home opener crowd   5,671, April 9 vs. Albany*

BATTING
Most runs in inning   10 at Canton on Aug. 8*
Most doubles   6 at New Britain on April 19*
                        6 at New Britain on June 9*
                        6 at Binghamton on July 16*
Most triples   3 vs. New Britain on April 12*

SINGLE-GAME INDIVIDUAL RECORDS
BATTING
At-bats	7	Mike Hardge, June 19 at Reading
Triples	2	Rondell White, April 12 vs. New Britain
	2	Mike Hardge, July 31 at New Britain
Stolen bases	3	Cliff Floyd, June 30 vs. Canton*
	3	Mike Hardge, July 4 at London*

PITCHING
Strikeouts, LHP	13	Brian Looney, July 24 vs. New Britain
	13	Brian Looney, Aug. 5 vs. Bowie
Walks	7	Miguel Batista, May 12 vs. Canton*
	7	Miguel Batista, May 28 vs. Albany*
	7	Ugueth Urbina, Aug. 28 vs. Binghamton*
Runs	9	Miguel Batista, June 23 at Bowie*
	9	Reid Cornelius, July 25 vs New Britain*

FIELDING
Passed balls	2	Rob Fitzpatrick, May 18 vs. Binghamton

* Record since broken

303

POSTSEASON SINGLE-GAME TEAM RECORDS
BATTING

Hits	15	Game 4 finals, Sept. 14 at Canton
Doubles	4	Game 1 semifinals, Sept. 6 vs. Albany*
Triples	2	Game 2 semifinals, Sept. 7 vs. Albany
Stolen bases	4	Game 1 finals, Sept. 11 vs. Canton

PITCHING

Strikeouts for	20	Game 2 semifinals, Sept. 7 vs. Albany

FIELDING

Errors	3	Game 2, finals, Sept. 12 vs. Canton

POSTSEASON SINGLE-GAME INDIVIDUAL RECORDS
BATTING

At-bats	6	Tyrone Horne, Game 2 semifinals, Sept. 7 vs. Albany
	6	Glenn Murray, Game 2 semifinals, Sept. 7 vs. Albany
	6	Chris Martin, Game 4 finals, Sept. 14 at Canton
Hits	4	Tyrone Woods, Game 4 finals, Sept. 14 at Canton*
Steals	3	Mike Hardge, Game 1 finals, Sept. 11 vs. Canton
	3	Mike Hardge, Game 2 finals, Sept. 12 vs. Canton
Walks	3	Mike Hardge, Game 1 finals, Sept. 11 vs. Canton
	3	Mike Hardge, Game 2 finals, Sept. 12 vs. Canton
	3	Tyrone Horne, Game 3 finals, Sept. 13 at Canton
Ks	4	Shane Andrews, Game 2 semifinals, Sept. 7 vs. Albany

PITCHING

Ks	10	Reid Cornelius, Game 5 finals, Sept. 15 at Canton*
WPs	2	Reid Cornelius, Game 5 finals, Sept. 15 at Canton
Relief IP	4.1	Joe Ausanio, Game 2 semifinals, Sept. 7 vs. Albany*

POSTSEASON INDIVIDUAL RECORDS
BATTING

Hits in postseason	16	Glenn Murray vs. Albany and Canton
	16	Derrick White vs. Albany and Canton
	16	Tyrone Woods vs. Albany and Canton
Hits in one series	10	Glenn Murray vs. Canton
Steals, postseason	6	Mike Hardge vs. Albany and Canton
Steals, one series	6	Mike Hardge vs. Canton
Games with an RBI	9	Derrick White vs. Albany and Canton

* **Record since broken**

304

Major League Numbers

SEASONS IN MAJORS	
Miguel Batista	18
Cliff Floyd	17
Rondell White	15
Kirk Rueter	13
Curtis Pride	11
Ugueth Urbina	11
Gabe White	11
Joey Eischen	10
Yorkis Perez	9
Shane Andrews	7
Rick DeHart	4
Archie Corbin	3
Reid Cornelius	3
Brian Looney	3
Derrick White	3
Joe Ausanio	2
Rod Henderson	2
Oreste Marrero	2
Darrin Winston	2
Heath Haynes	1
Glenn Murray	1
Mike Thomas	1

JOEY EISCHEN

GAMES PLAYED	
Cliff Floyd	1,621
Rondell White	1,474
Miguel Batista	658
Ugueth Urbina	583
Shane Andrews	569
Gabe White	472
Curtis Pride	421
Kirk Rueter	340
Yorkis Perez	337
Joey Eischen	324
Derrick White	76
Rick DeHart	56

POSTSEASON GAMES	
Cliff Floyd	19
Ugueth Urbina	10
Kirk Rueter	8
Miguel Batista	7
Rondell White	4
Gabe White	3
Curtis Pride	2

WORLD SERIES RINGS	
1	Cliff Floyd, 1997 Florida
1	Miguel Batista, 2001 Arizona
1	Ugueth Urbina, 2003 Florida

CAREER EARNINGS

Cliff Floyd	$53.1 million
Miguel Batista	$47.6 million
Kirk Rueter	$38.3 million
Rondell White	$35.1 million
Ugueth Urbina	$25.8 million
Gabe White	$10.3 million
Joey Eischen	$ 4.9 million
Shane Andrews	$ 3.2 million

ALL-STAR GAMES

2	Ugueth Urbina, 1998, 2002
1	Cliff Floyd, 2001
1	Rondell White, 2003

PLATE APPEARANCES

Cliff Floyd	6,062
Rondell White	5,852
Shane Andrews	1,924
Curtis Pride	898
Derrick White	119
Oreste Marrero	104
Glenn Murray	104

CLIFF FLOYD

AT-BATS

Rondell White	5,357
Cliff Floyd	5,319
Shane Andrews	1,704
Curtis Pride	796
Derrick White	116
Glenn Murray	97
Oreste Marrero	89

BATTING AVERAGE

Rondell White	.284
Cliff Floyd	.278
Curtis Pride	.250
Oreste Marrero	.225
Shane Andrews	.220
Glenn Murray	.196
Derrick White	.181

HITS

Rondell White	1,519
Cliff Floyd	1,479
Shane Andrews	375
Curtis Pride	199
Derrick White	21
Oreste Marrero	20
Glenn Murray	19

ON-BASE PERCENTAGE

Cliff Floyd	.358
Oreste Marrero	.337
Rondell White	.336
Curtis Pride	.327
Shane Andrews	.298
Glenn Murray	.250
Derrick White	.202

SLUGGING PERCENTAGE

Cliff Floyd	.482
Rondell White	.462
Shane Andrews	.421
Curtis Pride	.405
Oreste Marrero	.348
Derrick White	.302
Glenn Murray	.289

SINGLES

Rondell White	991
Cliff Floyd	883
Shane Andrews	209
Curtis Pride	128
Glenn Murray	14
Derrick White	13
Oreste Marrero	12

DOUBLES

Cliff Floyd	340
Rondell White	296
Shane Andrews	76
Curtis Pride	39
Oreste Marrero	6
Derrick White	5
Glenn Murray	3

TRIPLES

Rondell White	34
Cliff Floyd	23
Curtis Pride	12
Shane Andrews	4
Oreste Marrero	1

HOME RUNS

Cliff Floyd	233
Rondell White	198
Shane Andrews	86
Curtis Pride	20
Derrick White	3
Glenn Murray	2
Oreste Marrero	1

CURTIS PRIDE

RUNS BATTED IN

Cliff Floyd	865
Rondell White	768
Shane Andrews	263
Curtis Pride	82
Derrick White	8
Glenn Murray	6
Oreste Marrero	5

STOLEN BASES

Cliff Floyd	148
Rondell White	94
Curtis Pride	29
Shane Andrews	7
Derrick White	3
Oreste Marrero	1
Glenn Murray	1

WALKS

Cliff Floyd	601
Rondell White	360
Shane Andrews	191
Curtis Pride	85
Oreste Marrero	15
Glenn Murray	7
Derrick White	2

STRIKEOUTS

Cliff Floyd	1,064
Rondell White	925
Shane Andrews	515
Curtis Pride	211
Glenn Murray	36
Derrick White	28
Oreste Marrero	19

BATISTA   **EISCHEN**   **PEREZ**

RUETER   **URBINA**   **WHITE**

GAMES PITCHED

Miguel Batista	658
Ugueth Urbina	583
Gabe White	472
Kirk Rueter	340
Yorkis Perez	337
Joey Eischen	324
Rick DeHart	56
Reid Cornelius	45
Joe Ausanio	41
Archie Corbin	37
Darrin Winston	34
Brian Looney	7
Rod Henderson	5
Heath Haynes	4
Mike Thomas	1

STARTS

Kirk Rueter	336
Miguel Batista	248
Reid Cornelius	33
Ugueth Urbina	21
Gabe White	15
Rod Henderson	2
Brian Looney	2
Darrin Winston	1

WINS

Kirk Rueter	130
Miguel Batista	102
Ugueth Urbina	44
Gabe White	34
Yorkis Perez	14
Joey Eischen	11
Reid Cornelius	8
Joe Ausanio	4
Darrin Winston	4
Archie Corbin, Rick DeHart	2

RELIEF APPEARANCES

Ugueth Urbina	562
Gabe White	457
Miguel Batista	410
Yorkis Perez	337
Joey Eischen	324
Rick DeHart	56
Joe Ausanio	41
Archie Corbin	37
Darrin Winston	33
Reid Cornelius	12
Brian Looney	5
Heath Haynes	4
Kirk Rueter	4
Rod Henderson	3
Mike Thomas	1

LOSSES

Miguel Batista	115
Kirk Rueter	92
Ugueth Urbina	49
Gabe White	26
Reid Cornelius	17
Yorkis Perez	15
Joey Eischen	9
Rick DeHart	3
Darrin Winston	2
Joe Ausanio, Archie Corbin	1
R.Henderson, Brian Looney	1

INNINGS PITCHED	
Miguel Batista	1,956.1
Kirk Rueter	1,918.0
Ugueth Urbina	697.1
Gabe White	570.2
Joey Eischen	296.1
Yorkis Perez	282.0
Reid Cornelius	211.0
Rick DeHart	63.0
Joe Ausanio	53.1
Archie Corbin	50.2
Darrin Winston	37.0
Brian Looney	12.2
Rod Henderson	10.1
Heath Haynes	3.2
Mike Thomas	1.1

EARNED-RUN AVERAGE	
Heath Haynes	0.00
Mike Thomas	0.00
Ugueth Urbina	3.45
Joey Eischen	3.67
Kirk Rueter	4.27
Archie Corbin	4.44
Yorkis Perez	4.44
Miguel Batista	4.48
Gabe White	4.51
Reid Cornelius	4.91
Joe Ausanio	5.57
Darrin Winston	5.84
Rick DeHart	6.14
Rod Henderson	9.58
Brian Looney	11.37

COMPLETE GAMES	
Miguel Batista	11
Kirk Rueter	4

SHUTOUTS	
Miguel Batista	5
Kirk Rueter	1

SAVES	
Ugueth Urbina	237
Miguel Batista	41
Gabe White	17
Joey Eischen	3
Yorkis Perez	2
Joe Ausanio	1
Rick DeHart	1
Darrin Winston	1

HITS ALLOWED	
Kirk Rueter	2,092
Miguel Batista	2,021
Gabe White	556
Ugueth Urbina	539
Joey Eischen	297
Yorkis Perez	251
Reid Cornelius	226
Rick DeHart	81
Joe Ausanio	58
Archie Corbin	50
Darrin Winston	39
Brian Looney	24
Rod Henderson	14
Heath Haynes	3
Mike Thomas	2

HOME RUNS ALLOWED	
Kirk Rueter	220
Miguel Batista	194
Gabe White	96
Ugueth Urbina	86
Reid Cornelius	30
Yorkis Perez	29
Joey Eischen	25
Rick DeHart	13
Joe Ausanio	12
Darrin Winston	11
Archie Corbin	4
Rod Henderson	3
Brian Looney	2

WALKS ALLOWED		STRIKEOUTS	
Miguel Batista	899	Miguel Batista	1,250
Kirk Rueter	582	Kirk Rueter	818
Ugueth Urbina	307	Ugueth Urbina	814
Yorkis Perez	147	Yorkis Perez	259
Gabe White	141	Gabe White	254
Joey Eischen	139	Joey Eischen	244
Reid Cornelius	85	Reid Cornelius	101
Archie Corbin	39	Joe Ausanio	51
Rick DeHart	32	Archie Corbin	51
Joe Ausanio	29	Rick DeHart	45
Darrin Winston	9	Darrin Winston	19
Rod Henderson	7	Brian Looney	11
Brian Looney	6	Rod Henderson	4
Heath Haynes	3	Heath Haynes	1
Mike Thomas	1	Mike Thomas	0

WALKS-HITS PER 9 IP		STRIKEOUTS PER 9 IP	
Ugueth Urbina	1.21	Ugueth Urbina	10.5
Gabe White	1.22	Archie Corbin	9.1
Darrin Winston	1.30	Joe Ausanio	8.6
Kirk Rueter	1.39	Yorkis Perez	8.3
Yorkis Perez	1.41	Brian Looney	7.8
Joey Eischen	1.47	Joey Eischen	7.4
Reid Cornelius	1.47	Gabe White	7.2
Miguel Batista	1.49	Rick DeHart	6.4
Joe Ausanio	1.63	Miguel Batista	5.8
Heath Haynes	1.64	Darrin Winston	4.6
Archie Corbin	1.76	Reid Cornelius	4.3
Rick DeHart	1.79	Kirk Rueter	3.8
Rod Henderson	2.03	Rod Henderson	3.5
Mike Thomas	2.25	Heath Haynes	2.5
Brian Looney	2.37	Mike Thomas	0.0

JIM TRACY'S MANAGERIAL CAREER IN THE MAJORS

Year	Team	Record	Year	Team	Record
2001	Los Angeles	86-76	2007	Pittsburgh	68-94
2002	Los Angeles	92-70	2009	Colorado	74-42
2003	Los Angeles	85-77	2010	Colorado	83-79
2004	Los Angeles	93-69	2011	Colorado	73-89
2005	Los Angeles	71-91	2012	Colorado	64-98
2006	Pittsburgh	67-95	**TOTAL (11 years)**		**856-880**

Judging History, Part 1

Minor League Baseball's Top 100 teams from 1901-2000, as compiled by historians Bill Weiss and Marshall Wright:

1.	1934	Los Angeles Angels (137-50)	51.	1902	Corsicana Oil Citys (86-22)
2.	1921	Baltimore Orioles (119-47)	52.	1920	London Tecumsehs (86-32)
3.	1937	Newark Bears (109-43)	53.	1932	Newark Bears (109-59)
4.	1924	Fort Worth Panthers (109-41)	54.	1952	Milwaukee Brewers (101-53)
5.	1924	Baltimore Orioles (117-48)	55.	1961	Reno Silver Sox (97-43)
6.	1920	St. Paul Saints (115-49)	56.	1931	Charlotte Hornets (100-37)
7.	1903	Jersey City Skeeters (92-33)	57.	1916	New London Planters (86-34)
8.	1937	Salisbury Indians (80-16)	58.	1933	Davenport Blue Sox (82-32)
9.	1920	Baltimore Orioles (110-43)	59.	1905	Columbus Senators (100-52)
10.	1925	San Francisco Seals (128-71)	60.	1975	Waterloo Royals (93-35)
11.	1981	Albuquerque Dukes (94-38)	61.	1950	Winston-Salem Cards (106-47)
12.	1939	Kansas City Blues (107-47)	62.	1983	Reading Phillies (96-44)
13.	1943	Los Angeles Angels (110-45)	63.	1906	Des Moines Champions (97-50)
14.	1920	Fort Worth Panthers (108-40)	64.	1949	Stroudsburg Poconos (101-36)
15.	1922	Baltimore Orioles (115-52)	65.	1941	Houston Buffaloes (103-50)
16.	1938	Newark Bears (104-48)	66.	1910	Joplin Miners (90-34)
17.	1922	Fort Worth Panthers (109-46)	67.	1949	Pensacola Fliers (98-42)
18.	1923	Kansas City Blues (112-54)	68.	1939	Sanford Lookouts (98-35)
19.	1923	Baltimore Orioles (111-53)	69.	1980	Nashville Sounds (97-46)
20.	1922	Enid Harvesters (104-27)	70.	1978	Visalia Oaks (97-42)
21.	1920	Toronto Maple Leafs (108-46)	71.	1909	San Francisco Seals (132-80)
22.	1911	Denver Grizzlies (111-54)	72.	1992	Columbus Clippers (95-49)
23.	1992	Greenville Braves (100-43)	**73.**	**1993**	**Harrisburg Senators (94-44)**
24.	1927	Buffalo Bisons (112-56)	74.	1980	Peninsula Pilots (100-40)
25.	1954	Waco Pirates (105-42)	75.	1979	Saltillo Saraperos (95-40)
26.	1931	Hartford Senators (97-40)	76.	1902	Toronto Maple Leafs (85-42)
27.	1902	Indianapolis Indians (96-45)	77.	1921	Independence Producers (103-38)
28.	1929	Kansas City Blues (111-56)	78.	1966	Spartanburg Phillies (91-35)
29.	1903	Los Angeles Angels (133-78)	79.	1955	Fresno Cardinals (104-43)
30.	1955	Keokuk Kernals (92-34)	80.	1910	Sioux City Packers (108-60)
31.	1906	Portland Beavers (114-58)	81.	1951	Hazard Bombers (93-33)
32.	1921	Memphis Chicks (104-49)	82.	1941	Wilson Tobs (87-30)
33.	1925	Fort Wayne Panthers (103-48)	83.	1932	Tulsa Oilers (98-48)
34.	1952	Norfolk Tars (96-36)	84.	1946	Montreal Royals (100-54)
35.	1919	Baltimore Orioles (100-49)	85.	1948	Indianapolis Indians (100-54)
36.	1951	Charlotte Hornets (100-40)	86.	1941	Newark Bears (100-54)
37.	1980	Denver Bears (92-44)	87.	1960	Toronto Maple Leafs (100-54)
38.	1970	Hawaii Islanders (98-48)	88.	1922	St. Paul Saints (107-60)
39.	1926	Toronto Maple Leafs (109-57)	89.	1990	West Palm Beach Expos (92-40)
40.	1952	Miami Sun Sox (104-48)	90.	1946	Scranton Red Sox (96-43)
41.	1907	Wichita Jobbers (98-35)	91.	1923	St. Paul Saints (111-57)
42.	1931	Houston Buffaloes (108-51)	92.	1947	Havana Cubans (105-45)
43.	1933	Columbus Redbirds (101-51)	93.	1978	Appleton Foxes (97-40)
44.	1922	San Francisco Seals (127-72)	94.	1946	Abilene Blue Sox (97-40)
45.	1918	Toronto Maple Leafs (88-39)	95.	1986	Puebla Angeles (88-41)
46.	1921	Fort Worth Panthers (107-51)	96.	1950	Quebec Braves (0͞
47.	1940	Nashville Vols (101-47)	97.	1947	Lubbock Hub͡
48.	1924	Memphis Chicks (104-49)	98.	1947	Stockto͡
49.	1924	Okmulgee Drillers (110-48)	99.	1944	Har͡
50.	1928	San Francisco Seals (120-71)	100.	1944	Mil͡

311

Judging History, Part 2

Just how well did the 1993 Harrisburg Senators rank against the Top 100 teams in the history of the minors? Consider this:

— Of the teams on Minor League Baseball's Top 100 list, only the '93 Senators had as many as eight of their players spend all or parts of at least 10 seasons in the majors after first playing with them. The 1937 Newark Bears, who were ranked third on the list, and 1992 Columbus Clippers, at No. 72, were next with seven each.

— Of the 72 teams ranked ahead of the '93 Senators, 53 played before Jackie Robinson broke organized baseball's color barrier in 1946, when he played for Brooklyn's top farm team in Montreal.

— Of the 19 teams ranked ahead of the '93 Senators after Jackie Robinson joined the Class AAA Montreal Royals in 1946, fewer than two-thirds of them — 12 of 19, to be exact — won their league championship. Among the seven who failed to win in the playoffs were the 1983 Reading Phillies, who at 96-44 were the only other Eastern League team ranked higher in the Top 100 with more victories than the '93 Senators. Reading, though, lost in the first round of the 1983 playoffs to the New Britain Red Sox, who received a late-season boost from a 21-year-old, first-year pro pitcher named Roger Clemens.

— The 1953 Reading Phillies, who finished that season with a Eastern League-record 101 wins and a record the '93 Senators spent much of their season chasing, did not make the Top 100 list.

— Only two other Eastern League teams won more than 90 games in the regular season since the '93 Senators won 94 — the 2002 Akron Aeros, who went 93-48; and the 2017 Trenton Thunder, who were 92-48. Unlike the Senators of 1993, though, neither Akron nor Trenton won the title. Ironically, Akron lost to the Senators in the first round of the 2002 playoffs, while the 2017 Trenton Thunder were managed by Bobby Mitchell, who in 1993 was one of the Montreal Expos' roving instructors and talent evaluators.

After The 'Burg

Within hours of returning from Canton with the Eastern League trophy they always believed would be theirs, the Senators of 1993 scattered across North America, the Caribbean and Latin America.

They were out of Harrisburg faster than Curtis Pride or Rondell White could run from first to third.

The Senators finally were heading home after their six-month journey that began in mid-March at the dust bowl that was their spring training home in Lantana, Florida, and ended on Sept. 15 — at 9:49 p.m. to be exact — at Canton's Thurman Munson Memorial Stadium, where the Senators won their 100th game from the start of the regular season through the playoffs.

Individually, they had varying degrees of talent, just like any other team in professional baseball.

Together, though, they formed one of the greatest teams in the century-plus history of the minor leagues.

More than half of the players — 22 of 41 — would reach the majors with eight of those 22 staying there for 10 or more seasons.

Most of them had never before played above Class A prior to the '93 season. Some of them were barely old enough to legally have an adult beverage. Some were not even that old.

313

All that changed over a quarter-century for the Class of '93.
After their playing careers ended, some of them went into coaching or scouting. A couple ventured into broadcasting.

One started his own medical supply business.

One retired to live on a horse farm.

One now has a son playing quarterback in college, while another just became a father at 46.

Another spent five years in prison for attempted murder.

Sadly, one passed away from leukemia.

Others simply disappeared. Like the iconoclastic D-Day in the film "Animal House," their exact whereabouts were unknown.

For sure, none of them ever played for another team quite like the one they had in Harrisburg that summer so long ago, yet a summer that only seemed like last week.

THE MANAGER

JIM TRACY: After leaving Harrisburg, Tracy spent the 1994 season managing the Expos' AAA team in Ottawa before becoming Montreal's bench coach in 1995. He eventually managed for 11 seasons in the major leagues, beginning in 2001 with the Los Angeles Dodgers and finishing in 2012 with the Colorado Rockies. Had three Top 4 finishes in voting for the National League manager of year award with the Dodgers before finally winning the award in 2009 with the Rockies. Career record in the majors was 856-880. Last seen living in Mason, Ohio, with his wife, Deb, and doting on their handful of grandchildren. Beside fishing and deer hunting, his hobbies now include bird hunting, a challenge he undertakes with his Labrador retriever. The pup's name? Ofor Four.

THE COACHES

CHUCK KNIFFIN: Returned in 1994 as the pitching coach for the Expos' Class A affiliate in West Palm Beach. Eventually joined the Arizona Diamondbacks as a minor league coach before becoming their major league pitching coach in 2002, where he was reunited with Class of '93 pitcher Miguel Batista. Kniffin stayed in the majors until 2004, when he and manager Bob Brenly were fired in the midst of the Diamondbacks' rebuild. Was Colorado's Class AAA pitching coach from 2006-09, when he retired before his 60th birthday.

GREG FULTON: His gutsy May 2 cameo behind the plate was his last appearance as a player. Despite Jim Tracy's praise of him, Fulton was let go by the Expos after the 1993 season. Now lives with his family in Boston, Massachusetts.

THE PLAYERS

SHANE ANDREWS, third baseman: Spent the 1994 season at Class AAA Ottawa before reaching the major leagues in 1995 with the Montreal Expos. Played seven seasons in the majors with the Expos, Chicago Cubs and Boston Red Sox, batting .220 in 569 games with 86 homers and 263 RBIs. Last seen coaching Little League baseball in his hometown of Carlsbad, New Mexico.

JOE AUSANIO, Pitcher: A couple of months after that stellar relief appearance in Game 2 of the '93 semis against their Albany affiliate, Ausanio was picked by the New York Yankees in the minor league phase of the Rule V draft. He spent parts of the 1994 and '95 seasons with the Yankees, posting a 4-1 record and 5.57 ERA in 41 appearances. Also has dabbled in pro wrestling. Last seen as the head softball coach at Marist College, a 30-minute drive from his hometown of Kingston, N.Y.

TIM BARKER, shortstop: Spent the final half of his 10-year career in the minors from 1994-98 playing for Class AAA affiliates of the Milwaukee Brewers, New York Yankees and Colorado Rockies. Lifetime .273 hitter in 967 games in the minors. The native of Baltimore retired after turning 30 and was last seen working as a branch manager for the Bank of Delmarva.

MIGUEL BATISTA, pitcher: Lasted longer in the major leagues than any Senator from the Class of '93, retiring at age 41. Finished his 18-year career in the majors in 2012 with the Atlanta Braves, his 12th team. Posted a 102-115 career record in 658 games with a 4.48 ERA and 41 saves. The Dominican-born Batista was last seen as an author and poet, following up his first book of poetry with a novel on serial killers.

MARIO BRITO, pitcher: After Harrisburg, Brito played in Class AAA for the Milwaukee Brewers and Florida Marlins before pitching in Japan and, finally, Mexico and retiring after the 2000 season at the age of 34. Last seen in his native Dominican Republic, where he remains close friends with Class of '93 teammate Yorkis Perez.

MIAH BRADBURY, catcher: Never played again after walking away from his April 30, 1993 promotion to Class AAA Ottawa, retiring at 25 after four pro seasons and a .267 batting average in 279 games. The San Diego native was last seen living in Milford, Massachusetts, where he was the general manager of a Toyota dealership.

ARCHIE CORBIN, pitcher: Spent two seasons playing in Class AAA for the Pittsburgh Pirates before signing with Baltimore and reaching the majors with the Orioles in 1996. Was 2-0 with a 2.30 ERA in 18 appearances for Baltimore, but drifted back to the minors before returning to the majors for a final time with Florida in 1999. Finished with a 2-1 career record in the majors with a 4.44 ERA in 37 games. Last seen living in his hometown of Beaumont, Texas.

THE PLAYERS

REID CORNELIUS, pitcher: Put together a second straight healthy season in 1994 at Class AAA Ottawa before reaching the majors in 1995 with the Expos. Also pitched on and off again for the New York Mets and Florida Marlins before leaving the majors in 2000 with a career record of 8-17 record and 4.91 ERA in 45 appearances. Last seen coaching in the Atlanta Braves' farm system after serving as the Marlins' major league bullpen coach from 2010-16.

MIKE DANIEL, catcher: Spent two more seasons in the minors after playing in three games for the '93 Senators, splitting time with Class A and AA affiliates for Minnesota, Florida and Pittsburgh before retiring in 1995 at the age of 26. Last seen as a medical supply sales rep living with his wife and three children in Bixby, Oklahoma.

RAFAEL DIAZ, pitcher: Split the 1994 and '95 seasons between Harrisburg and Class AAA Ottawa before leaving organized baseball. Resurfaced in 2000 to briefly pitch in Japan. Last seen pitching in the Mexican League, where he spent four seasons before retiring in 2004 at the age of 34.

RICK DeHART, pitcher: Spent 1994 at Class A West Palm Beach before returning to Harrisburg in 1995. Integral member of the Senators' 1996 EL championship team. Reached the majors in 1997 with the Expos, going 2-1 over parts of three seasons with a 6.14 ERA in 56 games. Briefly returned to the majors in 2003 with the Kansas City Royals. Retired in 2008 after five seasons in the independent leagues. Last seen coaching for the independent league Kanas City T-Bones.

JOEY EISCHEN, pitcher: Made his major league debut with the Expos in 1994, but spent most of that season at Class AAA Ottawa. Traded early in the 1995 season to Los Angeles, beginning a dizzying three-year tour of the majors with 70 relief appearances for the Dodgers, Detroit Tigers and Cincinnati Reds. Bounced around the minors and independent leagues for next three seasons before returning to the majors in 2001 to begin a six-year stay with the Expos and then, after their relocation in 2005, the Washington Nationals. Retired after the 2006 season. Finished 10-year career in the majors with an 11-9 record, three saves and a 3.67 ERA in 324 appearances — all in relief. Now lives with his family in Lithia, Florida.

ROB FITZPATRICK, catcher: Returned in 1994 as the Senators' starting catcher, batting .251 in 95 games, throwing out 47 percent of would-be basestealers and helping Harrisburg reach the EL finals. Career derailed in 1995 when he refused the Expos' not-so-subtle request in spring training to become a replacement player for then-striking major leaguers. Retired after the 1995 season at the age of 27. Now teaching and coaching at the Westfield School in Perry, Georgia.

316

THE PLAYERS

CLIFF FLOYD, first baseman-left fielder: Finished the '93 season in the majors, where he batted .226 in only 31 at-bats. His first homer came in his 11th at-bat, a two-run shot to deep right field off the New York Mets' Dave Telgheder in Montreal's 9-3 loss on Sept. 26, 1993 at Shea Stadium. Floyd hit 232 more homers over the next 16 seasons, finishing his career in 2009 with the San Diego Padres. He hit 20 or more homers in six seasons and was a National League All-Star in 2001, when he batted .317 in 149 games for Florida with 31 homers and 103 RBIs. Won a World Series ring in 1997 with the Marlins, and was Tampa Bay's designated hitter in 2008 during the Rays' American League championship season. Last seen working as an analyst for the MLB Network; dabbling as an entrepreneur developing protective liners for baseball caps; and, in 2018, becoming a school superintendent with the opening of "Floyd's Academy" for children in Hazel Crest, Illinois.

MARC GRIFFIN, outfielder: Opened the '94 season in Harrisburg, batting .231 in 10 games and, at 25 years old, deciding to retire rather than accept a demotion to Class A West Palm Beach. Briefly tried to make a comeback in 1995 as a replacement player for major leaguers who were striking during spring training. He later worked as a color commentator on the Expos' French-speaking radio network.

MIKE HARDGE, second baseman: Spent all of the 1994 season in Harrisburg, where the Expos tried to turn him into a switch-hitter. The experiment did not end well for Hardge, who after leaving Montreal's organization in 1995 split another eight seasons between Class AA and the independent leagues. Retired after the 2002 season and now is the marketing director for Robinson Creek Home Health and Hospice in Austin, Texas.

HEATH HAYNES, pitcher: Reached the majors in 1994 with the Expos and did not allow a run in four appearances over an eight-day span in midseason. He never pitched again in the majors, drifting to Boston and then Oakland on waivers. Also pitched in the minors with the Anaheim Angels, Colorado Rockies, Florida Marlins and Houston Astros before retiring after the 2000 season at the age of 31. Now living in Lake Havasu City, Arizona, where he is the founder and president of Haynes Investment Management.

ROD HENDERSON, pitcher: Started the '94 season in Harrisburg before making his major league debut that summer with the Expos. Pitched in three games for Montreal in 1994 and two more with the Milwaukee Brewers in 1998. Later pitched in the minors for the Seattle Mariners, New York Mets and Oakland Athletics before retiring after the 2001 season. Now a scout with the Pittsburgh Pirates, and living with his family in Lexington, Kentucky.

THE PLAYERS

TYRONE HORNE, left fielder: Always a threat in the batter's box, but never could find a spot in the majors. Returned to Harrisburg in 1994 and '95 before playing for six organizations and in the Korean and independent leagues and retiring in 2001 after 14 seasons. Made national headlines on July 27, 1998 while playing with Class AA Arkansas as he homered for the cycle with a solo homer, two-run homer, three-run homer and grand slam in a 13-4 victory over San Antonio in a Texas League game. Last seen living in Ammon, Idaho, and working as a case manager at Rehabilitative Health Services.

CHRIS JOHNSON, pitcher: Traded only days into the '93 season to the Chicago Cubs, who kept the right-hander at Class AA Orlando through 1995. Spent the 1996 season playing independent ball before retiring at 27. Last seen living in Hixson, Tennessee.

RON KRAUSE, second baseman: Was batting .288 and off to the best start of his pro career when he walked away from the Senators early in the '93 season and never played again, retiring at the age of 22. Last seen living in Avon Lake, Ohio.

BRIAN LOONEY, pitcher: Reached the majors with the Expos at the end of the 1993 season, pitching in three games for Montreal before making four appearances for the Expos and Boston Red Sox over the 1994 and '95 seasons. Played for 11 organizations from 1996-2003 before splitting his final four seasons between the independent Atlantic League and the fledgling Italian Baseball League. Founder and owner of the Hamden Yards youth baseball academy in Hamden, Connecticut.

ORESTE MARRERO, first baseman: Played 32 games in the majors for Montreal after his late-season promotion from Harrisburg, but did not return again to the majors until 1996 with, albeit briefly, the Dodgers. Spent his final six seasons in the independent Atlantic League, finishing in 2005. Last seen living in Brooklyn and working for UPS.

CHRIS MARTIN, infielder: After playing three seasons in Harrisburg, Martin spent three more seasons with the Expos' Class AAA team in Ottawa from 1994-96 before signing with the expansion Tampa Bay Devil Rays. Never played higher than AAA for the Rays, retiring in 1999 at the age of 31. Last seen living in Los Angeles and working as the talent acquisition director for Fair, an automotive buyer and seller.

GLENN MURRAY, outfielder: Traded by Montreal late in spring training 1994 to Boston for minor league outfielder Derek Vinyard. Traded again two years later to Philadelphia, where he played 38 games for the Phillies in 1996 before spending two seasons in the Cincinnati Reds' system. Spent eight of his final nine seasons in the independent Atlantic League, retiring in 2008 at the age of 37. Now lives with his family in Nashua, New Hampshire.

THE PLAYERS

YORKIS PEREZ, pitcher: Played briefly for the Chicago Cubs in 1991 before reviving his career with the Senators in 1993. Signed with Florida after the '93 season and spent eight of the next nine seasons in the majors with the Marlins, Mets, Phillies, Astros and Orioles. Retired after the 2002 season and now lives with his family in Santo Domingo of the Dominican Republic.

CURTIS PRIDE, outfielder: Made his major league debut with the Expos late in the 1993 season, becoming the big leagues' first deaf player since outfielder Dick Sipek played 82 games for Cincinnati in 1945. Ended up playing 421 games in the majors with six teams from 1993-2006. Now the baseball coach at Gallaudet, the predominately deaf university in Washington, D.C. Ironically, Pride, who as a child learned to read lips but never to sign, first had to learn sign language before he was hired at Gallaudet. In 2016, he also was appointed as one of Major League Baseball's Ambassadors for Inclusion.

ED PUIG, pitcher: Already a nine-year pro when he arrived on City Island in '93 as the Senators' oldest player at 27. Lasted two more seasons after the Senators' championship run and retired after the 1995 season at the age of 29. Last seen living in Denver, Colorado, working for the United States Postal Service and coaching high school baseball.

LANCE RICE, catcher: Returned to Harrisburg in 1994 as a player-coach before playing two more seasons in the minors for Detroit and Baltimore, and retiring at the age of 29. Last seen living with his wife and two children on a horse farm in Northern Virginia, where he also has been coaching youth travel baseball.

KIRK RUETER, pitcher: The first of the '93 Senators to reach the majors, where he promptly went 8-0 in 14 starts for Montreal. Won 12 of 18 decisions over the next two seasons before being traded in July 1996 to San Francisco for pitcher Mark Leiter. While Leiter went 4-2 in just 12 starts for Montreal, Rueter with the Giants became one of the majors' most consistent left-handers. In 2002, when he won his 100th game in the majors, his .622 career winning percentage trailed only Randy Johnson, Andy Pettitte, Tom Glavine and John Tutor as the best since 1980 among lefties with 100 decisions. Retired in 2005 with a 130-92 record and 4.27 ERA. Now lives in Nashville, Illinois, where his home includes a 4,500 square-foot "shed" filled with sports memorabilia.

MATT RUNDELS, Utility player: Returned to Harrisburg in 1994 and '95, but could not duplicate the early success he had with the Senators and watched his batting average fall nearly 100 points from his .342 mark in 1993. Played the 1996 season in the independent Northern League before retiring at the age of 26. Last seen living with his family in Wellington, Florida, where he is an investment advisor.

THE PLAYERS

MITCH SIMONS, infielder: Never played again in Harrisburg after '93, spending his final eight seasons in the game playing on the Class AA and AAA levels for six organizations before retiring in 2001 at the age of 32. Last seen being inducted into the Oklahoma State University Hall of Fame.

MIKE THOMAS, pitcher: Joined Milwaukee's organization after the 1993 season. Had the briefest time of any member of the Class of '93 who reached the majors, pitching in only one game for the Brewers in 1995 against the Chicago White Sox. The last of the six batters he faced in that game was Hall of Famer Tim Raines, whom Thomas retired on an infield pop-up. Retired after the 1995 season at the age of 26. Last seen living in Cabot, Arkansas.

EDGAR TOVAR, shortstop: Returned to Class A West Palm Beach in 1994, but was back for 81 games with the Senators in '95 before playing the final 10 years of his career in the independent leagues and retiring at the age of 31. Later spent five seasons as the Chicago Cubs' bullpen catcher from 2007-11 before becoming a youth baseball instructor in Palm Beach County, Florida.

UGUETH URBINA, pitcher: Returned to the Senators in 1994 and went 9-3 in 21 starts before reaching Class AAA Ottawa and the majors with Montreal in 1995. Moved exclusively to the Expos' bullpen in 1996 and saved 125 games for them from 1997-2001, when he was traded to Boston for pitchers Tomo Ohka and Rich Rundles. Saved another 112 games for the Red Sox, Texas, Florida, Detroit and Philadelphia before leaving the majors after the 2005 season at the age of 31. Twice named an All-Star — in 1998 with Montreal and 2002 with Boston. Won a World Series ring in 2003 with Florida. Alas, life after baseball did not go well for Urbina, who served more than five years in a Venezuelan prison after being found guilty of trying to kill five workers on his family's ranch in his native Caracas. He was released from prison in 2012. Last seen living in Caracas.

DERRICK WHITE, first baseman: The Expos never made the call White said was promised to him when he was demoted late in the '93 season. Instead, the Expos sent him to Class AAA Ottawa to start the '94 season before releasing him. White signed a minor league contract with the Marlins and after the season signed with Detroit. He played in 39 games for the Tigers in 1995 and did some more touring of the minors before returning to the majors in 1998 to split 20 games between the Chicago Cubs and Colorado Rockies. Spent the final 11 years of his pro career hopscotching from the minors to the indy leagues to Korea, Japan and Mexico, retiring in 2009 at the age of 39. Last seen as the director of international scouting for the Rakuten Eagles of Japan's Pacific League.

THE PLAYERS

GABE WHITE, pitcher: Reached the majors in 1994 with Montreal and appeared in 26 games over two seasons with the Expos before being traded to Cincinnati for minor league infielder Jhonny Carvajal, who became a mainstay on Harrisburg's Eastern League championship teams from 1996-98. While Carvajal helped the Senators to three more titles, White became one of the majors' most heavily used left-handers, first with the Reds and then Colorado. White later pitched for the New York Yankees and St. Louis before retiring in 2005 at the age of 33. Post-playing career included competing in truck races with his beloved Ford, the aptly named "High N Tite." Last seen living in Georgia and, at 46 years old, entering the world of fatherhood.

RONDELL WHITE, center fielder: Made his major league debut with the Expos on Sept. 1, 1993. He stayed with the Expos for the next six-plus seasons before being traded to the Chicago Cubs in the middle of the 2000 season for pitcher Scott Downs. Eventually played for the Yankees, San Diego, Kansas City, Detroit and Minnesota before retiring after the 2007 season at the age of 35. Played in one All-Star Game, pinch-hitting for Barry Bonds in the 2003 game in Chicago. Last seen living with his family in Davie, Florida.

RANDY WILSTEAD, first baseman: Returned to Harrisburg in 1994, batting .294 and helping the Senators reach the EL finals. His career, though, was derailed in 1995 by a lingering shoulder injury and his refusal to become a replacement player for striking major leaguers. He retired at 27 and went home to St. George, Utah, where he still lives today with his wife and three sons. Owns a medical supply firm, and is known to occasionally sit in on an operation. His middle son, Kody, was recruited as a fleet-footed Division I college quarterback. Wilstead quickly noted that Kody did not inherit any speed from his father.

DARRIN WINSTON, pitcher: Split the 1994 season between the Senators and Class AAA Ottawa before joining Pittsburgh as a minor league free agent. Reached the majors in 1997 with Philadelphia, where over two seasons he went 4-2 in 34 appearances. Spent his final four pro seasons with Somerset in the independent Atlantic League, retiring in 2002 at the age of 36. He died on Aug. 15, 2008 at his home in Freehold, New Jersey, only days after being diagnosed with leukemia. He was 42, leaving behind his wife, six children and one grandchild.

TYRONE WOODS, outfielder: Played 38 games in 1994 for the Senators before spending two seasons in Class AAA for the Baltimore Orioles and Boston Red Sox, and then 11 more seasons in the Korean and Japanese leagues. He was 39 when he finally retired in 2008 with 478 homers in 21 pro seasons. Last seen living with his family in his hometown of Brookville, Florida.

THE GENERAL MANAGER

TODD VANDER WOUDE: Named The Sporting News' minor league top executive in 1993. Grew accustomed to ordering championship rings as he oversaw the Senators' record run of four straight Eastern League titles from 1996-99. The championship rings for the '93 team were different, though. Up to that point, no team in the minors had a larger ring than the Senators. He traveled to West Palm Beach in March 1994 to distribute the bling. "On the plane ride down to spring training, I had all of the rings in my briefcase," he said. "I felt I needed to have it cuffed to my wrist." He remained the Senators' GM through 2007, when the team's new owner, Michael Reinsdorf, forced out longtime assistant GM and broadcaster Mark Mattern, prompting Vander Woude to resign. Now leads the non-profit Harrisburg Downtown Improvement District, and still lives with his family in Harrisburg's historic Shipoke section.

THE BROADCASTER

MARK MATTERN: Was the on-air voice of the Senators for more than 2,300 games from 1987 through 2007, when new owner Michael Reinsdorf unceremoniously purged the front office. Still lives with his family in suburban Harrisburg, and now is the associate director of York Habitat For Humanity.

THE CLUBBIE

STEVE PURVIS: Baseball sometimes has silly names for serious positions. To wit: "Clubbie" for clubhouse manager. The nickname is the only short part of the tireless position, which Purvis held from 1990-97. He worked home games from 3:30 in the afternoon to 1 or 2 a.m., and that on top of working full-time for the federal government. For the Class of '93, if they needed something, Purv made sure they had it.

THE BALLPARK

The creaky, mayfly-infested, heat-retaining Erector set that was the Senators' home in 1993 underwent a $45.1 million makeover in 2007-08.

The Class of '93 may not recognize the place today, but they still would own the joint.

Snapshots Over The Years

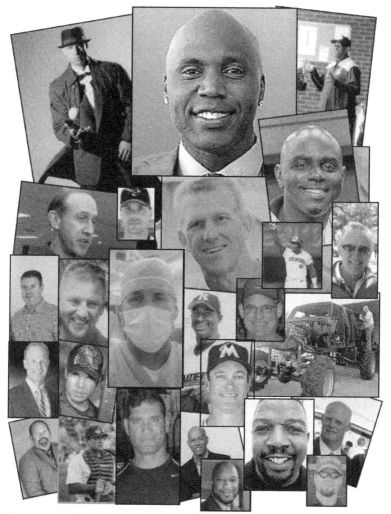

From top row left: Miguel Batista, Cliff Floyd, Curtis Pride, Kirk Rueter, Rick DeHart, Jim Tracy, Rondell White, Tyrone Woods, Matt Rundels, Rod Henderson, Lance Rice, Randy Wilstead post op, Glenn Murray, Greg Fulton, Gabe White with his truck "High N Tite," Marc Griffin, Ugueth Urbina, Reid Cornelius, Joe Ausanio, Edgar Tovar, Oreste Marrero, Chris Martin, Mike Hardge, Tyrone Horne, Joey Eischen and Rob Fitzpatrick.

ACKNOWLEDGMENTS

In many ways, the story of the 1993 Harrisburg Senators was easy to tell. The trick in writing their story was knowing how to stay out of the way of the story itself, to let the men of the Class of '93 tell their own story as it happened, to let the momentum created by their successes carry that story from spring training through the playoffs.

Hopefully, that was accomplished here.

The Harrisburg Senators of today once again were kind enough to supply many of the photos of their more famous predecessors from the Class of '93.

This book could have been done simply by sifting through old newspaper clips, notebooks and a well-worn scorebook that long ago lost its covers and, after 25 years, now is a scorebook held together by a wire and a prayer.

Those basics provided the template for this book.

The best parts, though, came from many of those who lived the tale, from folks whose memories remained as clear a quarter-century later as when those moments occurred.

Helping tell the tale were then-Senators general manager Todd Vander Woude, broadcaster Mark Mattern, clubhouse manager Steve Purvis and, of course, the players. Especially players like Rod Henderson, Curtis Pride, Ed Puig, Lance Rice and Randy Wilstead who all graciously took time to answer a slew of questions from a formerly well-caffeinated newspaper writer who told them they could not leave Memory Lane until they answered all of those questions. Same with Jim Clark, the longtime Canton, and now Akron, broadcaster who graciously relived his suffering through the final three games of the 1993 Eastern League finals.

My greatest thanks goes to manager Jim Tracy, who spent a whole bunch of hours — with Trace, no one ever really keeps track of the actual time — providing insights into that special season. He was the perfect choice in 1993 to run the Senators and, 25 years later, his was the perfect voice to tell their story.

Finally, I am forever grateful to my wife, Michelle, and our daughter, Annie, who both survived another book, even though at times they not so secretly wanted to relocate my office to the barn behind our house.

ABOUT THE AUTHOR

Andrew Linker is an award-winning sports writer who has spent more than 35 years working for newspapers and magazines up and down the Susquehanna River. Much of that time has been spent writing about the Harrisburg Senators since their return to City Island in 1987.

He and his wife Michelle and their daughter Annie live in Palmyra, Pa., exactly 19.8 miles from home plate on Harrisburg's historic City Island.

He has authored three other books on Harrisburg's rich baseball history — *One Patch of Grass,* which was published in 2012; *Clippings: All of the Other Cool Stuff That Didn't Fit Into the First Book* (2013); and *30 For The Books, By The Numbers: The Harrisburg Senators 1987-2016* (2017).

91395951R00186